S0-BAK-731

Moral Issues in Military
Decision Making

Moral Issues in Military Decision Making

Second Edition, Revised

Anthony E. Hartle

University Press of Kansas

© 2004 by the University Press of Kansas
All rights reserved

Published by the University Press of Kansas (Lawrence, Kansas
66049), which was organized by the Kansas Board of Regents and is
operated and funded by Emporia State University, Fort Hays State
University, Kansas State University, Pittsburg State University,
the University of Kansas, and Wichita State University

Library of Congress Cataloging-in-Publication Data

Hartle, Anthony E., 1942–
    Moral issues in military decision making / Anthony E. Hartle.—2nd ed.
    p. cm.
Includes bibliographical references and index.
    ISBN 0-7006-1320-x (cloth : alk. paper) — ISBN 0-7006-1321-8 (pbk. : alk. paper)
    1. Military ethics. I. Title.
    U22.H38 2004
    174'.9355—dc22   2003020021

British Library Cataloguing-in-Publication Data is available.

Printed in the United States of America
10 9 8 7 6 5

The paper used in this publication meets the minimum requirements of the
American National Standard for Permanence of Paper for Printed Library
Materials Z39.48-1984.

Contents

Preface

When the first edition of this book appeared in 1989, the United States was engaged in a costly arms race with the Soviet Union. Nuclear weapons threatened humanity as a whole. The strategic policy of both countries sought to avoid nuclear war through deterrence and to advance national interests by threatening the indiscriminate slaughter of millions of innocent people. That policy raised troubling ethical questions for military officers and civilian decision makers alike, and all conventional engagements took place in the shadow of apocalyptic possibilities.

The world of the twenty-first century is dramatically different. Major ethical issues exist for the profession of arms today, but the most prominent are clearly different from those of the Cold War. The demise of the USSR has left the United States as the most powerful nation on Earth by far, but despite the military and economic might of the United States, or in part because of it some might say, the world is now more chaotic and more complex in terms of the responsibilities of American military forces. Unable to oppose the United States with conventional weapons, various countries strenuously seek to achieve nuclear capabilities that can provide a deterrent to the U.S. pursuit of national interests. The increase in the responsibilities of American military forces has made the role of military ethics and the performance of the professional military leader ever more critical. Today the protection of vital national interests and the values of American society depend upon men and women in uniform having a clear understanding of their obligations as members of the military profession.

As a profession, the American military has made progress in that regard. In 1989 the argument that the professional military ethic for

Americans in uniform had its core in the functional requirements of military service and the obligations incurred by the commitment to the Constitution was not a familiar one. Today the proposition is the assumption behind discussions of professional responsibility for members of the military services. Each of the American military services published a set of core values during the decade of the 1990s. Although the value sets are different in terms of labels and terminology, the behavior called for is essentially the same.

Military interventions, usually under the auspices of the United Nations, became frequent in the last decade of the twentieth century. Service as a member of a multinational force brought its own professional issues, some of them morally challenging. As a profession, the military has focused attention on these issues and attempted to find appropriate answers. Various studies of the military have raised awareness and provided insights concerning the nature of service to the nation.

That service takes place in an increasingly complex environment within the American military, which in the early twenty-first century is attempting to transform itself from a massively powerful military force into one that is both lethal and flexible in the face of rapidly shifting circumstances. "Small wars" and the fight against terrorism require such changes. Remarkable advances in communication and information technology call for innovation and adaptation that do not come easily to hierarchical organizations that value tradition and seek to minimize risk and uncertainty.

In view of the changes wrought by the end of the Cold War, the proliferating practice of military intervention, the pervasive role of the United Nations in peace operations, the emphasis on human rights, and the new context of the war on terrorism and homeland defense are moral issues in military decision making that merit a careful re-examination. This revision focuses on understanding moral aspects of the role of the military officer in the current affairs of the nation.

Chapter One

The Hardest Place

For war is the hardest place: if comprehensive and consistent moral judgments are possible there, they are possible everywhere.
—Michael Walzer, *Just and Unjust Wars*

The environment in which members of the military must operate poses a severe threat to consistent moral behavior. In addition to the inevitable stresses of leadership in the profession of arms,[1] men and women in uniform in the twenty-first century face a confusing variety of inconsistencies in national policy, government practice, and social behavior. The state, defended by the military professional, champions the cause of peace while pursuing an open-ended global war on terrorism, supporting protracted military involvements abroad, and providing massive quantities of arms to potential belligerents around the world. The United States government adheres to a strategic nuclear policy that supports nonproliferation but uses nuclear weapons as a threat in pursuing national interests. Defense of American values constitutes the soldier's fundamental purpose, but government officials of the state that embodies those values sometimes deem it necessary to operate pragmatically rather than on the basis of principle. Although society may be ethically better than it was a century ago in that we have more social freedom, more political stability, and a greater degree of equality before the law along with many other desirable features, we have become a juridical society where trust is minimal and social relations are based on entitlements and legalities.[2] Society demands an ethical military but provides few institutional examples to emulate. Members of the military services swear to support and defend a constitution structured by values, but in our capitalistic society "The 'laws' of the market have . . . no ethical norms, and corporations have no consciences."[3]

There is another aspect of the contemporary world that increases concern about the conduct of American military forces. The United States, reacting to the crippling terrorist attack on New York City and the Pentagon in September of 2001, continues to expand military capabilities already vastly superior to those of any potential rival while scaling back foreign aid. In 2001 American military spending was on the order of five times larger than that of Russia, the next largest spender.[4] American military spending in 2002 exceeded that of all other NATO states, Russia, China, Japan, Iraq, and North Korea combined.[5] In 2003, American expenditure increased again, becoming six times larger than Russia's and more than twenty times larger than the combined military budgets of the "rogue states" (Cuba, Iran, Iraq, Libya, North Korea, Sudan, and Syria).[6] The United States arguably possesses more power in relation to the rest of the world than any nation in history—and yet perhaps for the first time Americans across the country feel seriously threatened. Security has risen in priority with respect to our humanitarian values.

In such an environment, confusion multiplies rapidly. Thus, for practical reasons alone, the professional military ethic becomes a matter of particular concern. The ethic needs to be a workable guide that cuts through such confusion and illuminates the standards properly applied to moral decisions. Confusion hinders effectiveness, and the effectiveness with which the military services perform their primary function—the systematic application of force—can have momentous consequences for the state they serve. In an age marked by both American hegemony and the proliferation of weapons of mass destruction, the effectiveness of the United States armed services affects populations around the globe.

For the American military, the professional military ethic is also a matter of concern for an additional reason: members of our armed forces make a moral commitment through their commissioning or enlistment oath. They make a commitment to a set of values, which provides a depth and complexity to the ethic that requires more than a superficial examination if the ethic is to be understood and properly applied. A group of soldiers could make a commitment to defend a certain piece of ground, for example, and such a commitment might well be construed as a choice involving a distinct moral obligation on their part. Considerable conceptual complexity is added, however, if a group makes a moral commitment to adhere to and support a set of values that itself has extensive moral implications. Such a situation exists when new members of the military swear to "support and defend the Constitution" against all enemies.[7]

My discussion will examine the complexity of the existing American professional military ethic and the justification for the ethic. I hope to clarify the moral framework within which moral decisions must be made, both in time of peace when such decisions are often quite difficult, and in time of war, which is indeed "the hardest place."

The nature of that place eludes accurate description in ordered prose on a written page, but the testimony of those who endure war nonetheless suggests the savage quandaries that inevitably arise. James McDonough relates a typically trying situation he encountered as a young lieutenant in the Vietnam War. With part of his platoon, he rushed to the assistance of a stay-behind ambush that had initiated a firefight. In the action, one of the members of the small element had been seriously wounded and needed medical help, but at the base of the hill on which the injured man was located, Lieutenant McDonough encountered a minefield that effectively blocked him from moving to the assistance of the stay-behind group. Desperately casting about for a way to proceed, he discovered a frightened local farmer cowering nearby. Through his interpreter, McDonough demanded that the farmer show them how to get through the minefield, only to be refused.

"Ask him again, Nhan," I ordered.

Again the farmer refused, his eyes widening in fear. I took out my knife. "Nhan, tell him I'll kill him right now if he doesn't tell us."

I had crossed the line. I wouldn't have killed him, but he didn't know that, and the threat itself was criminal. But I weighed that against the bleeding soldier and the others who might bleed if we didn't get through to them quickly. A leader has no one to look to for advice on such decisions. He must do what he thinks is best, but he must not fool himself as to the consequences of his choice. War is not a series of case studies that can be scrutinized with objectivity. It is a series of stark confrontations that must be faced under the most emotion-wrenching conditions. War is the suffering and death of people you know, set against a background of the suffering and death of people you do not.[8]

Lieutenant McDonough reached the group under fire and evacuated the wounded man, whose life was saved by the action. Does that justify his treatment of the farmer? In some instances, can one justifiably violate the laws of war in order to achieve specific ends? If so, how can we identify such circumstances? Once we accept the principle that "in this case" the end justifies the means, how do we limit the application? Such situations, repeated with terrible frequency, corrode the soul and warp moral sensibilities.

On a more massive wartime scale, the responsibility of deciding who is to live seems more than should be asked of any conscientious person. General Omar Bradley faced such a decision at St. Lô during World War II, when the fate of millions hung in the balance. That situation, suggestive of the kind of moral dilemma that senior officers must be prepared to face today, further illustrates why the maelstrom of war becomes the hardest place.

In July 1944, American forces poised for what General Bradley called "the most decisive battle of our war in Europe."[9] After three weeks during which the Germans bottled up the invasion forces in Normandy, Allied forces were committed to a major breakthrough in the area of St. Lô, where armored forces would be able to operate on solid ground beyond the hedgerows. Michael Walzer has pointed out one difficult moral aspect of that operation that illustrates the severe stress on conscience that unavoidable military decisions can create.[10] Part of the plan for the breakout, dubbed Operation COBRA, was a relatively new concept called carpet bombing. At the point of attack in the enemy lines, an area of five square miles was to be pulverized by an overwhelming force of 350 fighter planes and 1,500 heavy bombers. The infantry units would then secure the penetration to allow a breakthrough by armored elements.

When General Bradley briefed a group of journalists, however, just before the battle was to begin, one asked about the French citizens of St. Lô, who would be subjected to the Allied bombs along with the Germans. Would they be warned somehow? General Bradley, having already wrestled with that question, painfully shook his head, "as if to escape the necessity for saying no."[11] Warning the civilians would jeopardize the operation, and the stakes were too high.

But the fate of French civilians was not the only morally agonizing issue in this offensive. An important part of Bradley's plan was to use a road running parallel to the American front as a guide for the huge air armada that would launch COBRA. The major artery, clearly visible from the air, would allow the bombing to proceed with a reasonable degree of security for the infantry units in attack positions. Bombers were seldom used in support of ground operations because they were notoriously inaccurate; much too often bombs landed on friendly troops rather than on the enemy. On 23 July the long chains of aircraft launched from airfields in England, only to be turned back by a heavy cloud cover that necessitated postponing the attack twenty-four hours. One group of bombers, however, flew on to the target and dropped their bombs—on the U.S. 30th Infantry Division, one of the assault units. When Bradley investigated, he found that the bombers had approached over the heads of friendly troops, perpendicular to the front rather than parallel to it. That approach made error by the bombardiers much more likely.

After a lengthy, frustrating series of indirect communications, General Bradley's headquarters discovered that the air forces indeed planned to use a perpendicular approach to the front, despite the general's initial insistence on the parallel course during the planning phase. The lone group of bombers had not been mistaken in its route. General Bradley then had to make yet another dispiriting moral decision in COBRA. Changing the approach of the long parade of bombers that were timed almost to the second—as aircraft taking off from dozens of airfields consolidated into one striking arm—meant yet another postponement, possibly making the plan of attack evident to the Germans. Proceeding with the plan meant almost certain U.S. casualties. General Bradley decided the attack must begin on schedule.

After considerable difficulty, the breakout succeeded in spectacular fashion, launching Patton's Third Army on its famous race across Europe. The early hours of the offensive were particularly difficult, however, because the COBRA bombers did hit American units in attack positions. The misguided bombs severely pounded the 9th and 30th Divisions, resulting in several hundred dead and wounded. One of the dead was Lieutenant General Lesley J. McNair, considered one of our great combat leaders. General Bradley was probably fortunate that the press of combat allowed little time to dwell on the burdens of conscience that are unavoidable for those in command.

Between conventional war and uneasy peace, we now have the ongoing war on terrorism, a shifting blend of operations by conventional units, by law enforcement agencies around the world, and by clandestine organizations that use clandestine means ranging from sophisticated technology to agents who infiltrate shadowy terrorist groups. The global scale of the conflict has generated new challenges and new moral quandaries that call for military professionals with wider knowledge, deeper insight, and stronger conviction.

Profound moral questions are clearly at issue in the complexity of decisions necessitated by war, but views concerning the status of morality differ widely. Some consider morality mere social convention; some view it as no more than a system of persuasion; others argue for moral absolutes to which all persons should conform. But all recognize it as a factor that regulates social behavior. If morality is to be effective in that function, it should be as free from internal contradiction as possible. Commitment to values and moral principles provides reasons for acting. Consistent, effective action will follow only from a coherent set of principles of action and rules for conduct, whereas general moral principles will provide the foundation for specific guides for action. The consistency with which we follow such guides, then, will necessarily be a function of the coherence of and justification provided for the general principles. Accordingly, my examination of the American professional military ethic will concern its content, its coherence, and its rational justifiability.

In my discussion of these aspects of the professional military ethic, I examine the claim that the military role is what sociologists sometimes refer to as a "differentiated role." Various writers, among them Alan Goldman, Richard Wasserstrom, and Robert Veatch, have been concerned with the special norms of professional groups in terms of role-differentiated behavior. Under this concept, we classify roles based on the degree to which various considerations that otherwise would be relevant or even decisive in moral evaluations are disregarded or weighted less heavily.[12] If the military operates under rules of conduct or even general principles different from those that apply to society in general, we need to understand that status. If the rules for conduct and general principles are the same for both the

military and American society, we need to understand how that constraint affects war fighting, the core military function.

Examining other professions can illuminate the subject of professional ethics. The profession of law, an important part of our legal
institution, recognizes the *Code of Professional Responsibility* established by the American Bar Association. The code articulates the
professional ethic and establishes the differentiated rules (some of
which also have legal force) that most state codes incorporate. Under
that code, one provision requires lawyers to give a client their best
efforts in furthering the client's interests. Sometimes those interests
are immoral, but so long as they are legal, the professional code en-
joins lawyers to do their best to realize those interests. That is one
sense in which we say that a lawyer's role is differentiated, meaning
that the moral guidance for lawyers in their professional role may call
for actions that are different from those appropriate for a general
member of society. Rules that specify different actions for lawyers are
said to be justified because the service provided to members of society
is so critically important that certain apparent violations of society's
moral rules for conduct are justified if they are necessary to maintain
the institution of law. That is, the role-differentiated behavior of
lawyers finds justification in the claim that such behavior is necessary to realize the fundamental values of society. Thus, the fundamental values that generate moral rules requiring general members
of society to act one way in normal day-to-day life might call for
lawyers to act quite differently in their professional role.[13] Understanding that the profession of arms has a similar role-differentiated
character can help clarify the moral nature of the professional military ethic.

A particular case that occurred in 1973 manifests the concept of
differentiation.[14] A mechanic from Syracuse, New York, killed four
persons camping in the Adirondacks. He apparently chose his victims at random. During the next month, authorities captured the
murderer, Robert Garrow, and indicted him for the murder of one of
the four persons, a college student. Police had recovered one additional body, but at the time of Garrow's arrest, no one knew the fate
of two of the victims. One of those was a young Illinois woman; the
other a teenage runaway. The court appointed two lawyers to defend
Garrow, who told them of raping and killing the Illinois woman and
subsequently hiding her body in a mineshaft. The lawyers investi-

gated and found the body, but left it and did not report their discovery. About a month later, following Garrow's instructions, they found the second body, which they also did not report.

The father of the Illinois woman, learning that the lawyers were defending a man accused of killing a camper in the Adirondacks, traveled to Syracuse and asked the lawyers if they had any information that might shed light on the whereabouts of his missing daughter. They said no. Later, in court testimony, Garrow implicated himself in the other three murders. Amid general outrage, the lawyers explained that because their knowledge of the other murders and the location of the bodies was privileged information received from their client, their professional ethical code prohibited revealing the facts. And however cruel and unfeeling that choice may seem, the lawyer-client privilege is one of the foundational principles of our adversary legal system in which both defense lawyers and prosecutors present the strongest cases possible. The assumption is that justice will best be served when that happens. If clients cannot be completely honest with their lawyers and be assured that the communication will go no further, lawyers cannot present the most effective defense. The lawyers in the Garrow case followed this rule: "Lawyers should never reveal information gained in the confidential lawyer–client relationship, unless the information is necessary to prevent a crime or to save a life."[15]

The Garrow case illustrates that the moral rules lawyers must follow are exactly the same as those members of the general population must follow, unless different standards are justified by the benefit that society would receive by adherence to differentiated rules. Because society benefits enormously from a stable and consistent legal system that incorporates fundamental values, our society considers that the differentiated rules necessary to maintain such a system are justified. At least, that is the theory. And from this view, lawyers are said to have a differentiated role in society. That differentiation serves society's interests because it promotes the successful pursuit of justice. With that model in mind, I want to ask whether the role of the military officer is indeed a differentiated role, and how we might justify the professional military ethic that exists.

Society grants to members of the military possession and control of an elaborate array of weaponry: weapons of great power and technological complexity forbidden to general members of society. In addition, military leaders have the authority to order other persons into situations of great danger, sometimes when death is likely. And, of course, soldiers are authorized to use deadly force in ways that general members of the society are not. In certain situations, combatants claim justification for putting the innocent at risk during the use of deadly force. These factors suggest a differentiated role for the military.

Society benefits in a straightforward sense. The world of nations in some ways has long resembled Thomas Hobbes's state of nature, in which every individual seeks his own interest and must guard against all others.[16] No higher authority exists despite the dramatic increase in the peacekeeping and intervention operations of the United Nations during the 1990s. At best, the United Nations can provide limited protection, as in Kosovo; enforcement through sanctions, as in Iraq; and legal proceedings, notably the International Criminal Tribunal for the Former Yugoslavia. The United Nations has no military power of its own. The simple fact is that we must have competent military forces if we are to maintain our way of life. The military services exist to protect the state with armed force as necessary.

The needs of society appear to justify the existence of the military profession, then, just as the needs of society justify the existence of the legal profession. And the military has a professional code governing the conduct of its members, just as the legal and medical professions do. The military code in the United States, however, is not a formally codified set of rules.[17] The product of tradition and experience, it can be explained in terms of three primary influences.

The three primary factors that have shaped the American professional military ethic are the functional requirements of military service, the international laws of war, and the core values of American society. In the pages ahead, we will examine the relationship among these primary influences and the application of the resulting professional military ethic by military professionals. In doing so, we will explore each of the factors as well as some of the institutional characteristics of the military profession. We will also have to consider how to articulate the provisions of the American professional military ethic that prevails as we embark on the twenty-first century.

Chapter Two

The Military as a Profession

The Nature of Professions

The sociologist Andrew Abbott notes that "the professions dominate our world. They heal our bodies, measure our profits, save our souls,"[1] and, I would add, wage war in our defense. My addition raises the question: what characteristics identify a particular activity as a profession? Alan Goldman, in *The Moral Foundations of Professional Ethics*, says, "We may take it as definitional of professions that they involve the application of a specialized body of knowledge in the service of important interests of a clientele,"[2] echoing one of the initial studies in the field that describes a profession as an organized body of experts who apply "esoteric knowledge to particular cases."[3] Specialized knowledge appears to be a necessary condition, though a gangland hit man might qualify as a professional if we accept this characteristic as sufficient. So would harbormasters and Alaskan hunting guides, which suggests some additional discriminating characteristics are necessary. Even so, I contend that under any of the authoritative definitions available, a distinct segment of the armed forces clearly qualifies as a professional group.[4] The officer corps constitutes that group. In addition, the senior noncommissioned officer corps and many dedicated Department of the Army civilians meet most of the criteria. Modern theorists have largely agreed on what professions are and what needs explanation, specifying that the term refers to an "occupational group with some special skill," usually an abstract skill requiring extensive training. The knowledge and skill are not applied in a routine fashion but require "revised application case by case."[5] The sense of the term "profession" that I cite refers to an occupation involving advanced study and

10

specialization, not the sense that includes activity in which skill is rewarded by money in contrast to amateur or volunteer activity, e.g., hockey players in the National Hockey League and professional artists, among others.

Huntington's View

Samuel Huntington, despite his difficulties with the National Academy of Sciences, remains a classic voice on the sociology of professions. His book *The Soldier and the State* continues to be an important source for anyone seeking to understand the military profession. Although subsequent studies have called into question some of his conclusions and have revealed complexities that Huntington ignored,[6] his model is still influential and insightful. It provides a useful starting point in examining the status of the American military. Huntington identified three characteristics as necessary for any activity to achieve the status of a profession: expertise, corporateness, and responsibility.[7] He contends that career military service possesses all three characteristics and concludes:

The modern officer corps is a highly professional body. It has its own expertise, corporateness, and responsibility. The existence of this profession tends to imply, and the practice of the profession tends to engender among its members, a distinctive outlook on international politics, the role of the state, the place of force and violence in human affairs, the nature of man and society, and the relationship of the military profession to the state.[8]

Huntington's "expertise" involves the satisfaction of a significant social need, which provides one argument for the justification of the profession's ethic (a subject I touched upon in Chapter 1 and to which I will return in Chapter 8). Medicine, for example, concerns the need to preserve human life and minimize suffering. One gains professional expertise through a lengthy period of formal education. In Huntington's words, "Professional knowledge . . . is intellectual and capable of preservation in writing."[9] Usually, the profession itself controls and perpetuates professional education through its own facilities.

A particular profession sees itself as a corporate body distinct from laymen as a result of its expertise and the nature of its activity. The profession generates and adheres to its own criteria of competence, and it normally controls admission to its ranks. Most activities recognized as professions enforce the standards of performance by this means and may also terminate membership when the standards are not maintained. The authority to police its own ranks is one of the distinctive characteristics of a profession.

The sense of corporateness results partially from the social responsibility borne by the profession. The expertise is one deemed critical, or at least necessary in some sense, by society. The professional gains special status and in return is expected to recognize a social obligation to provide a special expertise, so that commitment to the role entails a "profession" of obligation to society. The nature and substance of the obligation are normally articulated through a written code governing conduct, a statement of the professional ethic that establishes standards for behavior within the profession. One of various functions served by the code is that of safeguarding the relevant interests of society, which is of particular interest with respect to justifying the ethic. (That is not to deny, of course, that the ethic of a profession may serve the personal interests of members of the profession. It often does.) In some situations, society can realize the desired benefits only if the professional operates under special norms,[10] or so it is claimed; those cases concern us here.

Expertise

Huntington argues persuasively that the military institution has the three characteristics—expertise, corporateness, and social responsibility—to qualify it as a profession. He points out that the members of most professions have a diversified basic education supplemented by a formal, substantial period of advanced education that qualifies them in their occupation. The profession of arms indeed exemplifies this pattern. Military officers begin with a bachelor's degree (or complete one shortly after commissioning) and then progress through a series of military schools at different points in their careers if they remain on active duty. Those in leadership positions in the services have gone through a program of education that typically extends over a period of twenty years.

In the Army's system of professional education, junior officers complete a basic course that teaches fundamental skills and small unit tactics. After several years of professional experience, officers complete a lengthy course tailored to the officer's branch of service—infantry, artillery, signal corps, and so on. All U.S. Army officers of field grade rank must complete the Command and General Staff college course before being eligible for promotion to lieutenant colonel. Finally, between sixteen and twenty years of service, officers selected on the basis of merit attend a senior service college such as the Army War College at Carlisle Barracks, Pennsylvania, where the curriculum concentrates on strategy and international relations. At some point, most officers also receive an advanced degree from a civilian institution at the direction of the Army. The other military services pursue programs of professional development similar in nature.

The extensive educational programs of the armed forces focus on the unique character of military service and the peculiar sphere of military competence: the systematic application of force for political purposes. An effective commander of an army division must have a high degree of competence that requires extensive training, wide experience, and special abilities. The same is obviously true of the captain of an aircraft carrier or a group of ships in the navy. An understanding of the relationship between tactical alternatives and organizational capabilities is essential to competent performance, as is a comprehensive knowledge of the technological aspects of training for and conducting combat operations. Leaders in all the services must develop the interpersonal skills that allow them to motivate and command others. The direction of complex staff procedures and the command of large numbers of people in the stress of battle require capabilities normally achieved only after years of dedicated application and thorough study. One detailed analysis of command identifies four "learning objectives" for military leaders:

1. *Knowledge.* Information, data, facts, theories, concepts [includes military tactics, weapons capabilities, and logistical requirements].
2. *Skills.* Abilities that can be developed and manifested in performance, not merely in potential. . . . Includes technical, communications, information-retrieval, and some analytical skills.

3. *Insights.* Ideas and thoughts derived internally from an ability to see and understand clearly the nature of things. Necessary part of making judgments, of deciding, of "putting it all together," of "being aware," of wisdom, far-sightedness. . . . Cannot be taught directly, but can be induced by qualified teachers. Generally a product of education [and long experience] rather than training.
4. *Values.* Convictions, fundamental beliefs, standards governing the behavior of people. Includes attitudes towards professional standards such as duty, integrity, loyalty, patriotism, public service, and phrases such as "take care of your people" and "accomplish your missions." . . . The individual must derive values, like insights, if they are to have meaning.[11]

Thus, to be prepared for his responsibilities, a commander must be proficient in a variety of areas. He must be a "tactician, strategist, warrior, ethicist, leader, manager, and technician.[12] Another long-time student of the military profession notes that as a strategist alone, a soldier must be prepared for the following tasks:

1. Understand and support political *goals,* to insure effective coordination of policy and strategy.
2. Select military *objectives* that will lead logically to the achievement of political aims.
3. Allocate military *resources* and establish correct priorities.
4. Conduct war in a way that sustains *support* of the home front.
5. Maintain a proportional *balance* between the application of violence and the value of the political goals.[13]

A military professional prepared for high command is necessarily a person of unusual expertise, one carefully selected and one in whom the country has made a major investment.

At the turn of the century, during the Boer War in South Africa, a situation developed that provides a telling insight into the responsibilities of a military commander.[14] The case emphasizes both the strategic aspects noted in the previous list and the issue of moral responsibility that will concern us in the chapters ahead.

In South Africa, Britain faced a particularly unpleasant war against the Boers. The rapid defeat of the Boers had not come about as expected, so to hasten the event Britain placed in command its most distinguished soldier, the hero of Khartoum, Lord Kitchener. He was determined to bring the war to a rapid and successful conclusion, but he found some daunting obstacles. Many heads of Boer households and the able-bodied men of the Boer families had left home to join the Boer commandos, leaving behind the wives, children, and the infirm. Those remaining on the farms, where the rugged pioneers faced daily hardship in normal times, suffered greatly as the war dragged on. Perhaps of even more concern to Lord Kitchener was the fact that they also provided logistical support and intelligence to the Boer fighters. Kitchener ordered all the families removed from the farms and placed in great concentration camps, the infamous laagers, both to provide protection for the noncombatants and to further Britain's war effort. Unfortunately, the British failed to make adequate provisions for medical care, administration, or even food in the camps. Whether adequate care was even possible in view of the constrained resources and the ongoing war effort is uncertain, but in the months that followed, over twenty thousand Boer women and children died.

The brutal conditions in the camps were widely reported in British papers, and many people in England came to question the war and the actions of the British forces (a development similar to America's experience in Vietnam), making prosecution of the war much more difficult for the British government. Kitchener had made what he believed was a logical military decision in wartime, but he failed to give adequate consideration to the logistical and the concomitant moral dimensions of his decision. The results of establishing the concentration camps affected the achievement of political goals and changed the strategic situation. Kitchener failed to sustain the support of the home front. The disastrous results also raise the issue of a professional soldier's social responsibility.

Social Responsibility

The abilities of a professional officer corps are essential to the security of national interests in a world of shrinking resources and ideologically competitive states. That, at least, is the clear consensus of the American people, whose elected representatives have created and maintain the authorization for such an organization. That a strong and capable military force is considered essential to national interests seems undeniable since World War II, if one considers the huge budgetary appropriations for defense expenditures. As we have seen in recent years, any failure of the military is viewed with considerable alarm accompanied by demands for more effective training and improved leadership. Despite wishes to the contrary, the prevailing view in Western society seems to be that the use of force is an inherent aspect of the human condition.

Recent history certainly supports such a view. In 1987, under the narrowest definition, over thirty wars were underway around the world. Using a broad definition, we could have counted over one hundred. While the narrowly determined number decreased to about twenty-five in 1995, it rose again in 2000 to thirty-eight.[15] Modern society, curiously, does not seem greatly alarmed by the fact that people around the world face a much greater likelihood of destruction from conventional warfare than they do from the re-emerging threat of a nuclear holocaust.[16] An external observer of world affairs might well conclude that we have accepted the inevitability of armed conflict in world affairs. Although the twenty-first century opened with the United States as the overwhelmingly dominant military power on the globe, and despite the manifest benefits of peace, American power projection "wears a military uniform."[17] The end of the Cold War brought even more instances of conflict rather than recognizable progress toward peace.

The likelihood of armed conflict strongly suggests that military forces are essential to the defense of national interests. Nonetheless, historically a powerful military has also been a distinct threat to representative government. The history of struggles in Latin America provides many examples. American society since the Revolutionary War has manifested an antipathy toward the concept of a standing army and has traditionally harbored a deep-seated distrust of military professionals that has abated only in the last few decades. As a result, with very few exceptions, civil-military relations have been stable and unambiguous. In general, military forces and military leaders have always been an obedient arm of the state and strictly subordinate to civilian authority. The American military, reflecting the attitude of American society, has placed particular emphasis on the concept of social responsibility—the idea that professional officers must use their expertise only for society's benefit. More importantly, the civilian authority determines measures necessary to achieve that benefit. These observations support Huntington's contention that a particularly strong sense of social responsibility characterizes the profession of arms in the United States. Despite the trend of the 1990s toward a bureaucratic organization that regards military duty as a job, the idea of service to the nation remains a pervasive feature of career military officers.

Military professionals must also be competent to perform their duties. Sociologists observe that "expertise and the knowledge that underlies it are the coins of the professional realm."[18] The obligation to be competent constitutes another facet of the social responsibility borne by all military professionals. The criticality of their role as the ultimate bulwark of society, called upon to protect the nation, makes competence a moral imperative.[19] Here again, the parallel with other professions such as medicine and engineering seems obvious. The disastrous effects of incompetence generate continuous concern within the profession about individual skills and performance. The military's complex systems of schooling and individual evaluation, both of which continue throughout every member's career, reflect that concern.

During the 1990s, the demands on competence grew. The dramatic increase in United Nations peacekeeping operations, which always involved the United States military, made managing the peace a central concern of the U.S. Army. Subsequently, Afghanistan and the Second Gulf War provided the arenas for the application of new technological capabilities and unprecedented levels of integrated joint activity by the military services. The new challenges also brought intense discussion within the military about the jurisdiction of the services. Besides internal competition between the U.S. Army and the U.S. Marine Corps, the military services struggled with the definition of their proper roles. External jurisdictional competition resulted from the more complex requirements of peacekeeping and nation building in which mission success required expert knowledge in politics, civil affairs, cultural relations, law enforcement, and humanitarian relief as well as combat operations.[20] The U.S. military found itself cooperating with a variety of professions and organizations in a cascade of deployments—and sometimes competing with other agencies ostensibly pursuing the same ends. Both competence and professional legitimacy required more than the traditional warrior skills.

Corporateness

Few will question the argument for the corporateness of the military leadership. The officer corps itself evaluates and judges the conduct and competence of individual members. Huntington accurately describes the corporate nature of the organization in these words:

> The functional imperatives give rise to complex vocational institutions which mold the officer corps into an autonomous social unit. Entrance into this unit is restricted to those with the requisite education and training and is usually permitted only at the lowest level of professional competence. The corporate structure of the officer corps includes not just the official bureaucracy but also societies, associations, schools, journals, customs, and traditions. The professional world of the officer tends to encompass an unusually high proportion of his activities. He normally lives and works apart from the rest of society; physically and socially he probably has fewer nonprofessional contacts than most other professional men. The line between him and the layman or civilian is publicly symbolized by uniforms and insignia of rank.[21]

The foregoing, in brief, presents Huntington's argument for the claim that military career officers are members of a profession. Though it relies on a traditional approach to the analysis of professions, the case is persuasive. But just who fits into the category of military professional is not as clear as it might seem at first glance. Are naval ensigns professionals? Civilian ammunition logisticians in the Pentagon? Marine Corps master sergeants? Army nurses?

The military services have become highly complex organizations. The functions and traditions of the Air Force, the Army, the Navy, and the Coast Guard vary widely.[22] As is the case with even the paradigm professions such as medicine and law, the functions and jurisdictions of the occupation have changed over time. Andrew Abbott notes that professions claim authority over particular work, particular tasks, and that they compete with other professions.[23] He places emphasis on professional jurisdiction, the domain of social life "within which members of a profession try to solve particular problems by applying the special knowledge at their command."[24] Just as chiropractors, psychiatrists, neurologists, and homeopaths once competed for jurisdiction in the health profession, and sought protection of jurisdiction under the law, the military profession has distinct subdivisions that compete, even as the occupation as a whole competes with other professions and activities (e.g., various law enforcement and intelligence agencies). The tasks at hand in pursuing homeland defense provide an example of competition with external agencies. The long-standing jurisdictional disputes among the military services provide examples of internal turf battles. The Marine Corps and the U.S. Army have a shifting boundary with respect to appropriate missions. Both have infantry soldiers and thus present options for missions requiring the rapid deployment of light forces. Both have armored forces as well. The U.S. Air Force and the U.S. Army have often disagreed about the development of aviation assets where jurisdictions are unclear. Both see close air support as a professional task for its own units. In one recent study, the authors claim that we should think in terms of the army profession, the maritime profession, and the aerospace profession.[25] These occupational groups compete with each other for missions and funding.

Within each of these major divisions of the American military, the vast majority of soldiers, sailors, marines, and airmen are in the lower ranks. They are not clear-cut professionals under the qualifying characteristics given above, primarily because they do not acquire and apply a significant body of theoretical knowledge and they lack self-direction and self-regulation. A distinctive evaluation system emphasizes the particular corporate character of the officer corps, as do the special authority and responsibilities noted in the commission and the oath of office. The senior noncommissioned officers of the services, however, show strong attributes of professionalism. To further complicate the picture, among the officers of the services are many supporting specialists, many of them professionals in other areas. Included are doctors, lawyers, veterinarians, finance experts, and a host of others necessary for the support and maintenance of a large, modern military force. An army doctor is a medical professional working in support of a military force. A navy lawyer is a legal professional working in support of a military organization. A practical distinction thus exists between the purely military professional and the supporting cast that provides services not wholly peculiar to the military.

Thus the lines demarcating the professional component of the military services are difficult to fix. Actually, a spectrum exists. To the degree that various rank levels and positions in the military possess those characteristics sufficient for classification as "professional," they should be considered professionalized. In general terms, the following appears to be true:

> There is no absolute difference between professional and other kinds of occupational behavior, but only relative differences with respect to certain attributes common to all occupational behavior. . . . [On this view] the medical profession is more professional than the nursing profession, and the medical doctor who does university research is more professional than the medical doctor who provides minor medical services in a steel plant. Professionalism is a matter of degree.[26]

I will focus on the officer corps, by and large, because the officer corps possesses to the greatest degree the characteristics usually cited for a profession. Officers constitute a clearly defined group, though obviously not all officers are professionals with respect to expertise and career commitment.[27] Officers comprise the most critical group in terms of decision-making responsibility, and the military ethic applies most forcefully and most significantly to them.

Another perspective that also suggests a focus on the officer corps is that of noblesse oblige.[28] The term refers to the obligations to act honorably that come with a conferred station. Under this view, the more power and authority conferred by a societal role, the more stringent are the moral requirements and responsibilities of the role. Because power corrupts, society's demands for moral conduct and character increase as the importance of the position increases. The principle is not a new one, as John Adams's comment concerning the public's "right to know" indicates: "They have a right, an indisputable, inalienable, indefeasible, divine right to that most dreaded and envied kind of knowledge—I mean, of the characters and conduct of their rulers."[29]

In the military sphere, the concept of noblesse oblige has nowhere been captured more dramatically than by the Israeli war hero, Nahum Arieli, who commanded an isolated unit on a critically important hill during the early struggle for Israeli independence. When the unit was overrun by a much larger Arab force, he ordered a retreat. To have any chance of success, however, the retreat had to be protected by covering fire, which meant a portion of the unit had to remain in position as the retreat commenced. The Israeli commander issued an order that has come to represent the ethos of the Israeli officer corps: "All enlisted men are to withdraw; the officers will cover the retreat." Only one officer survived.[30]

The concept that officers must meet higher moral requirements also supports my focus on the moral obligations of the officer corps. Here is where we will find the essence of military professionalism.

Other Views of Professionalism

The sociological approach to professionalism is one that views a profession as an organized group that is constantly interacting with the society that forms its matrix, which performs its social functions through a network of formal and informal relationships, and which creates its own subculture requiring adjustments to it as a prerequisite for career success.
  —Ernest Greenwood, "Attributes of a Profession," in *Man, Work, and Society*

This rather technical definition certainly fits the military, for of all groups in society it is one of the most obviously organized elements. Interaction with society occurs constantly, from recruiting programs to the reality of the military-industrial complex. The military performs its social function through a prescribed set of formal relationships and a vast, intricate set of informal relationships involving both governmental leadership (from the local to the national level) and the business community. As a corporate entity, the military is one of the largest consumers in American society. Military activities involve extensive purchasing, contracting, and interaction with business firms of all sizes. The military services have also produced a distinctive subculture with stringent demands for achieving success. All these observations support the contention that we do in fact have a military *profession* (or professions).

The military can also be included under general descriptions of professionalism such as:

Professionals are expected to be persons of integrity whom you can trust, more concerned with helping than with emptying your pockets; they are experts who by the use of their skills contribute to the good of society, in a variety of contexts, for a multitude of purposes; they are admired and respected for the manifold ways they serve the growth of knowledge and advance [or protect] the quality of human existence. . . . [P]rofessionalism [is] an ideal defining a standard of good conduct, virtuous character, and a commitment to excellence going beyond the norms of morality ordinarily governing relations among persons.[31]

As we shall discuss shortly, members of the military frequently see themselves as answerable to a higher standard than members of the general population.[32] They also recognize that they possess unique expertise and that they are to employ it only for society's benefit.

But we need to consider an even wider perspective. Most authorities would accept the following five elements as those constituting the distinguishing structural attributes of a profession:[33]

1. Systematic theory
2. Authority
3. Community sanction
4. Ethical codes
5. A distinct culture

The American military services appear to possess all five attributes, but that observation requires support. First, a specialized body of knowledge organized as systematic theory clearly exists. The areas of military expertise are leadership, strategy, tactics, weaponry, and logistics. The military educational system teaches these subjects in a progressive education program that extends throughout an officer's career, as we noted earlier. And, in their areas of expertise, military figures are accepted as authorities; the military organization, maintained and supported by a representative government, is clearly sanctioned by society. The nation supplies the military not only with the extensive material support necessary to an essentially "non-producing" activity (the military does not provide material goods or services for use by general members of society) but also with the people necessary to fill its ranks and accomplish its functions.

The ethical code is the subject we will turn to in the next chapter. Despite its uncodified status, a set of guidelines for conduct unquestionably exists for members of the armed forces. Whereas "culture" is a less precise term, we are all familiar with the concept of the military environment, which does indeed consist of specific "values, norms, and symbols." Special guides to behavior in social situations certainly exist in the military. The guidelines are not as rigid now as they were in previous generations, but they are extensive enough to fill books such as *The Officer's Guide* and *Service Etiquette*. Beyond the social rituals are the deeper norms of service with honor. And indeed the military probably finds its identity in symbols to a greater extent than any other group that might be termed a profession, especially if we accept that by symbols we mean "insignias, emblems, and distinctive dress; . . . heroes and villains; and . . . stereotypes."[34]

We have long associated one additional characteristic with professional activity—the idea that professionals are committed to their work in a special way. In Ernest Greenwood's words, "The term *career* is, as a rule, employed only in reference to a professional occupation. . . . A career is essentially a calling. . . . Professional work is never viewed as a means to an end; it is the end in itself."[35] Although Greenwood's claim is questionable (the phrase "a career on the stage" is certainly familiar), the point about a professional occupation being a calling is worth noting. This characteristic is an ideal attribute, of course. It goes without saying that many lawyers go into the legal profession as a means of attaining social position or further opportunity. Otherwise, so many lawyers would not forsake their practices for administrative or corporate positions, or for the pursuit of political activity. Just as obviously, some medical practitioners are more concerned with financial benefits and social pursuits than the practice of medicine per se. As many career military officers probably find their occupation an end in itself as do members of the traditional professions. Because of the relative lack of financial and social rewards, the military may qualify on this account more clearly than a number of other commonly recognized professions.

Professor Allan Millett has given careful consideration to the status of the military as a profession. As a result of historical analysis, he concludes that

> by the time the United States entered World War I, the professionalization of American naval and army officers had taken observable form in the organizational sense. Both services provided line officers with mid-career training in fleet and army operations at the Naval War College (1884), the Army School of the Line and Staff (started as the Infantry and Cavalry School in 1881), and the Army War College (1901).[36]

Millett notes that while there is no fixed set of attributes of a profession, the following seem to be included in most analyses:

1. The occupation is a full-time and stable job, serving continuing social needs.
2. The occupation is considered a life-long calling by the practitioners, who identify themselves personally with their job subculture.
3. The occupation is organized to control performance standards and recruitment.
4. The occupation requires formal, theoretical education.
5. The occupation has a service orientation in which loyalty to standards of competence and loyalty to clients' needs are paramount.
6. The occupation is granted a great deal of collective autonomy by the society it serves, presumably because the practitioners have proven their high ethical standards and trustworthiness.[37]

In the preceding discussion, we established that the military meets the first five criteria of our list. That the last criterion applies forcefully to the military is perhaps most obviously indicated by the responsibility and authority granted to the military organization to administer a large percentage of public funds and resources, and by the fact that the military services have been granted the authority to operate separate judicial systems.

Despite the points raised so far, a critic might say that a military career officer does not fit the tradition in which doctors or lawyers "hang out their shingle" and make their services available. The professional tradition is one in which a practitioner, possessing special knowledge and unique skills, is sought out by individual clients who put themselves in his or her hands. In this respect, the military professionals of today do not fit the pattern, because a single corporate client actually directs their activities. In fact, however, other professionals also increasingly depart from the traditional paradigm. Lawyers work for corporations, a situation in which the client becomes the directing employer. For many medical specialists, working for a salary or working for a hospital or medical organization is now the rule. Professionals frequently work with particular institutional groups and in corporate settings in which all capital goods are owned by the organization. Today fewer than fifty percent of doctors and lawyers are in independent practice. The traditional two-party arrangement—the professional and the client—no longer prevails in the public image as it did in the past.[38] That traditional aspect of the professional practitioner was never the distinguishing characteristic of professions in any event. Tailors, swordsmiths, and cobblers all hung out shingles as well.

In addition to the structural considerations already discussed in some detail, members of a profession accomplish three functions: they identify a problem and gather information concerning it; they reason about possible ways to resolve the problem; and they decide what to do (diagnose, infer, respond).[39] In the core competence of the military, which is the use of force, *diagnosis* consists of recognizing the situation at hand. That *diagnosis* can take many forms depending upon the service and the scope of responsibility of the service member involved, but the need to act against an enemy presents the starting point. An admiral might recognize the need to protect a major shipping lane and resupply route for a theater of war; a general might discern the need to attack cut lines of supply and communication, as General MacArthur did when he approved the Inchon landings during the conflict in Korea. A lieutenant might recognize the need to seize high ground that overlooks his attacking unit; and a fighter pilot might need to determine the best route to take to a heavily guarded objective. *Inference*, or reasoning about a problem, brings to bear all of the professional's expertise. Military leaders employ particular forms of analysis and decision making to reveal all the possibilities in responding to a requirement and accomplishing a mission. The *response* is the action that the unit selects to carry out the mission and thus solve the problem. Military leaders can select from a great array of forms of maneuver or formations that they have learned in the military education system or that they have learned through training and experience. Although the three steps can involve a complex and varied application of expertise, there is no doubt that military activity fits this functional model as well as the structural models noted previously.

Sociologist James Burk provides an additional consideration when he defines a profession as "a relatively 'high status' occupation whose members apply abstract knowledge to solve problems in a particular field of endeavor."[40] As a minimum, the designation as a "high status" occupation means the public has particular respect for the activity and holds the occupation in high regard. Burk goes on to say,

> My definition identifies three prescriptive factors that, when found together, mark an occupation as a profession. One is mastery of abstract knowledge, which occurs through a system of higher education. Another is control—almost always contested—over a jurisdiction within which expert knowledge is applied. Finally is the match between the form of professional knowledge and the prevailing cultural belief or bias about the legitimacy of that form compared to others, which is the source of professional status. We can refer to these simply as expertise, jurisdiction, and legitimacy.[41]

Moral Considerations

The security of the state was a continuous concern throughout the twentieth century. In the late twentieth century, security issues became such a concern that at times members of the government cited the goal of protecting national interests as sufficient justification for systematic deception of the public and lying to members of the House and Senate.[42] This is a point to which we will return when we examine the professional military ethic itself. For the United States, the devastating attack on the World Trade Center in New York on 11 September 2001 made security a major concern for every American. The destruction of the World Trade Towers revealed not only domestic vulnerability but also the necessity of combating extremist enemies abroad before they could organize and press the attack against American cities, the prime targets of terrorists.

The wars of the twentieth century had already firmly established the need for highly capable military forces led by a professional officer corps. The threat of global terrorism starkly underlines the necessity for a highly flexible, lethal defense capability. The hallmark of professional leadership for such military forces is the establishment of objective personnel management criteria based on ability, education, and experience rather than the considerations of birth, social position, and politics that prevailed in many armies of the nineteenth century, and in some even more recently. Morris Janowitz notes that "a professional group is more than a group with special skill, acquired through intensive training. A professional group develops a sense of group identity and a system of internal administration. Self-administration—often supported by state intervention—implies the growth of a body of ethics and standards of performance."[43]

Military professionals unquestionably have a strong sense of identity, reinforced by a certain alienation from the society they serve. The military services have developed extensive systems of self-administration, and they profess a set of ethical standards and rules that have developed over time. These characteristics relate directly to requirements for accomplishing the mission of the armed forces. Some members of the profession also see the military as guardians of deep values rooted in national character.

If we accept that career military officers constitute the members of a profession in American society, moral questions concerning conduct in warfare and in preparation for war become more pointed and possibly more manageable. We can then identify morally troubling activity and morally ambiguous circumstances as situations appropriately analyzed in terms of role differentiation. Alan Goldman has shown that professional roles can be surveyed in terms of the degree to which the professional ethic renders permissible, required, or forbidden actions that would be judged otherwise under the criteria applying to society in general. Such differentiation can then be examined in search of justification. As I have indicated previously, one of the more plausible means of justification appears to be an argument in terms of the fundamental values of society. That justification begins with the contention that professions exist to serve society's vital interests.

Examining professional ethics in terms of role differentiation appears to be a reasonable way to reveal the moral structure within which military professionals work. I will apply this analytical technique in the discussion that follows. For those who believe professional ethics are grounded in moral truth in some sense, examining the justification of role differentiation may seem to be beside the point. I contend, however, that we can better understand the limitations on conduct imposed by the professional ethic by understanding the concept of role differentiation as it applies to the military.

Let me review briefly points I have already made. The reasoning is as follows. The professional serves a social need in the performance of his or her function. One can thus argue that the status of being a professional, granted through society and its institutions, is a function of social needs. The fundamental values of society reflect these needs (though that is not to say that values are reducible to needs). In any particular society, special norms required by professional functions should be justifiable in terms of the society's basic values. That is perhaps the most significant aspect of being a professional and a professional group—the consequent existence of a particular moral relationship between the professional and the society within which he or she functions.

Because professions are social institutions, the most obvious source of justification for professional activity lies in the values of society. In other than repressive totalitarian states, such values primarily determine social institutions. As the values of society govern the modes of social activity, so too the values of a particular group within society establish modes of activity for the group. One major feature of professional groups is that they have distinctive values generated by the professional activity that tend to produce an explicit ethic. In many cases, such as those of lawyers, doctors, judges, and the military, special norms do govern the activity. To be rationally justifiable, the moral norms must be internally consistent, they must be necessary for the performance of the professional function, and they must be consistent with the values of the society that the profession serves. I think it is reasonable to maintain that if the moral norms possess such coherence, then, within the context of the given society, sufficient moral grounds exist for the special norms involved.

Chapter Three

The Nature of Professional Ethics

Other Professions

How does the American professional military ethic compare with other professional ethics that play important roles in regulating spheres of activity in our society? Before we examine more closely the influences that have shaped the American professional military ethic and the set of standards that now guide the conduct of members of the military profession, we need to consider further the nature of professional ethics in general.

The concept of professional ethics presents no mystery. A professional ethic is a code that consists of a set of rules and principles governing the conduct of members of a professional group.[1] The code may be a formally published written code, or it may be informal, consisting of standards of conduct perpetuated by training and example. Although descriptions of what constitutes a profession may vary somewhat, all conceptions include the characteristic of self-regulation: "Every profession has a built-in regulative code which compels behavior on the part of its members."[2] And most professions recognize an ethic that is part formal and part informal.

Formally published codes are certainly common today, partly because any activity that desires the status of a profession appears to believe that having a formal code of ethics is necessary to achieve that recognition. One professional code mentioned earlier, about which we hear frequently, is the lawyer's *Code of Professional Responsibility*, which consists of a set of "Canons," "Ethical Considerations," and "Disciplinary Rules." Published by the American Bar Association, the code provides a model for state versions, most of which have the force of law. The disciplinary rules establish clear-cut, minimum standards of conduct. Violation of the disciplinary rules is often punishable under law. The ethical considerations establish interpretations of principles of conduct. They are aspirational in character and represent objectives toward which every lawyer should strive, but they also apply to many specific situations. The canons are very general normative statements concerning the standards of professional conduct expected of lawyers. All members of the profession should unstintingly serve justice, but how that is to be done in particular cases requires moving from the statement of broad ideals to the specific, concrete, grainy facts of particular circumstances. The ethical considerations and the disciplinary rules help serve that purpose.

The pattern for the lawyer's code is repeated in many other professions, including the *Code of Ethics for Engineers* published by the National Society of Professional Engineers and the standards established through the American Institute of Certified Public Accountants.[3] The engineer's code consists of five "Fundamental Canons," five "Rules of Practice," and eleven "Professional Obligations."[4] Its familiar structure follows the pattern of codes that consist of a statement of fundamental ideals, interpretations in terms of operating principles, and a listing of specific rules whose transgression is punishable through sanctions imposed by the profession. Altruism and social responsibility are not the only concerns reflected in codes. Some of the rules do not appear to have any broadly moral purpose, such as the engineer guideline that prohibits engineers from entering competitions for designs for the purpose of obtaining commissions for specific projects unless compensation is provided for all designs submitted. Such rules appear to further the self-interest of members of the profession.

Perhaps the medical profession has the longest tradition of adherence to a professional ethic, and we are all familiar with the existence of the ancient Hippocratic Oath. In the United States, the American Medical Association publishes the authoritative *Principles of Medical Ethics of the A.M.A.*[5] that establishes general standards for the conduct of members of the profession. Section 1, for example, states that "the principal objective of the medical profession is to render service to humanity with full respect for the dignity of man." Section 9, which states the principle of confidentiality, is more specific: "A physician may not reveal the confidences entrusted him in the course of medical attendance, or the deficiencies he may observe in the character of patients, unless he is required to do so by law or unless it becomes necessary in order to protect the welfare of the individual or the community."

In the medical profession, an extensive informal code exists as well concerning day-to-day interactions among doctors, ranging from the handling of consultations and referrals to the medical competence of colleagues. Doctors learn those standards through the process of professional socialization.

Codes of professional ethics such as those I have mentioned serve at least three distinct purposes: (1) they protect other members of society against abuse of the professional monopoly of expertise, (2) they "define the professional as a responsible and trustworthy expert in the service of his client,"[6] and (3) in some professions they delineate the moral authority for actions necessary to the professional function but generally impermissible in moral terms. The first and third purposes are accomplished primarily through defining the rights and obligations of the professional in relation to clients, colleagues, and the public. Broadly worded references to responsibilities to humanity are common in the statements of general principles.

The professional ethical code may thus both prohibit and permit various morally significant actions. The medical code professes high ideals, making adherents appear worthy of respect and trust, and identifies certain uses of medical knowledge as unacceptable. In many cases, the value to society of the professional function is such that, within the constraints established by (1) and (2) above, society authorizes the professional to perform actions forbidden to a general member of society. Doctors are entrusted to prescribe dangerous and addictive drugs, for example, and lawyers are allowed to conceal the facts of a crime when the crime was committed by a client. In an oft-quoted statement, Lord Brougham indicated the special status of the legal advocate more than a century and a half ago:

An advocate, in the discharge of his duty, knows but one person in all the world, and that person is his client. To save that client by all means and expedients, and at all hazards and costs to other persons, and, among them, to himself, is his first and only duty; and in performing this duty he must not regard the alarm, the torments, the destruction which he may bring upon others. Separating the duty of a patriot from that of an advocate, he must go on reckless of consequences, though it should be his unhappy fate to involve his country in confusion.[7]

Members of the military profession also have a special status. Officers routinely initiate actions that will cause death and destruction. They are also permitted to constrain the exercise of fundamental rights in certain situations. We will have to examine such issues carefully in Chapter 8, when we will consider the extent to which role differentiation in terms of moral norms can be justified for members of a profession. At present, I wish only to observe that a professional ethic will generally perform the three critical functions already noted: it protects society from exploitation, it enhances the image of the professional, and it may articulate a warrant for certain actions morally impermissible for a nonprofessional. The American professional military ethic, which we will discuss in the next chapter, serves all three purposes.

Formative Influences on the Professional Military Ethic

The institutions of society are not formed in isolation. The concerns, interests, and objectives of the people involved with the institution will mold its nature. Once established, of course, a continuing institution such as the law, the government, or the military in turn influences the society that gave it birth. However, there is no question that society shapes the institutions it generates. Thus, one of the major factors that has affected the American military institution is the set of values that fundamentally characterizes American society. The Prussian army of the nineteenth century possessed quite distinctive characteristics, as did the military forces of France when Napoleonic power was at its height. Members of the Japanese military leadership played major roles in Japanese politics until the end of World War II. Their attitudes and perspectives were strikingly different from those of the military services of the United States, even though essentially the same functional requirements affected their development.

Quite dissimilar rules and standards of conduct govern the military forces of different nations, which is to say that the military ethic varies significantly from one society to the next. While hardly an original insight, this fact is important because the most critical variable in each case is the culture of the society concerned. As values vary among societies, so, to some degree, do the codes of the professional military ethics involved. Accordingly, examination of the values of the society concerned is necessary in analyzing a particular professional military ethic, for the values of society constitute one of the three major influences that mold a professional military ethic. In the case of the American professional military ethic, the values of society play an even more important role than they do in many other nations.

Guidance concerning professional conduct begins, logically, with requirements imposed by the nature of the activity itself. With that in mind, we might disagree with the following claim: "It is my contention that the military cannot bestow legitimacy upon itself. This must come from society. If this is so, then the profession and professional values must be generally congruent with the values held by society."[8] Although the military certainly cannot bestow legitimacy upon itself, this position appears to be too strong if "congruence" means complete agreement. Congruence is unlikely, particularly in terms of *priorities* among values, because of the exigencies of the profession; that is, because of the functional requirements involved in the systematic application of force. These are essentially constant from one society to the next, and their influence probably produces professional values that are not congruent with those held by society. Compatibility, or noncontradiction, appears to be sufficient for legitimacy in the sense involved in this discussion—that of being sanctioned by society.

A study in the late 1970s revealed that most American military professionals felt that discipline, patriotism, and sacrifice are found "to a greater or much greater extent" in the military than in society in general.[9] If anything, that attitude has strengthened in the intervening years. Such a belief is not surprising if the military function imposes certain requirements concerning conduct. Samuel Huntington makes this point in his frequently quoted study, *The Soldier and the State*:

The military profession exists to serve the state. To render the highest possible service the entire profession and the military force which it leads must be constituted as an effective instrument of state policy. Since political direction only comes from the top, this means that the profession has to be organized into a hierarchy of obedience. For the profession to perform its function, each level within it must be able to command the instantaneous and loyal obedience of subordinate levels. Without these relationships, military professionalism is impossible. Consequently, loyalty and obedience are the highest military virtues....[10]

Without discipline, of course, obedience will not be achieved. We can conclude that the requirements of the profession demand loyalty, obedience, and discipline without referencing any particular social values. Today, members of the military are even more likely than in the 1970s to perceive the military as a more disciplined, more sacrificing group as compared to the larger society. Without dwelling on the justification of such views, we can reasonably claim that the exigencies of the profession influence, perhaps most pervasively, the content of any professional military ethic.

The third major influence arises from international law. Within little more than the last century, the laws governing the conduct of war have been codified and accepted by the states of the international community. The laws apply to all national military forces and thus constitute limitations on the conduct of their members. The regulatory guidance for American military forces specifically incorporates the laws, and the moral guidance makes adherence to the laws of war a duty. Moral principles provide the foundation for the laws of war themselves, and those principles are specifically integrated into the professional military ethic through the incorporation of the laws of war. Thus, if such moral principles were not already incorporated into the foundation of the professional military ethic, they would be through the relationship between the professional military ethic and the international laws of war.

Given such disparate influences, can the resulting ethic be one that makes logical sense? If the ethic is to be practically useful in providing moral guidance for action, the provisions of the ethic must not contradict one another. Otherwise, application of the ethic will produce statements that a given action is both right and wrong, permissible and impermissible. Any such code will be incoherent and hence counterproductive in terms of regulating activity within the profession.

The coherence of the American professional military ethic is thus, in part, a function of the compatibility of the three factors I have identified as the most important in the formation of the professional military ethic: the values of society, the exigencies of the profession, and the laws of war. These three factors have largely shaped the professional ethical code that guides the conduct of members of the American military.

A Partially Differentiated Role

The professional military ethic resulting from the interplay of the three major factors reveals the differentiated status of professional activity. The American military professional fills what might be termed a partially differentiated role—one in which professional considerations will be given additional weight, so that in evaluating such considerations in conjunction with general moral criteria the moral balance may be shifted. To take an obvious example, general members of society would not sacrifice their neighbors on orders from the mayor. On the orders of superiors, military leaders may send their subordinates into combat situations that make death certain for some, perhaps many; and their role as military professionals is clearly a factor in decisions to obey such directives. For the military professional, the central goal of the profession remains the security of the state, and the actual or potential use of force constitutes the means of attainment. In contrast, for doctors, the central goal is the health of patients; for lawyers, it is the guarantee of justice insofar as the exercise of the legal rights of clients allows.

In pursuit of the central goal of the profession, members of the military in combat straightforwardly kill the uniformed enemy and directly cause widespread destruction of both government and private property. As a society, we consider such actions, within certain constraints, not only justifiable but obligatory. Underlying this fact, in our society, is the contention that in many cases the rights to autonomy and individual dignity represent higher values than the right to life itself.

Legally and morally permissible actions of organized military forces at times unquestionably override the rights of individuals. Enemy soldiers and civilians need not even be considered in coming to this conclusion. The rights to liberty and self-direction of an unwillingly drafted military recruit are subordinated to the interests of society when the interest concerned is military security and it must be sought through conscription and mandatory military service. The legal right to free speech embodied in the First Amendment to the Constitution, generally regarded as a formalization of a moral right, is suppressed in peace as well as war for members of the armed forces. In such constraint, however, the right of free speech is not set aside. The right is still considered, but the decision maker gives greater weight to considerations involving security, morale, and discipline.[11] And during wartime, society justifies noncombatant deaths and widespread destruction of private property (our own as well as the enemy's) so long as we honor the constraints of the laws of war.

Acts of violence, possession of enormously destructive weapons, the imposition of discipline, and other aspects of military activity are morally and often legally impermissible for general members of society unless they are forced into a military role (e.g., a *levée en masse* or partisan warfare). Since certain actions expected of members of the military are morally impermissible for general members of society, the role of the military must be either fully differentiated (in which case only the professional ethic is to be considered in making moral decisions in the context of professional activity) or partially differentiated. If the military role were fully differentiated on the basis of functional requirements alone, and such differentiation were somehow morally consistent with serving society's interests, analysis of the ethical dimensions of the profession and application of the professional military ethic would be relatively clear-cut. For the American military, however, military necessity and the demands of warfare are not the sole basis of the professional military ethic, which will be obvious when we articulate the provisions of the ethic. Both the values of society and the moral principles underlying the laws of war have affected the content of the professional military ethic. Because it appears unreasonable at first glance to conclude that the professional military ethic includes the entire structure of the American value system and the moral principles underlying the laws of war, one suspects that it is best described as partially differentiated. Thus, while role-specific considerations may be given additional weight in making moral decisions, other moral considerations apply as well. This point is easily misunderstood, but I would argue that the American value system (which *does*, I think, include the principles underlying the laws of war) involves considerably *more* than the specifiable values, standards, and rules that constitute the professional military ethic. Although a professional code should help resolve certain kinds of moral conflicts generated by the professional activity, the provisions of the professional code and individual understanding of the code will sometimes be inadequate. Other moral considerations may apply in such situations, which again suggests partial differentiation.

The officer corps, American society in general, and the Supreme Court, as reflected in decisions concerning military authority, recognize that those in the military role do indeed act with special moral authority in applying force on behalf of society. If that is so, partial differentiation indeed appears to be the appropriate classification for the professional role. In any case, the professional military ethic reflects the assumption that the differentiated role is justified. Whether the partially differentiated role actually is rationally defensible is a question we will have to consider further in Chapter 8.

In summary, the military professional, in the preparation for and conduct of war, takes actions that would not be permissible outside the role. The function of the military could not otherwise be achieved by the armed forces. Because of their special responsibility to society, however, military decision makers weigh the significance of their actions in terms of general moral criteria that derive from the basic values of society.

When individual moral rights are subordinated, some claim that preserving the fundamental values of society provides sufficient justification. Thus, if the foundational values of self-determination (freedom) and individual choice are subverted or constrained by specific alternatives, and officers weigh their special obligations and their functional requirements against the violations of individual rights, such role performance constitutes partial differentiation. This, I contend, is the case with respect to the American military; within the context of American society, the military considers such differentiation justifiable.

Military Values

That a professional ethic serves at least the three functions discussed earlier appears to be a reasonable claim: (1) protecting society's interests, (2) enhancing professional status, and (3) identifying special norms. These three functions together should facilitate the achievement of the purpose of the profession, so long as the profession in fact serves society (and if an activity or institution did not, in terms of our discussion it would not be a profession). The three functions also appear characteristic of the American professional military ethic. A revealing 1970 Army War College study supports this view: " 'Ethical behavior' and 'military competence' (knowledge of assigned duties) are closely interrelated, and inadequate performance in one area contributes to inadequate performance in the other. This observation demonstrates the importance of professional ethics to long range mission accomplishment."[12] The long-range mission is to protect American society and preserve the state under the Constitution. The professional military ethic thus facilitates this purpose, and the War College study suggests that the professional military ethic is essential to the primary mission. The quotation also suggests that certain types of behavior enhance the military function. We can describe such behavior in terms of "military values."

Concerns with the functional aspects of military activity have thus contributed to the formation of the professional military ethic. Huntington maintains that, over time, performing a certain role will produce distinctive habits of thought that give those who fill the role "a unique perspective on the world."[13] He defines "professional military ethic" very broadly as the "attitudes, values, and views of the military man,"[14] whereas I am using the professional military ethic in reference to a recognized set of rules and standards. Huntington's definition suits his purpose of sociological analysis, and he goes on to establish a model of behavior in terms of the "military mind."[15] Because that term today suggests a hidebound, doctrinaire mentality that lacks imagination, indeed even the capacity for independent thought, I prefer "military perspective," a more neutral term. Military values, themselves products of functional exigencies, shape the military perspective in critical ways.

And what are "military values"? Are they values that presumably affect all military organizations? No one questions the military's responsibility for national defense, which is the primary function of the armed forces and the reason for their existence. According to the analysis of Bengt Abrahamsson, a respected sociologist, this responsibility produces the following in any military organization:

- A view in which the state is considered the basic unit of political organization.
- A stress on the continuing nature of the threats to the military security of the state and the continuing likelihood of war.
- An emphasis on the magnitude and immediacy of the threats to national security.
- Advocacy of strong, diverse, and ready military forces.[16]

Huntington's research produces the same conclusion concerning the first item on Abrahamsson's list: "The military man . . . tends to assume that the nation state is the ultimate form of political organization. The justification for the maintenance and employment of military force is in the political ends of the state."[17] The idea of the military as an agent of the state is central to the professional military establishments in both Europe and the United States. From such a belief, Huntington says, it follows that, for the military professional, "The military security of the state must come first. Moral aims and ideological ends should not be pursued at the expense of that security."[18] Although we need to explore further the relationship between moral aims and military security, it is clear that Huntington identifies state security as one of the primary values of a modern military force.

As one would expect, Abrahamsson's study of various national military institutions reveals them to be inherently conservative. "Military conservatism in part reflects dominant elements in 'classical' conservatism. It tends to emphasize order, hierarchy, and the 'stabilizing' institutions of society (church, family, private property). It maintains a pessimistic view of human nature and is dubious of the prospects for avoiding war. . . ."[19] Abrahamsson concludes that the most prominent characteristics of the military profession are the following:

- Nationalism
- Alarmism (the belief that armed conflict cannot be avoided indefinitely)
- Pessimism about the nature of mankind

Attributing pessimism to the military perspective is logical as well as empirically accurate, for, as Huntington points out, the military is charged with security. Viewing man's behavior from a perspective that focuses on threats to security produces an emphasis on the acquisitive, egoistic, nationalistic, and aggressive aspects of human behavior. Such behavior constitutes the threat to security and stability that generated the creation of the military institution, and that behavior necessitates, in both society and the military, organization and discipline in protecting society's interests. Thus it should come as no surprise that obedience and discipline are also primary values in the professional military ethic.

The military perspective reveals national sovereignty as a fundamental concept as well. The state, which legitimizes the professional military function, provides the ultimate moral and political ideal in the context of professional service. We commonly refer to this conception, of course, as nationalism. Although today many view nationalism as a relic of a Hobbesian world that is passing, it remains a distinctive feature of international relations and the military perspective. As Richard Falk notes, "the rise of global market forces is challenging the centrality of the state in the construction of the world order" and "transnational social actors are playing increasingly significant roles."[20] The United Nations struggles to prevent conflict and moderate human suffering. Interventions in the affairs of various states in the 1990s under the auspices of the United Nations have generated debate about limitations on state sovereignty, but the international community, despite progress in globalization, still functions on the paradigm of a community of independent states. Both NATO and the United Nations have employed the national forces of various countries in multinational operations, but the ultimate purpose of such collective actions remains the security of the international system—the community of sovereign states.

Such are the reasons, in brief compass, for saying that the following aspects of the military perspective are directly traceable to the exigencies of the profession. Empirical data supporting this view are highly persuasive.[21]

- Nationalism
- Pessimism concerning human nature
- Pessimism concerning the possibility of eliminating war

- Conservatism (emphasis on order, hierarchy, and social stability)
- Authoritarianism (stereotyped obedience given and expected)

Within this military perspective, the functional requirements of military activity make certain character traits essential for sustained and effective operations.[22] These are the traits identified previously: loyalty, obedience, and discipline. Physical courage, or bravery, is another such character trait, and, as we will discuss, honesty or truth-telling in relationships within a professional group is a further essential characteristic. And no military force can be consistently successful against serious opposition unless it is technically proficient.

The exigencies of the profession, however, are but one of the three major factors influencing the formation and evolution of actual professional military ethics. The fundamental values of the given society will also affect the professional military ethic by changing emphasis and by establishing limitations on the determining influence of the purely "military" values in professional decisions. We will return to this issue in Chapter 8. Each professional military ethic may have a different relationship with the international laws of war as well, so an understanding of any particular professional military ethic requires that it be examined carefully on an individual basis in its social and cultural context.

Chapter Four

The American Professional Military Ethic

The Sources

Not all young officers give serious thought to the professional ethics taught by the military education systems. Most simply accept the "rules" as established fact and either attempt to abide by them or choose to violate them for reasons of their own. After a certain period of time, those who make the military a career begin to identify themselves in terms of their role, which often makes objective analysis of "the rules" even more difficult and less frequent. That, at least, was true in my case. It seemed obvious to me that military decisions involving moral issues were appropriately governed by the precepts that structured the role of the professional military officer. The general precepts of the code guiding behavior were embedded in my moral awareness as a result of immersion in a firmly structured environment at West Point. The only issue was that of ensuring that one knew and understood just what the rules were. The education at the Military Academy had placed great emphasis on the rules.

Two years of combat service in Southeast Asia, however, generated numerous morally ambiguous situations, some of them deeply troubling, and the answers provided by the code as I understood it were sometimes incompatible with my intuitions of conscience. In some of those situations, the code provided a rationale for overriding such intuitive misgivings. At some point in my experience, though, the code itself was no longer enough and justification of the code became necessary. The nature of the conflict in Vietnam brought many soldiers to that point, I believe, and reactions to the

experience varied widely. Disillusionment, cynicism, and resent-
ment were not unusual ways of responding to the agonizing conflicts
that abruptly and consistently confronted both willing and unwilling
soldiers.

Men and women in uniform sometimes fail to recognize that
being a member of a profession imposes moral obligations. We will
explore those obligations in detail in this chapter, but we should
remember that the profession of arms makes a vital contribution to
society and to civilization. The philosopher Thomas Hobbes claimed
that people need society to escape from the state of nature, where life
is "solitary, poore, nasty, brutish, and short."[1] In an imperfect world,
armed forces are necessary to preserve society and the state. For
while the state brings order to existence, and in Hobbes's view makes
moral existence possible, international society remains a dangerous
arena. Despite the role of the military in deterring war and defending
with force when necessary, in the words of a thoughtful Army officer,
"if the [armed forces] merely replicate the state of nature, as in societies run by warlords, [they cease] to be useful to society."[2] The
armed forces may be quite useful to an individual, a particular leader,
but they will be marginally useful at best to the community. The
state of nature cannot defend against the state of nature; it can only
struggle for survival.[3] The armed forces must reflect the demands of
morality if they are to be consistently useful to society—indeed, if
they are not to be a danger to it. Military officers need to understand
that their commitment to professional activity brings a commitment to moral constraints. When we face enemies who accept no
such constraints, that covenant can be difficult to maintain. The
Second Gulf War was fortunately brief. Had it continued for some
time, fighting against an enemy that ignored the laws of war would
have placed great pressure on the conduct of Coalition forces. In
some instances, moral constraints would have been difficult to
maintain.

The military services today seek to deepen understanding of professional commitment by explaining what it means to be an officer.
The U.S. Army discusses the practice of being a commissioned leader
in terms of four interrelated identities: servant to the nation, member of a profession, warrior, and leader of character. The oath of office
that officers take upon commissioning sets the parameters for the

role of servant to the nation. The commission itself provides the foundation for service as a military professional, though the implications of being a member of a profession are complex.[4] The qualities necessary to lead men and women in carrying out missions that impose both great responsibility and great danger shape what it means to be a leader of character. The skills and attributes necessary to be successful in combat establish what it means to be a warrior. These identities clarify the application of the professional code that guides and inspires the conduct of men and women in uniform.[5]

My own experience suggests that a necessary step in preparing career professionals for the kinds of problems that soldiers faced in Vietnam is to make clear the code of the profession and its typical applications. The American professional military ethic has not been formally and systematically codified. The formal aspects of the code are found primarily in the oath of enlistment and the oath of commissioning (the wording of the commission actually awarded to officers), and the codified laws of war, though a variety of official publications contribute to the accepted guidelines for conduct. Informal elements of the ethic are taught through professional socialization. For commissioned and noncommissioned officers, that process takes place most obviously in the structured programs of the military's professional development system. However, the day-to-day activities in military units and the examples set by superiors provide the most telling influences. The role of military leaders at all levels is a critical element in the overall process of professional socialization. For example, the official policy of the military services concerning sexual harassment may be quite clear and specific, but if unit commanders indicate that sexual harassment is an unimportant issue or that they will condone harassment, their perspective will dominate in the understanding of the informal code governing their unit's conduct. As the U.S. Army War College study noted as the war in Vietnam drew to a close, however, a definite consensus existed within the American military concerning professional ideals that applied to the military services.[6] A consensus exists thirty years later as well, though many people in uniform would be hard pressed to articulate the professional military ethic as such. Most would probably refer to the published "core values" of the services and discuss how those values apply to the conduct of men and women in the military. For any of them, the oath would be a good place to start in searching for the professional military ethic.

The Oath of Office

Broad parameters are established in the oath of office itself:

I do solemnly swear (or affirm) that I will support and defend the Constitution of the United States against all enemies, foreign and domestic; that I will bear true faith and allegiance to the same, and that I take this obligation fully, without any mental reservation or purpose of evasion; and that I will well and faithfully discharge the duties of the office on which I am about to enter. So help me God.

The oath requires two commitments. First, the Constitution is the object of allegiance, to be upheld whether its authority is challenged from within or from without. Secondly, the officer is committed to perform the duties required in the professional role. Though the commitment appears straightforward, many officers give insufficient consideration to the implications of the political and moral principles manifested in the Constitution. Because the nature of the duties required in the role is open-ended, the professional officer's explicit commitment to support and defend the Constitution becomes particularly important. (In Chapter 8, I will contend that this commitment circumscribes the nature of the duties required in the professional role.) Commitment to the Constitution entails a commitment to the values and principles represented by the Constitution. Accordingly, the substance of those principles and values is critical to an adequate understanding of the American professional military ethic.

The Meaning of the Commitment to the Constitution

While it may be generally accepted, as I will argue, that characteristic values endure for any particular society, it is just as clear that values do change, even if exceedingly slowly. If we consider the Constitution as the manifestation of the fundamental values of American society, we might be tempted to conclude that the values and principles that it represents change with disturbing regularity. Analyzing the varying interpretations of the Constitution in court opinions has long provided a vocation for legions of legal scholars. As the political, economic, and social environment of our rapidly developing American republic changed, applications of constitutional law inevitably changed as well. Only through adaptation to new and unforeseeable circumstances could the Constitution continue as a viable blueprint for government. Aside from this obvious fact, however, the Supreme Court has been accused of imposing contemporary and transitory conceptions of morality in interpreting the Constitution. Such accusations appeared in Franklin Roosevelt's day and reached a crescendo during the era of the Warren Court.

Despite such changing views, certain fundamental principles and values are as clear today as they were when the Founding Fathers wrote the Constitution.[7] Interpretations concerning various aspects have changed—such as the authority of and relationships among governmental agencies—but basic principles and values have not. Constitutional scholars such as Leonard Levy support this contention: "Questions of constitutional law involve matters of public policy which should not be decided merely because of the original meanings in the Constitution. They must be read as revelations of the general principles that are expansive and comprehensive in character. Those principles and purposes are what was intended to endure."[8] The professional officer is particularly concerned with these principles. When officers commit themselves to the support and defense of the Constitution and acknowledge its fundamental authority as the basis of government, these basic principles and values constitute the object of their pledge. A brief examination of the way constitutional law changes will support the contention that the basic principles and values underlying the Constitution are essentially constant. As one commentator points out, "The Constitution was not fixed for all time in 1789," but rather "is a set of fundamental ideas by which orderly change can take place in a stable society."[9] The point is that whereas the circumstances in which constitutional law is applied may change, the guiding principles do not.

The watershed era of the Warren Court probably represents the most significant shift in interpretation of constitutional law. It provides the most obvious test of the contention that the basic constitutional principles change in application, but not in essence. The Warren Court believed that the government's obligation to take affirmative action to secure individual rights and liberties required positive constitutionalism. That term refers to the thesis that the Constitution is not a fixed, unchanging document, but is instead a guide to principles of justice. To defend those principles, the Warren Court imposed new law. Before the New Deal changed American life, and before civil rights became a national preoccupation, a different view of the government's role predominated.

Both the Fourteenth and Fifteenth Amendments contain sections granting Congress the power to implement the Amendments' guarantees "by appropriate legislation." It had been a principle of constitutional law since 1883, however, that this Congressional power was negative and corrective, rather than affirmative and preventive. In other words, nineteenth century Supreme Court decisions had established the doctrine that Congress' power was limited to the enactment of legislation to correct state actions which had already occurred, and which the Court found in violation of the Amendments' guarantees.[10]

The Warren Court introduced a momentous change from this view that altered the character of American life in important respects, but the principle of individual rights itself has not changed. The major innovation of the Warren Court concerned how the principle of individual rights was to be implemented. The 1954 *Brown v. Board of Education* decision might have ended the long-standing precedent of "separate but equal" decisions and begun the "affirmative action" era, but the content of the basic constitutional moral principles was unchanged. Whether individuals in general had certain rights was not the issue; rather, the question was the extent to which government at all levels must secure such rights against circumstances and events not in the scope of direct government responsibility.[11]

Rights and liberties are at the center of any analysis of the Constitution. The various political principles that structure American government (such as the allocation of powers between state and federal government, the separation of powers at the federal level, the checks and balances system, and representative legislation) all ultimately concern creating a system that protects the rights and liberties of individuals.[12] Discussion of rights can become confusing and ambiguous because rights can take various forms, so we should note that the rights under scrutiny here are both legal and normative. We are all quite familiar with legal rights or positive rights, those for which there is both social recognition and legal protection. They are empirical and contingent. Normative rights are those for which there is a moral justification. Constitutional rights are those that the Framers of the Constitution and subsequent generations have held to be not only normative and legal but also universal and indefeasible. The Constitution has consistently been described as a document created to protect fundamental rights: "Logically, the document is less a willful assertion of power than an act of sovereign self-restraint in behalf of a hierarchy of values that would find us willing to adjust our notions of economic well-being and national security as needed to honor constitutional rights."[3] The status of those rights and their significance beyond our borders are subjects we will address in the next chapter.

The concept of constitutionalism itself certainly belongs among the basic, unchanging principles represented by the central political document of the United States. The familiar preamble to the Constitution states that

WE THE PEOPLE OF THE UNITED STATES, in order to form a more perfect union, establish justice, insure domestic tranquility, provide for the common defense, and secure the blessings of liberty to ourselves and our posterity, do ordain and establish the Constitution of the United States of America.

The preamble makes it clear that the purpose of the Constitution is to secure liberty, justice, and the general welfare. The principle of constitutionalism holds that a written, comprehensible constitution that limits the power of government and of individuals and agencies in government is necessary for the maintenance of civilized society in which citizens can enjoy liberty, justice, and equality. The body of the Constitution both establishes and limits the power of the specified branches of a republican form of government, and in doing so, reveals a profound wariness of the power of government. Because agencies of the government have command over extensive resources, the potential for the abuse of power is always present, as we know all too well from repeated incidents during the last three decades of the twentieth century. The "checks and balances" of the Constitution are an overt attempt to preclude or minimize such abuses. The principle of constitutionalism maintains that, in the interests of liberty, justice, and equality, the constitution must be the final authority in the affairs of the state, embodying the fundamental values of the society in which it functions and reflecting the ultimate source of authority in republican government—the people. As established in the U.S. Constitution, the people—and only the people—have the indefeasible right to change their government. An understanding of the principle of constitutionalism helps clarify the critical importance of an officer's oath to support and defend the values and principles represented in our founding document.

The principle of individual rights is another of the fundamental values manifested in that document. It concerns those rights of man that are not to be denied by the government itself or by the desires of the majority. The principle is reflected most obviously in the amendments to the Constitution and in the function of the Supreme Court, which is why nominations to the Court are so closely examined. The Bill of Rights, the first ten amendments to the Constitution, embodies the doctrine of natural rights, which was the "hard core of Revolutionary political theory."[14] The Constitution forbids the majority or even the entire House and Senate to pass laws that impair the fundamental rights of individuals. The strength of this prohibition is clear in the First Amendment: "Congress shall make no law respecting an establishment of religion, or prohibiting the free exercise thereof; or abridging the freedom of speech, or of the press; or of the right of the people peaceably to assemble and to petition the Government for a redress of grievances." An examination of the wording of the first ten amendments supports the well-documented claim that the Bill of Rights was originally "intended to render certain rights immune from abridgement by legislative majorities."[15]

In addition to specifying the rights of individuals to certain basic freedoms, the Constitution created the institution of the Supreme Court. It is not implausible to claim that the powers granted the Supreme Court are primarily for the purpose of protecting individual rights, even, to a certain extent, against the will of the majority. Through this institution, the mechanism of government and law has a "limited mandate to correct mistakes made by State and natural majorities."[16] In so doing, the Court serves to protect the rights of individuals. The institution of the Supreme Court, of course, will eventually affect the will of the majority, but it ensures that action will be taken only after deliberate, reflective, considered study. Both the amendments to the Constitution and the institution of the Supreme Court embody the principle of individual rights within the framework of the Constitution.

During the 1990s, human rights emerged as a prominent factor in international affairs. United Nations interventions in Bosnia, Kosovo, East Timor, and other areas of conflict were in response to massive human rights violations. Recognition of human rights in the United States and around the world makes it necessary to understand how they fit into our discussion of the professional military ethic. Whereas the preceding discussion makes reference to natural rights and the equality of all persons before the law, our Constitution governs but one nation—the United States. It applies to the regulation and protection of American society and the conduct of American citizens. Increasingly, dialogue about rights occurs in the context of universal human rights.

Discussions abound in which such rights are assumed to be self-evident, beginning with the seminal human rights document, the 1948 Universal Declaration of Human Rights produced by the United Nations. As we will see in our discussion of the laws of war, human rights have become increasingly prominent in this century via considerations of the moral limitations of governmental actions (though disturbingly paralleled by increasing violations of such rights). In its most general form, the doctrine of human rights holds that there are certain individual rights that obtain quite independently of any particular states, societies, or periods. Although we will explore that doctrine in some detail in the next chapter, some initial considerations will be useful here.

In any discussion of rights, specific elements become important: the holder of the right, the object of the right (that to which one has a claim), and the duty-bearers of the right (those against whom one makes the claim). Human rights are distinctive with regard to two of these three elements. Every human being qualifies as a right holder, and the objects of human rights include all other human beings and all human agencies. The identity and obligations of the duty-bearers vary depending on circumstances and relationships, but claims to at least noninterference apply to all.

Another core element of the concept of human rights is that human beings, the right holders, are all equally entitled to such rights because of their status as autonomous beings who are responsible for what they do. They have both equal moral worth and equal moral responsibility. Responsibility is important because what people merit in terms of treatment is a function of how they act, how they manage moral responsibility. When individuals—or states—act in ways that fail to respect the rights of others, they fail in their moral responsibility and they are accountable. Thus the murderer who has wrongfully taken the life of another person has failed in moral responsibility and is appropriately punished by society.

If we examine the nature of state sovereignty on the basis of the domestic analogy, famously applied by Michael Walzer,[17] we can say that states have rights as well, by virtue of being states. As Walzer put it, "As with individuals, so with sovereign states: there are things that we cannot do to them, even for their own ostensible good."[18]

The Peace of Westphalia, a treaty signed by the major European powers in 1648, inaugurated the modern state system in the Western world and heralded the principle of sovereignty that dominated world affairs until the end of the Cold War. The rights of states under this system "are summed up in law books as territorial integrity and political sovereignty." Walzer finds the foundation—and justification—for those rights in the rights of citizens: "The duties and rights of states are nothing more than the duties and rights of the men who compose them."[19] But we can make an even stronger claim today: the legitimacy of the state, and thus its authority to exercise rights in the international community, is a function of its credibility in protecting the rights of its citizens and the corresponding support of the citizens for the state and its political structure. The fundamental moral and political rights of the citizens of a state are, in this view, everywhere the same. They are the human rights possessed by all human beings.

Whether we focus on natural rights, civil rights, or human rights, an independent judiciary and reliable law enforcement provide the means to secure individual rights and social order. If people are to live together in some regulated fashion, government must have the authority to restrict liberty, to regulate property, and to protect the pursuit of happiness—though such interference is permissible only under and within the rule of law. We find the principle of the rule of law clearly reflected in the Constitution and in its applications; one need look no further than the Due Process Clause of the Fifth and Fourteenth Amendments for evidence. Additional consideration reveals the interesting fact that while the President as Commander in Chief controls overwhelming military power, and while Congress controls the power of the purse, the power of the Supreme Court consists entirely in the principle of the rule of law established by the provisions of the Constitution.[20] Thus, we can reasonably claim that individual rights secured by law constitute the central value reflected in the Constitution.

Though we can categorize the provisions of the Constitution in a variety of ways, the principle of constitutional authority is indisputable. Closely allied with it is the rule of law that we have discussed. The object of both, it appears, is to secure the principle of individual rights, itself a basic moral principle. Of preeminent concern are moral rights. David Richards claims that "[t]he Founding Fathers believed that the rights guaranteed . . . in the Bill of Rights were natural moral rights which government had no right to transgress. Man, they supposed, was foremost a moral person, and secondarily a member of a political union."[21] While natural law doctrine and the related concept of natural rights may no longer be the basis of legal theory in many cases, the idea of universal, inalienable human rights remains.

And indeed, this universal sense remains fundamental in the Constitution. The moral rights with which the Constitution is concerned "constitute moral reasons for action of a special weight and urgency."[22] They are "moral claims to kinds of individual needs and concerns which must be satisfied prior to other kinds of moral claims and which justify the use of force, other things being equal, in support of the moral urgency these claims involve."[23] Through the Constitution, these moral rights become legal rights as well. In that form, they are protected from unjust actions by the majority. Accordingly, "[m]ajority rule is not the basic moral principle of the Constitutional order. The basic moral principle is the principle of greatest equal liberty. Majority rule is justified only to the extent that it is compatible with this deeper moral principle, which constitutes a standard of criticism for majority rule."[24]

This conclusion, supported firmly by the content of the amendments to the Constitution, establishes the relationship between the concept of fundamental freedoms and moral rights. The latter take precedence within the constraint of greatest equal liberty for all. The principle of greatest equal liberty guides us in moving from the abstract principle of both the rule of law and of individual rights to actual practice.[25]

Although interpretations and applications of constitutional law are perpetually in flux, firm ground exists for maintaining that the broad principles of constitutionalism, representative democracy, individual rights, the rule of law, and greatest equal liberty are fixtures in our national understanding of the Constitution. Also evident in our national history and implicit in the provisions of the Constitution, which authorizes the raising of armed forces, is the firm belief that these ennobling values are worth fighting for and that the use of force in their defense is fully justified. That is the soldier's purpose. When military members pledge their commitment to the support and defense of the Constitution, they commit themselves, by logical extension, to the principles and values that form the basis of its provisions.

The Commission

The commission provided to military officers begins with the following: "Know ye, that reposing special trust and confidence in the patriotism, valor, fidelity, and abilities of [named officer]. . . ." The commission from the commander in chief continues, stating that "this officer is to observe and follow such orders and directions, from time to time, as may be given by me, or by the future President of the United States of America." The fundamental law of the United States is the Constitution, so that the commission confirms the supremacy of the Constitution in the commitment of military officers. Were the President or any other superior to issue an unlawful order, military officers would be obligated by their role requirements to disobey it. That obligation finds its moral basis in the commissioning oath.

During President Nixon's last, bitter days in office, some people were concerned that the military might support an attempt by the President to remain in power despite the demands of Congress and the courts. Anyone who understood the commitment of the officer corps to the Constitution, however, would not have taken the possibility seriously. An officer's loyalty is to the principles and values manifested in the Constitution, not to the person of the commander in chief.

The oath and the commission provide the foundation for the traditional idealistic code of the United States armed forces, the code I have been calling the professional military ethic. The Armed Forces Code of Conduct, promulgated after the Korean Conflict, also provides guidance for members of the military, but it has limited application because it concerns actions appropriate for those taken prisoner.

One note of caution may be in order at this point. The professional military ethic and actual behavior are two separate areas of consideration. That observation appears obvious, but frequently I find that discussions of what ought to be done in a specific situation appeal both to prevailing forms of conduct and to ideal standards of conduct. Sometimes those discussing the issue confuse the two arenas and make the issue more difficult. The relationship between standards and behavior is complex; its study provides a fruitful subject for sociology and psychology, but it is not our direct concern here. One reason the U.S. Army War College *Study on Military Professionalism* caused such concern was the revelation of the gap perceived by members of the military between recognized standards of professional ethics and actual behavior. At some point, institutional pressures that require behavior that is inconsistent with the traditional professional ethic will result in a change in the content of the ethic itself. That will occur, that is, if the professional military ethic and behavior are in fact mutually influencing. Elaborately formal codes in some professions sometimes appear to be designed for public consumption rather than self-governance.

The officers surveyed in the War College study, however, indicated the "present climate" was at odds with the existing ethic and the exigencies of the profession. Moreover, I would contend that, in some respects, it was also at odds with society's expectations of the military. To what degree we can attribute the problems of the early 1970s to the protracted conflict in Southeast Asia is a subject of debate, but most Army officers accepted the study as an argument for institutional reform rather than modification of the ethic. And reform followed, slowly, continuing into the 1980s. The U.S. Army War College study summarized the issues in this fashion:

It is impossible to forecast future institutional climates with any degree of reliability. Nevertheless, it is not unreasonable to state consequences of the present climate: it is conducive to self-deception because it fosters the production of inaccurate information; it impacts on the long-term ability of the Army to fight and win because it frustrates young, idealistic, energetic officers who leave the service and are replaced by those who will tolerate if not condone ethical imperfections; it is corrosive of the Army's image because it falls short of the traditional idealistic code of the soldier—a code which is the key to the soldier's acceptance by a modern free society; it lowers the credibility of our top military leaders because it often shields them from essential bad news; it stifles initiative, innovation, and humility because it demands perfection or the pose of perfection at every turn; it downgrades technical competence by rewarding instead trivial, measurable, quota-filling accomplishments; and it eventually squeezes much of the inner satisfaction and personal enjoyment out of being an officer.[26]

The Army did in fact recover from the running sores of Vietnam and, with the other military services, performed in spectacular fashion in the First Gulf War in 1991. The high operational tempo of the 1990s, however, made heavy demands on men and women in uniform. The result was a re-emergence of a number of the concerns presented in the 1970 War College Study. Studies at the turn of the century revealed that service members were again concerned with a variety of issues that could undermine effectiveness. Prominent among them were the trustworthiness of senior leaders, quality of life issues, and micromanagement by superiors. Information technology made possible dramatic advancements in battle effectiveness, but it also made extensive information available to higher headquarters and gave commanders the means to make a zero-defects mentality pervasive. Excessive operations tempo, under-funded training, and shortages of materiel and resources raised issues of quality of life and personal satisfaction.[27] These factors and others, such as inconsistent leadership in units, led to a dysfunctional level of distrust of senior leadership in the military services.[28] A study of attitudes among junior U.S. Navy officers in 1998 provides this summary:

> The reason that 88 percent of the junior officers we listened to do not aspire to command is that command doesn't look satisfying anymore. . . . Among the top issues identified by the JOs [junior officers] we listened to were: loss of job satisfaction, self-inflicted pain, micromanagement and the zero-defect mentality, erosion of benefits, and lack of confidence in leadership.[29]

Such developments make a focus on the professional military ethic even more important than it would otherwise be. The erosion of trust and confidence in officers in senior leadership positions will inevitably have a corrosive effect on military operations. The professional military ethic provides a set of standards for judgment that can correct misunderstandings or reveal necessary measures of reform.

Duty—Honor—Country

The discussion that follows focuses on the "traditional idealistic code" against which institutional actions are measured. We will examine the standards of behavior that military professionals feel they ought to meet, not conduct that fails to meet such standards or institutional pressures of a particular period that contribute to the failure to meet them.

To understand the code as it exists today, we need to remember its historical roots. In Europe prior to the nineteenth century, military officers came from the nobility. The tradition of the armed forces in America—where all men are considered equal—has been quite different.[30] The emphasis has been on ability and competence, which have been closely identified with character:

> Washington, almost from the moment of his death, became a legend symbolizing (among other things) the 'superiority' of American military leaders over foreign officers because of their greater strength of character. Conversely, this rationale declared that officers who proved unworthy were probably so because of some character deficiency.[31]

General Sir John Hackett, in his study of the American military, revealed another aspect of the professional officer corps. His comments also indicate that the pessimistic view of the nature of man and the likelihood of war has long been a feature of the development of the American military:

The years between 1860 and World War I saw the emergence of a distinctive American professional military ethic, with the American officer regarding himself as a member no longer of a fighting profession only, to which anybody might belong, but as a member of a learned profession whose students are students for life. With this view went the acceptance of the inevitability of conflict arising out of the unchanging nature of man.[32]

The distinctive American professional military ethic that Hackett discusses is customarily referred to in a brief, simplistic motto. "The traditional standards of the American Army officer may be summarized in three words: Duty—Honor—Country. The officer corps of today espouses this statement of professional ideals."[33] Analysis of what this motto means to the American military profession reveals considerable emphasis on individual character and certain virtues.

Duty. Duty incorporates the concepts of obedience and self-discipline previously noted in discussing the exigencies of the profession. Whereas self-discipline would apply to most professions, it is of fundamental significance to the military professional, for the demands of duty can be particularly heavy. They may require the sacrifice of one's own life and those of others—an aspect of daily existence in a combat environment. The professional commitment is one of "ultimate liability." The requirement for both physical courage and the courage to make difficult decisions is implicit. In light of such demands, members of a military organization recognize that obedience is essential for effective functioning. As one long-time student of military sociology put it, "Integrity and instant obedience are the *sine qua non* of the military institution."[34]

In the American tradition, the oath of commissioning indicates that an officer's duty is to the state and, in particular, to the Constitution. Duty assumes the subordination of personal desires to the requirement generated by the oath; that of defending the Constitution and through it the state, in a specific form. "As a member of a service, an individual accepts a series of narrowly defined duties to superiors and subordinates consistent with his responsibilities to uphold that oath."[35]

Honor. For American military officers, honor connotes integrity, not military glory or prestige.

> Its underlying values are truth-telling, honesty, and integrity. Implicit in "honor" is a sense of trust within the officer corps. Subordinates must be able to trust their leaders implicitly. The trust must be mutual if the unity and cohesion which are so crucial to combat effectiveness are to be developed. Requirements of combat demand high standards of honor, integrity, loyalty, and justice. The same applies to the military institution as a whole in carrying out the heavy responsibilities entrusted to it by the host society.[36]

The experience of recent decades sorely tested this aspect of the American professional military ethic. The substitution of appearance for substance, emphasized in the distant War College study and highlighted again in recent surveys of men and women in uniform, remains a concern for the profession and the public alike. The allegiance of military professionals was not doubted in 1970, nor the general devotion to duty. The integrity of the officer corps, however, appeared problematic. The armed services recovered from that experience, but the re-emergence of such concerns at the turn of the century not only provides reason to question military leaders but also confirms the central position of personal honor in the American professional military ethic. The actions of the two most visible military figures in the Iran-Contra affair of the 1980s, Lieutenant Colonel Oliver North and Admiral James Poindexter, troubled many because they appeared to betray the professional military ethic. The arena of national policy in which the two men operated was considerably removed from the normal range of activity of a military officer, but they were still presumably committed to the professional military ethic. In that context, personal honor remains nonnegotiable. The following analysis states the position clearly:

At the daily working level, an atmosphere of trust and confidence is essential for military organizations to operate effectively. . . . Mutual confidence and esteem are essential to a unit's esprit de corps . . . high standards of personal integrity must be nurtured so that mutual confidence can survive long periods of stress.

When orders imply substantial sacrifice and risk on the part of subordinates, they must have no lingering doubts of the commander's true motivations. To execute the orders effectively, they must accept his personal integrity without question.

Of course, the most obvious and perhaps the unique requirement for high standards of honor in the military profession has to do with the necessity of accurate reporting in combat. The danger of unnecessary loss of life in such situations is too obvious to warrant elaboration. . . . The advice of the military professional to military or civilian superiors must accurately reflect current situations; otherwise, the consequences can be severe.[37]

While Lieutenant Colonel North, in deliberately misleading members of Congress and others in government about U.S. activities in relation to Iran and the Contra movement, was acting in the capacity of a presidential advisor rather than that of a military officer, the last paragraph quoted above seems nonetheless forcibly applicable. Recent studies do not reveal an institutional crisis comparable to the Iran-Contra affair, but they do show that the leadership of the Army did not enjoy the trust of younger members of the profession to the degree that the health of the profession needed. National security suffered from the actions of Lieutenant Colonel North and Admiral Poindexter when they departed from their professional roles, especially the aspects highlighted by the motto, "Duty—Honor—Country."

Country. The country is the objective to which the performance of duty and the maintenance of honor are devoted. The third element of the motto "Duty—Honor—Country" re-emphasizes the concept that no particular government administration or individual commands the allegiance of the military. The country itself (the state) is the beneficiary of the services of the armed forces. Further, members of the profession subordinate personal welfare to the welfare of the nation. This principle follows from the fundamental purpose of the armed forces. Since successful accomplishment of assigned missions often means that lives must be expended, the exigencies of the profession obviously demand that the means employed in combat, including the expenditure of human lives, are precisely that—means. Because of the criticality of the function of the organization, its welfare must have priority over the welfare of individual members. Here again, however, the American professional military ethic is modified from the straightforward requirements of military activity, in which mission goes before all (which is to say that the security of the state justifies all). If functional requirements alone provided the basis for moral decisions, the accomplishment of assigned missions would have priority over all other considerations. That, however, is not the case in the American military, as the discussions of the laws of war and the values of American society will illustrate.

The commissioning oath makes clear that the values of American society as exemplified in the Constitution give substance to the American professional military ethic. While human rights are not referred to as such in the document, it establishes the political system in which individual freedoms, representative democracy, and equality are to be optimized. The amendments to the Constitution reflect many of what we think of as human rights, and the specifics of the Bill of Rights can be justified in terms of the fundamental human rights highlighted in the Declaration of Independence. The commitment to the country is thus constrained by conceptions of morality and "guided by an overwhelming commitment to constitutional process."[38]

Traditional Values

Within the context established by "Duty—Honor—Country," four more specific principles have developed that are also fundamental to the American professional military ethic. The principle of *professional competence* influences all professional activity in the American military. To the extent that any military organization becomes professionalized, technical competence becomes a central concern. Lewis Sorley argues that this characteristic of professions applies with special emphasis to the armed forces: "The nature of the military profession, and the responsibilities of the profession to the society it serves, are such as to elevate professional competence to the level of an ethical imperative."[39] To be capable of conscientiously striving to perform in accordance with the precepts of "Duty—Honor—Country," an officer must be competent to perform assigned tasks. The more capable officers are, the more successful they will be in living up to the other principles in the professional military ethic. Given the weight of responsibility shouldered by the military, no degree of competence short of the maximum possible can be declared acceptable in terms of the professional ideals.

Another fundamental principle is *civilian control of the military* by the elected representatives of the people. From this principle derives another that is far from unique to the American military but nonetheless basic to it. "The professional soldier is 'above politics' in domestic affairs."[40] If the integrity of the military is to be beyond reproach, *professional officers must not directly involve themselves in domestic politics.* On the surface, such a position appears somewhat naive. The military establishment is the largest institutional complex in the government of the United States, and the extension of the "military-industrial complex" in economic terms is most difficult to assess just because it includes so much.[41] Functional influence, however, is one matter; overt participation by an individual is another. The code forbids the latter. While the distinction is one of degree in practice, the services maintain the distinction with surprising effectiveness. Certainly, the military as an institution traditionally observes political neutrality.

A fourth principle that is basic to the American professional military ethic concerns *the importance of the welfare of the individual soldier,* which goes beyond utilitarian concerns. Such a principle might be expected in a society that traditionally has placed great emphasis on individualism. This principle is firmly embedded in the ethic as well as explicitly stated in the law. Article 5947, Title 10, U.S. Code, states that "commanding officers and others in authority shall take all necessary and proper action—to promote and safeguard the morale, physical well-being, and general welfare of the officers and enlisted men under their command and charge." Two aspects of combat in the Vietnam era also reflect this concern for the individual. It was not unusual in the jungles of the Cambodian border area or in the mountains of the central highlands to find American soldiers in the field eating ice cream flown in by helicopters. While such actions might reveal logistical mismanagement, they also reveal the extent to which the system attempted to "take care of" soldiers. The second aspect was tactical. The massive use of firepower reflected the concern (at times perhaps undue) with friendly casualties. Arguments continue concerning the degree to which manifestations of the concern about the welfare of uniformed members of society hindered the pursuit of military objectives, but the basis for that concern is firmly embedded in the American professional military ethic. In the southwest Pacific in 1944 during World War II, Japanese resistance on the coral island of Biak was intense, with the Japanese soldiers well protected in deep caves.[42] One such emplacement was an area about 500 by 800 yards referred to as the Ibdi Pocket, defended by about 1,000 Japanese. Instead of ordering casualty-heavy attacks, the U.S. commanders continuously shelled and bombed the Pocket from 1 June until 21 July. Although casualties were still significant, they were much lower than they would have been had the commanders not expended huge amounts of ordnance in reducing the enemy capabilities. In Vietnam, the attitude was epitomized by the dictum, "Spend bullets, not bodies." That policy was a function of public and Congressional relations at some level, of course, but "politics" was not the primary motive. Soldiers are members of American society who have value in their own right as persons. Lives of men and women in uniform are not to be risked without compelling cause.

The phrase "Duty—Honor—Country" thus represents the content of the American professional military ethic. Each term has particular connotations in the American context. The broad principles of civilian control of the military and that of political neutrality overarch these connotations, and the obligation to promote the physical and psychological welfare of the individual military member to the maximum extent possible within the context of mission accomplishment permeates all aspects of the motto. Lastly, in each of these principles, the concept of professional competence is required and assumed.

Provisions of the American Professional Military Ethic

The Uniform Code of Military Justice (UCMJ) constitutes a specific body of rules supported by sanctions that apply to the military.

Some might suggest that these rules are part of the professional military ethic. The UCMJ, however, applies to all members of the military, not just members of the most obviously professional component. It is more comparable to the laws of the state in relation to other professionals, which apply to professionals and laymen alike.[43] Nonetheless, the UCMJ defines honorable conduct in a negative sense by establishing what members of the military will *not* do. The professional military ethic, on the other hand, emphasizes ideals and positive aspects of conduct. Without question, the morality that shapes the professional military ethic also underlies the UCMJ, but the two guides for conduct are quite different.

The *Joint Ethics Regulation* (JER)[44] "provides a single source of standards of ethical conduct and ethics guidance, including direction in the areas of financial and employment disclosure systems, post-employment rules, enforcement, and training."[45] The document does in fact provide a code for all federal employees, which presents a set of principles for conduct:

CODE OF ETHICS FOR GOVERNMENT SERVICE

Any person in Government service should:

I. Put loyalty to the highest moral principles and to country above loyalty to persons, party, or Government department.

II. Uphold the Constitution, laws, and regulations of the United States and of all governments therein and never be a party to their evasion.

III. Give a full day's labor for a full day's pay; giving earnest effort and best thought to the performance of duties.

IV. Seek to find and employ more efficient and economical ways of getting tasks accomplished.

V. Never discriminate unfairly by the dispensing of special favors or privileges to anyone, whether for remuneration or not; and never accept, for himself or herself or for family members, favors or benefits under circumstances which might be construed by reasonable persons as influencing the performance of governmental duties.

VI. Make no private promises of any kind binding upon the duties of office, since a Government employee has no private word which can be binding on public duty.

VII. Engage in no business with the Government, either directly or indirectly, which is inconsistent with the conscientious performance of governmental duties.

VIII. Never use any information gained confidentially in the performance of governmental duties as a means of making private profit.

IX. Expose corruption wherever discovered.

X. Uphold these principles, ever conscious that public office is a public trust.[46]

The JER explains that the code has as its foundations a set of values, which are also specified in the document.

PRIMARY ETHICAL VALUES

Honesty. Being truthful, straightforward, and candid are aspects of honesty.

a. Truthfulness is required. Deceptions are easily uncovered and usually are. Lies erode credibility and undermine public confidence. Untruths told for seemingly altruistic reasons (to prevent hurt feelings, to promote goodwill, etc.) are nonetheless resented by the recipients.

b. Straightforwardness adds frankness to truthfulness and is usually necessary to promote public confidence and to ensure effective, efficient conduct of Federal Government operations. Truths that are presented in such a way as to lead recipients to confusion, misinterpretation or inaccurate conclusions are not productive. Such indirect deceptions can promote illwill and erode openness, especially when there is an expectation of frankness.

c. Candor is the forthright offering of unrequested information. It is necessary in accordance with the gravity of the situation and the nature of the relationships. Candor is required when a reasonable person would feel betrayed if the information were withheld. In some circumstances, silence is dishonest, yet in other circumstances, disclosing information would be wrong and perhaps unlawful.

Integrity. Being faithful to one's convictions is part of integrity. Following principles, acting with honor, maintaining independent judgment and performing duties with impartiality help to maintain integrity and avoid conflicts of interest and hypocrisy.

Loyalty. There are many synonyms for loyalty: fidelity, faithfulness, allegiance, devotion and fealty. Loyalty is the bond that holds the nation and the Federal Government together and the balm against dissension and conflict. It is not blind obedience or unquestioning acceptance of the status quo. Loyalty requires careful balancing among various interests, values and institutions in the interest of harmony and cohesion.

Accountability. DoD employees are required to accept responsibility for their decisions and the resulting consequences. This includes avoiding even the appearance of impropriety, because appearances affect public confidence. Accountability promotes careful, well thought out decision-making and limits thoughtless action.

Fairness. Open-mindedness and impartiality are important aspects of fairness. DoD employees must be committed to justice in the performance of their official duties. Decisions must not be arbitrary, capricious or biased. Individuals must be treated equally and with tolerance.

Caring. Compassion is an essential element of good government. Courtesy and kindness, both to those we serve and to those we work with, help to ensure that individuals are not treated solely as a means to an end. Caring for others is the counterbalance against the temptation to pursue the mission at any cost.

Respect. To treat people with dignity, to honor privacy and to allow self-determination are critical in a government of diverse people. Lack of respect leads to a breakdown of loyalty and honesty within a government and brings chaos to the international community.

Promise keeping. No government can function for long if its commitments are not kept. DoD employees are obligated to keep their promises in order to promote trust and cooperation. Because of the importance of promise-keeping, it is critical that DoD employees only make commitments that are within their authority.

Responsible citizenship. It is the civic duty of every citizen, and especially DoD employees, to exercise discretion. Public servants are expected to engage personal judgment in the performance of official duties within the limits of their authority so that the will of the people is respected in accordance with democratic principles. Justice must be pursued and injustice must be challenged through accepted means.[47]

The values established by the Department of Defense (DoD) in the JER clearly encompass a larger set of people than the military services alone and are worded accordingly. Nonetheless, as one would hope, none of these values are in conflict with the guidance published by the military. All of the current core value sets of the military services, to which we will turn next, were framed with a knowledge of the DoD *Code of Ethical Conduct,* but each service felt it necessary to identify values that specifically structure its particular military activity, narrowing the focus from the wider category of government activity.

In practice, the JER provides a *legal* guide for the conduct of all members of the Department of Defense. For its implementation, the military services have initiated education programs and appointed "ethics officers"—almost always lawyers—at every installation and in all large organizations. Although the JER provides the broad guidance noted and some of the rules to which military officers are committed, it functions as a legal code more similar to the UCMJ than to an ethical guide. When one goes to a legal office with a question about the JER, the issue does not concern what the professional military ethic requires, or even what the (little known) *Code of Ethical Conduct* requires: it concerns what the regulation allows and prohibits, with emphasis on the latter. The following comment indicates why reliance on regulations and legal rulings makes corresponding emphasis on a professional ethic critical.

The complete juridification of ethics would be a dangerous procedure—even if it were possible. In respect to much of the ethical conduct and the corresponding relations between people it is not even possible, for the fine play of scruple and discretion that is often invoked in ethical judgments cannot be reduced to rules or promulgated as unambiguous laws. Where the law attempts to do this, it often only succeeds in rendering the original ethical norm into a crude regulation that can have the opposite effect to that intended.[48]

The JER provides guidance for legally acceptable actions, but to conclude that an action not prohibited under the JER is therefore ethically acceptable is a corruption that members of the military professions should avoid. A firm grasp of the professional military ethic will make such a conclusion less likely. We cannot legislate morality or professional ethics.

The U.S. field manual, *The Army*, FM 100-1, establishes the U.S. Army's position concerning the conduct of soldiers by identifying seven core values central to service in the American military. Each of the values serves as a guide for both character and conduct for soldiers. Doctrine about soldier development in the army discusses the triad of *be, know, do*, which refers to a model that presents what kind of person a soldier should be, what the soldier should know, and what conduct is appropriate for men and women in uniform. The army's seven values apply to both character and behavior.

ARMY VALUES

1. Loyalty
   Behavior: bearing true faith and allegiance to the U.S. Constitution, the Army, one's unit, and other soldiers.
   Trait: unwavering allegiance to the Constitution of the United States of America, the Army, and fellow soldiers.
2. Duty
   Behavior: fulfilling one's military obligations.
   Trait: commitment to fulfilling all aspects of one's professional responsibilities.
3. Respect
   Behavior: treating people as they should be treated.
   Trait: the controlling conviction that all people possess inherent dignity and worth.
4. Selfless Service
   Behavior: putting the welfare of the nation, the Army, and your subordinates before one's own.
   Trait: steadfast adherence to placing the welfare of the nation, the Army, and subordinates before one's own.

5. Honor

Behavior: living up to the Army values.

Trait: reverence for truth (honesty), faithfulness to one's word (fidelity), commitment to justice (fairness), and internalization of the other Army values.

6. Integrity

Behavior: doing what is right, legally and morally.

Trait: the character trait of consistently adhering to the dictates of personal and professional principles.

7. Personal Courage

Behavior: facing fear, danger, or adversity (physical or moral).

Trait: the state of mind that allows one to fulfill professional responsibilities with self-possession and resolution despite personal risk, danger, criticism, and uncertainty.

Each of the services has published a list of core values. Those of the U.S. Navy and the U.S. Air Force are shorter, three values each, but the explanations reveal that the ideas are quite similar to those of the U.S. Army.

NAVY VALUES

Honor: I will bear true faith and allegiance . . .[49]

Accordingly, we will: Conduct ourselves in the highest ethical manner in all relationships with peers, superiors and subordinates; be honest and truthful in our dealings with each other, and with those outside the Navy; be willing to make honest recommendations and accept those of junior personnel; encourage new ideas and deliver the bad news, even when it is unpopular; abide by an uncompromising code of integrity, taking responsibility for our actions and keeping our word; fulfill or exceed our legal and ethical responsibility in our public and personal lives twenty-four hours a day. Illegal or improper behavior or even the appearance of such behavior will not be tolerated. We are accountable for our professional and personal behavior. We will be mindful of the privilege to serve our fellow Americans.

Courage: I will support and defend . . .

Accordingly, we will have courage to meet the demands of our profession and the mission when it is hazardous, demanding, or otherwise difficult; make decisions in the best interest of the navy and the nation, without regard to personal consequences; meet these challenges while adhering to the highest standard of personal conduct and decency; be loyal to our nation, ensuring the resources entrusted to us are used in an honest, careful, and efficient way. Courage is the value that gives us the mental strength to do what is right, even in the face of personal or professional adversity.

Commitment: I will obey the orders . . .
Accordingly, we will: Demand respect up and down the chain of command; care for the safety, professional, personal and spiritual well-being of our people; show respect toward all people without regard to race, religion, or gender; treat each individual with human dignity; be committed to positive change and constant improvement; exhibit the highest moral character, technical excellence, quality and competence in what we have been trained to do. The day-to-day duty of every Navy man and woman is to work together as a team to improve the quality of our work, our people and ourselves.[50]

AIR FORCE VALUES

1. *Integrity first.* Integrity is a character trait. It is the willingness to do what is right even when no one is looking. It is the "moral compass"; the inner voice; the voice of self-control; the basis for the trust imperative in today's military. Integrity is the ability to hold together and properly regulate all of the elements of a personality. A person of integrity, for example, is capable of acting on conviction. A person of integrity can control impulses and appetites. But integrity also covers *several other moral traits* indispensable to national service.
   • *Courage.* A person of integrity possesses moral courage and does what is right even if the personal cost is high.
   • *Honesty.* Honesty is the hallmark of the military professional because in the military, our word must be our bond. We don't pencil-whip training reports, we don't cover up tech data violations, we don't falsify documents, and we don't write misleading operational readiness messages. *The bottom line is we don't lie, and we can't justify any deviation.*

- *Responsibility.* No person of integrity is irresponsible; a person of true integrity acknowledges his or her duties and acts accordingly.
- *Accountability.* No person of integrity tries to shift the blame to others or take credit for the work of others; "the buck stops here" says it best.
- *Justice.* A person of integrity practices justice. Those who do similar things must get similar rewards or similar punishments.
- *Openness.* Professionals of integrity encourage a free flow of information within the organization. They seek feedback from all directions to ensure they are fulfilling key responsibilities, and they are never afraid to allow anyone at any time to examine how they do business.
- *Self-respect.* To have integrity also is to respect oneself as a professional and a human being. A person of integrity does not behave in ways that would bring discredit upon himself or the organization to which he belongs.
- *Humility.* A person of integrity grasps and is sobered by the awesome task of defending the Constitution of the United States of America.

2. *Service before self.* Service before self tells us that professional duties take precedence over personal desires. At the very least it includes the following behaviors:
- *Rule following.* To serve is to do one's duty, and our duties are most commonly expressed through rules. While it may be the case that professionals are expected to exercise judgment in the performance of their duties, good professionals understand that rules have a reason for being, and the default position must be to follow those rules unless there is a clear, operational reason for refusing to do so.
- *Respect for others.* Service before self tells us also that a good leader places the troops ahead of his/her personal comfort. We must *always* act in the certain knowledge that all persons possess a fundamental worth as human beings.
- *Discipline and self-control.* Professionals cannot indulge themselves in self-pity, discouragement, anger, frustration, or defeatism. They have a fundamental moral obligation to

the persons they lead to strike a tone of confidence and forward-looking optimism. More specifically, they are expected to exercise control in the following areas:

Anger. Military professionals and especially commanders at all echelons are expected to refrain from displays of anger that would bring discredit upon themselves and/or the Air Force.

Appetites. Those who allow their appetites to drive them to make sexual overtures to subordinates are unfit for military service. Likewise, the excessive consumption of alcohol casts doubt on an individual's fitness, and when such persons are found to be drunk and disorderly, all doubts are removed.

- *Religious toleration.* Military professionals must remember that religious choice is a matter of individual conscience. Professionals, and especially commanders, must not take it upon themselves to change or coercively influence the religious views of subordinates.
- *Faith in the system.* To lose faith in the system is to adopt the view that you know better than those above you in the chain of command what should or should not be done. In other words, to lose faith in the system is to place self before service. Leaders can be very influential in this regard: if a leader resists the temptation to doubt 'the system', then subordinates may follow suit.

3. *Excellence in all we do.* Excellence in all we do directs us to develop a sustained passion for continuous improvement and innovation that will propel the Air Force into a long-term, upward spiral of accomplishment and performance.

- *Product/service excellence.* We must focus on providing services and generating products that fully respond to customer wants and anticipate customer needs, and we must do so within the boundaries established by the tax paying public.
- *Personal excellence.* Military professionals must seek out and complete professional military education, stay in physical and mental shape, and continue to refresh their general educational backgrounds.

- *Community excellence.* Community excellence is achieved when the members of an organization can work together to successfully reach a common goal in an atmosphere free of fear that preserves individual self-worth. Some of the factors influencing interpersonal excellence are:

    Mutual respect. Genuine respect involves viewing another person as an *individual* of fundamental worth. Obviously, this means that a person is never judged on the basis of his/her possession of an attribute that places him or her in some racial, ethnic, economic, or gender-based category.

    Benefit of the doubt. Working hand in glove with mutual respect is that attitude which says that all co-workers are 'innocent until proven guilty.' Before rushing to judgment about a person or his/her behavior, it is important to have the whole story.

- *Resources excellence. Excellence in all we do* also demands that we aggressively implement policies to ensure the best possible cradle-to-grave management of resources.

- *Material resources excellence.* Military professionals have an obligation to ensure that all of the equipment and property they ask for is mission essential. This means that residual funds at the end of the year should not be used to purchase 'nice to have' add-ons.

- *Human resources excellence.* Human resources excellence means that we recruit, train, promote, and retain those who can do the best job for us.

- *Operations excellence.* There are two kinds of operations excellence: internal and external.

    Excellence of internal operations. This form of excellence pertains to the way we do business internal to the Air Force from the unit level to Headquarters Air Force. It involves respect on the unit level and a total commitment to maximizing the Air Force team effort.

    Excellence of external operations. This form of excellence pertains to the way in which we treat the world around us as we conduct our operations. In peacetime, for example, we must be sensitive to the rules governing environmental pollution, and in wartime we are required to obey the laws of war.[51]

The values of the profession, thus identified and described, are manifestations of the uncodified tenets of the professional military ethic that does in fact guide the conduct of members of the military. Although the U.S. military has not formally published a "professional ethic" as such, its components have no shortage of guidelines. As our discussion has noted, we have the Uniform Code of Military Justice; the Joint Ethics Regulation; the Code of Conduct; extensive regulations within every service; the core value explanations in publications of the Army, Navy, Marines, Air Force, and Coast Guard; and a variety of studies and publications that examine expectations about military performance. Although what should be included in the *complete* set of provisions of the professional military ethic remains subject to debate, American military professionals fully recognize some guidelines for conduct that apply to all in uniform. The following certainly apply to the professional identity of American servicemen and servicewomen.

- The Constitution is our first loyalty.
- Our highest priority is the performance of duty with maximum competence.
- We are persons of honor and courage.
- We place the welfare of subordinates before our own.
- We follow the orders of the country's civilian leadership.

Based upon our examination of the influences bearing upon the professional military ethic and our review of current publications (flourish of drums, please), I would articulate the "traditional ethic" of the American military profession as a set of principles. Military professionals

1. Accept service to country as their primary duty and defense of the Constitution of the United States as their calling. *They subordinate their personal interests to the requirements of their professional functions.*
2. Conduct themselves at all times as persons of honor whose integrity, loyalty, and courage are exemplary. *Such qualities are essential on the battlefield if a military organization is to function effectively.*
3. Develop and maintain the highest possible level of professional

knowledge and skill. *To do less is to fail to meet their obliga-*
tions to the men and women with whom they serve, to the
profession, and to the country.

4. Take full responsibility for their actions and orders.
5. Promote and safeguard, within the context of mission accomplishment, the welfare of their subordinates as persons, not
   merely as soldiers, sailors, or airmen.
6. Conform strictly to the principle that subordinates the military
   to civilian authority. *They do not involve themselves or their*
   subordinates in domestic politics beyond the exercise of basic
   civil rights.
7. Adhere to the laws of war and the regulations of their service in
   performing their professional functions.

Whether the American military professional should have a more
extensive and detailed self-generated set of standards, and whether
the Department of Defense should formally publish an officially
sanctioned code in addition to the current designation of the central
values of the military professions are subjects for debate within the
professional ranks. The seventh provision, however, represents a
modification of the professional military ethic in the twentieth century, the incorporation of the laws of war. The explanation for this
incorporation appears in the next chapter, but the implications of the
professional military ethic become more extensive and detailed as a
result. Coherence becomes a more problematic issue. Are the laws of
war consistent in themselves? And are they consistent with the
other principles of the American professional military ethic? In one
sense, the laws of war represent no more than another body of rules
such as the UCMJ. In another sense, however, the laws of war represent a set of rules for applying certain moral principles. By incorporating the laws of war, the American professional military ethic
has in fact incorporated the underlying moral principles. Accordingly, we must examine those principles if we are to understand the
professional military ethic.

In the chapters that follow, we will examine the compatibility
and consistency of the constraints on the behavior of military professionals created by the factors that molded the professional military
ethic: the exigencies of the profession, the fundamental values of

American society, and the laws of war. Most commonly, in recent discussion, beyond questions about the morality of military activity itself, critics challenge the moral coherence of the normative guidance for the military in terms of the laws of war. The prominent role of human rights since World War II has contributed to that concern. Fighting wars to defeat the enemy and respecting human rights appear to be uneasy companions.

Chapter Five

Human Rights and
the Just War Tradition

We have explored the influence of various factors on the formation of the American professional military ethic, primarily the exigencies of the profession, the laws of war, and the values of American society. We can clarify further the nature and functioning of the professional military ethic by examining its relationship to human rights and the just war tradition. The contemporary laws of war have their foundation in the just war requirements that have developed over centuries of Western history, which is why we will examine just war concepts as part of our consideration of moral issues affecting military professionals. Human rights come into play in this discussion because they are embedded in American values and our society's concept of the individual. They are also key aspects of the American understanding of the meaning and purpose of sovereignty. An additional link thus comes into view: the just war tradition protects the sovereign status of nations. The overlapping triad of constraints on war, individual rights, and the status of national sovereignty presents even more issues that we need to understand in analyzing factors that affect military decision making. Exploring these relationships will illuminate our discussion of the application of the professional military ethic.

Human Rights

Many people (including some in uniform) might nonetheless ask why a military officer would need to understand human rights. After all, death and destruction are the tools of the military trade. Some would say that concern about human rights should be left to humanitarian agencies and nongovernmental organizations, which should then address such issues during the period following a conflict. Concern with human rights appears to reflect a humanistic focus that could eviscerate the fierceness of the warrior ethos—an essential feature of effective combatants. My response is emphatically different: rights are a centerpiece in applying principles of conduct because they are a means of instantiating fundamental American values, to include freedom, equality, individualism, and democracy. Identifying and respecting rights is how we make values operative in daily activities. Understanding how fundamental American values translate into guidance for action involves discussing rights. Military officers must recognize the importance of such values and their implications if they are to be competent professionals serving American society.

Our contemporary focus on terrorist threats has highlighted the rights issue. As soon as Americans took up arms against terrorism, the role of necessity loomed large. To fight terrorists who were without compassion or scruples, stern voices claimed, we must set aside concern for human rights. First, we do what we must to *survive;* then we concern ourselves with the more abstract issues of privacy and human rights. National security requirements in the "war on terrorism," the realist argument declares, make necessary measures that would not be acceptable in times of peace. Citizens, soldiers, and political leaders all had to grapple with that issue in the aftermath of 9/11. The brief discussion of rights in the preceding chapter made clear that individual rights, as proclaimed in the American Declaration of Independence, represent the foundational values established by the Constitution of the United States. We deny those rights at the peril of our national self-identity. Further, however checkered our record of behavior may be, we maintain as a society that our foundational values and corresponding rights apply to all people—not just Americans. In both our domestic and our foreign policies, we oppose the infringement of fundamental human rights. The U.S. military defends our nation and its values; therefore, if those values are important to military ethics, human rights are important as well.

The rights that we claim all human beings possess provide the link for American society between abstract values and specific guidelines for behavior. We realize our fundamental values by respecting and protecting the rights of individuals. As philosopher Brian Orend explains, "Rights are enduring grounds for treating the right-holder in a respectful way."[1] As we discussed in Chapter 4, a right is "a justified claim to particular treatment by other people and institutions."[2] A positive right usually finds its justification in the fact that it is the formal result of legislative processes. A normative, or moral, right finds its justification in the nature and actions of the agent, and human rights are a further subset of moral rights that are shared by all humans. One way to describe them is to say that they derive from the inherent dignity of human beings. Although human rights language serves many purposes today and in various applications may be expressed as "claims . . . options, entitlements, benefits, or merely as aspirations,"[3] in this discussion we will focus on the core concept of rights as justified claims. On this view, rights are compelling reasons to treat people in certain ways. Because human rights provide a way to translate abstract values into specific behavior that applies to all people, they are of special concern to military officers sworn to defend the Constitution and the values it embodies.

Beginning in 1776, Americans fought to establish their independence, their freedom, their sovereignty as a people. The Constitution documents and structures the political autonomy of the United States. It establishes the three branches of government—the executive, the legislative, and the judicial—in relationships that balance the power of the three. Our founding document also delineates the federal government's authority with respect to the states and specifies the rights of individuals that the government may not infringe. The oath of office, in which officers swear to support and defend the Constitution, incurs a commitment to preserve the nation's sovereign status in accordance with that founding document.

Despite the clarity of the Bill of Rights, rights issues are deeply complex, particularly in the international arena. Rights-talk unquestionably provides a means for advancing political agendas, and more often than not, though perhaps with the "best of motives," people use it for just that purpose. Claiming to protect human rights, states can justify aggressive actions or punitive sanctions that serve self-interested political objectives. Human rights–talk, however, invariably asserts that justice and human dignity are the goals at issue. At their core, American values and national aspirations support—indeed, insist upon—those goals.

To talk of human dignity is to talk about the worth and importance of the individual. In Bill Moyers's PBS series *In Search of the*

Constitution, interviews with both Supreme Court Justice William J. Brennan, Jr., and Professor Ronald Dworkin "emphasized that the fundamental value affirmed by the Constitution, and especially the Bill of Rights, was the value of human dignity."[4] The philosopher Alan Gewirth claims, "It is because humans have dignity that they have human rights."[5] Dignity can have various meanings, as a trip to the dictionary will attest, but here it has the same meaning that Thomas Paine had in mind when he called for recognition of the "natural dignity of man."[6] It is the same sense in which Thomas Jefferson and his contemporaries used the term as their new nation forced its way onto the world stage following 1776. The philosopher William Parent describes the human dignity protected by the Constitution as "a clarion declaration that all citizens are equal before the law, that there is no superior, dominant class of human beings, that the government may not treat certain groups under its jurisdiction with arbitrary contempt by denying them protections, on morally irrelevant grounds like race or sex, that it vigorously secures to others."[7] Parent's discussion makes clear that equality does not mean that the fate of neo-Nazis should matter equally with their victims or that hired murderers are as worthy as those they victimize. Nor is it sufficient to say that persons receive equal treatment if they receive due process under the law, for they may receive unfair treatment because of mistaken beliefs or prejudices accepted as truth by judges and juries. In Parent's words, "Constitutional due process . . . condemns governmental denials of life, liberty, or property based on beliefs or feelings that have no factual support."[8] Besides making a connection with the value of equality, a subject reconsidered in Chapter 7 when I discuss American values, I present the preceding points to make it clear that when we talk about human dignity or individual worth, we most commonly express what it means in terms of human rights.

With these points in mind, it is reasonable to claim that the values of American society, the human rights regime, and the principles of just war are compatible. I add the principles of just war to this set of issues because all three factors constrain the use of national power. Even though national power—political, economic, and military—remains a blunt instrument, it is today the only feasible means of defending values and human rights. We will look more carefully at just war in the next chapter.

Respect for rights extends to both legal and moral rights, though moral rights clearly have top billing. All agree that legal rights are local and contingent. On the other hand, advocates contend that moral rights at their center at least, that arena to which we refer with the term *human* rights, apply across the borders of communities and cultures. If we accept the claim that people possess human rights, such rights have priority over legal rights. We need to know about them.

To place in context the role of rights with respect to American society, the laws of war, the just war tradition, and the professional military ethic, we will trace the historical development of rights that has brought us to the beginning of the twenty-first century. Our examination will not explore whether we can provide adequate justification for any particular theory of rights, though that is a subject of interest for many. American society presents a pluralistic approach to justification; whichever supporting argument one favors, Americans certainly believe that justification *does* exist and that to respect rights serves the cause of justice. If that were not the case, if support for human rights were simply an effective means of serving our self-interest, as "realists" claim, then we would abandon them when our self-interest so dictated. That view undermines the ethos of American culture, however, and runs counter to our national identity.

After reviewing the history of rights, we will examine the role of rights in international affairs and the relationship between human rights and the principle of sovereignty. Sovereignty comes into play in our discussion because some claim that human rights compromise the principle of sovereignty that has been the foundation of the relations between states since the Peace of Westphalia in 1648. If we can show that human rights and sovereignty do not necessarily conflict in the international arena, we can turn our attention in the next chapter to the moral character of the laws of war. We will then be able to identify additional ways to relate the laws of war (largely products of the just war tradition) and the values of our society, which are two of the major formative influences on the professional military ethic.

The Distant Past

To further our understanding of human rights and to be able to sort out behavior that respects such rights, we will examine the origins and development of the concept. We also need to understand how American values incorporated human rights. In pursuit of that understanding, we will trace the history of the development of human rights and what preceded the emergence of the concept. We begin in the ancient world.

If we go back as far as Homer's Greece, we will find nothing like our contemporary concept of human rights, primarily because the Greeks did not conceive of individuals as independent, autonomous beings. Every person existed as a member of a family, clan, or city. An individual derived any rights, privileges, and authority—indeed, identity—from that membership. No one conceived of rights that were "pre-political or pre-tribal."[9] Rights were specifically attached to one's station in life and were part of a conception of right order in the world, part of an objective right that one learned or discovered.

During the Roman period, the idea of a right order prevailed still, both as an aspect of the stoic view that whatever is, is right, and as the authority of Roman custom. The stoics maintained that the proper response for us is to accept the world as it is. As described by Gary Herbert, "Custom became, in effect, the Roman stoic substitute for nature; it became the unchallenged source of right and law in early Rome."[10] The idea of *individuals* having independence and liberty as moral entitlements apart from their status as Roman citizens had not yet appeared despite extensive thought and writing about natural law in later periods of the empire. The nature of that discussion appears in this excerpt from the *Institutes of Justinian* in the sixth century:

> The law of nature *(ius naturale)* is the law instilled by nature in all creatures. It is not merely for mankind but for all creatures of the sky, earth and sea. From it comes intercourse between male and female, which we call marriage; also the bearing and bringing up of children. Observation shows that other animals also acknowledge its force. The law of all peoples *(ius gentium)* and the law of the state *(ius civile)* are distinguished as follows. All peoples with laws and customs apply law which is partly theirs alone and partly shared by all mankind. The law which each people makes for itself is special to its own state. It is called "state law," the law peculiar to that state. But the law which natural reason *(naturalis ratio)* makes for all mankind is applied

the same everywhere. It is called "the law of all peoples" because it is common to every nation.[11]

The natural law or natural right that Justinian describes has no moral qualities and does not focus on individuals; it is simply an aspect of the natural order of existence, though clearly it applies universally. In that sense, the Roman concept of natural law laid the groundwork for the eventual emergence of the idea of an individual's natural rights. Rights that have a moral character, which is to say rights specifying what *ought* to be, did not appear until the Middle Ages.

Although generalization is dangerous in speaking of a period as various and extensive as the Middle Ages, we can reasonably say that the Catholic Church came to dominate many aspects of Western existence and certainly the considerations of natural law and the role of the individual. The Church guided the soul, and the sovereign guided civil existence. The sovereign ruled, of course, by the grace of God, though some sovereigns were more grateful for that fact than others. The Middle Ages generated deeply involved discussions of rights (e.g., the Franciscan/papal controversy over whether the right to property was a natural right or a civil right),[12] but such conceptions provided only the structure from which the idea of a universal right was to emerge in the seventeenth century. The Church leader Thomas Aquinas contributed part of that structure in explaining that human beings could come to know aspects of divine law through reason. Until the fourteenth century, God's will was known through revelation, primarily by means of the Bible and the Catholic Church hierarchy. Aquinas defended the thesis that through reason individuals could come to an understanding of divine truth by studying the world around them. God's creation itself could provide revelation to human reason. That development marked a shift to a focus on the individual and toward the idea of rights that we have today—a shift reinforced by the Protestant Reformation and its emphasis on the individual's direct relationship with God.

The profound change in attitudes cascaded in the Renaissance, the period beginning in the fifteenth century that brought a burst of creative expression and individual assertion. The end of feudalism, the invention of the printing press, the rediscovery of the Classical World, and many other momentous developments generated energy that transfigured the face of Europe. The remarkable achievements of Leonardo da Vinci, Michelangelo, Francis Bacon, and Copernicus in art and imagination led the way. Renaissance humanism represents the essential spirit of the many transformations in the social fabric, political structure, religious perspective, and art, that followed the end of the Middle Ages. Central to Renaissance humanism was the concept of human dignity and the role of man as the master of nature. Free inquiry and a new confidence in human possibilities arose that further prepared the way for the individualism that marked the Enlightenment period. As the Renaissance gave way to that era, the delineation of our modern conception of rights took a major step forward in the work of Thomas Hobbes (1588–1679) and John Locke (1632–1704).

The Modern Period

A great acceleration of change began in the seventeenth century. For the purposes of our discussion of rights, I will refer to it as the beginning of the "modern period," which extends from the mid-seventeenth century to the mid-twentieth century. It begins with Hobbes and Locke because they advanced the idea that human beings have rights grounded in their nature as persons, not just as members of a family or community, or as a gift from God. Or to state the case in other terms, until this time persons were right-holders by virtue of having specific social characteristics, such as being a member of a tribe, a Roman citizen, or an adult male landowner. Hobbes and Locke argued that natural rights are a feature of all human beings— independent of any contingent status and aside from any theological foundation. Although Locke was famously cautious to avoid conflict with religious authority, his rational arguments for the existence of natural rights to life, liberty, and property resonated powerfully in the American colonies a century later. Nonetheless, in the view of both Hobbes and Locke, rights were no more than principles of self-interest that relied upon sovereign power for their realization. That is, in the view of these two philosophers, rights were not moral entitlements that existed before any civil association. For them, *moral rights* were human artifacts, created by a "social contract" and made possible by the state and the sovereign power that provided order and stability. Hobbes argued that natural reason makes clear that life in society—the only place a secure life is possible—is much preferable to life in the state of nature, where security is unattainable. Rational people thus create or join society, thereby establishing an implicit social contract under which they cede the use of force to a sovereign power responsible for security. In fits and starts, that is the kind of process that occurred in the United States during the political discussion of federalism.

At the same time that the American colonies established their independence, a watershed event occurred in Europe: the French Revolution. The people of France overthrew the monarchy and the aristocracy, trumpeting a new doctrine. The Declaration of Rights of Man and Citizen in 1789 proclaimed, "Men are born, and always continue, free and equal in respect of their rights." Those rights include the right to "liberty, property, security, and resistance to oppression."[13] The people who spoke for the revolution articulated a belief in the freedom and dignity of the individual; they insisted that the rights of men were absolute and limited only by the requirement not to infringe the rights of others. The privileges and power of the monarchy and the upper classes were swept away in a wave of violence and retribution. Unfortunately for the movement, after the initial euphoria of liberty and idealism, the Committee of Public Safety assumed governmental authority in France and, ostensibly to protect the revolution, instituted what became known as the Reign of Terror. In the name of liberty, the Committee of Public Safety itself harshly repressed all persons suspected of opposition, and the revolution self-destructed. The revolt against the French sovereign generated the same difficulty that Hobbes and Locke had been unable to solve: the sovereign powers invoked to protect individual rights were also grave threats to the very rights they were intended to protect.[14]

As a result of the French Revolution, the concept of rights changed in Europe. In Hobbes's state of nature with limited resources, natural self-interest led to the war of all against all, dictating the creation of society under an all-powerful sovereign (the only way to achieve a reasonable level of security). The revolutionaries rejected the idea of a sovereign with absolute power and proclaimed that all persons are morally equal in possessing inherent and inalienable rights to freedom, dignity, and property. Although they failed to translate those beliefs into a practical political structure, they focused the moral spotlight on individuals whose claims concerning fundamental rights placed boundaries on the authority of the state.

In the nineteenth century, influential voices criticized and sometimes rejected the new concept of rights that had emerged from the French philosophers and the revolutions in France and America. In Britain the social reformer Jeremy Bentham (1748–1832) savaged the concept of natural rights and rejected the claims made in the American Declaration of Independence. In an essay entitled *Anarchical Fallacies*, he declared "that there are no such things as natural rights—no such things as rights anterior to the establishment of government—no such things as natural rights opposed to, in contradistinction to, legal. . . ."[15] The German philosopher G. W. F. Hegel (1770–1831) argued for rights—but he contended that the interests of the state always supersede the rights of the individual.[16] Karl Marx (1818–1883), the best known communist theorist, rejected rights utterly, calling them a bourgeois tool for suppressing and exploiting the working class—with the right to property at the center of the web. He declared that people have no rights "outside of, or prior to . . . social and political community."[17] Within communities, he saw rights as an obstacle to human progress, particularly the right to property:

> The right of property is . . . the right to enjoy one's fortune and to dispose of it as one will, without regard for other men, and independently of society. . . . None of the supposed rights of man, therefore, go beyond the egoistic man, man as he is, as a member of civil society; that is, an individual separated from the community, withdrawn into himself, wholly preoccupied with his private interest and acting in accordance with his private caprice.[18]

After these and other attacks from both the left and the right of the political spectrum, concern about rights other than legal and political rights faded to the background during the latter half of the nineteenth century and the beginning of the twentieth, even in philosophical discussion. It was not until the great atrocities of World War II, the reaction against colonialism, and the increasing global awareness created by modern communications that the concept of rights and concern for the status of the individual again gained widespread attention.

The Regime of Human Rights

After World War II this concern again appeared on center stage when the United Nations (UN) came into being. The establishment of the United Nations, the proceedings of the Nuremberg Tribunal, and the promulgation of the Universal Declaration of Human Rights were "watershed events" that inaugurated the human rights era and changed the complexion of sovereignty in international affairs.[19] Today scholars in the People's Republic of China straightforwardly note, "The concept of human rights has been accepted in almost all societies and governments in the world."[20] The international community moved to this acceptance very rapidly in a shift that accelerated after the fall of the Soviet Union. The USSR's fall brought an end to the bipolar world that had limited action by the United Nations Security Council, the only body that can authorize armed intervention in the domestic affairs of member states under the provisions of the United Nations Charter. When both the United States and the Soviet Union could exercise veto power over Security Council proposals, United Nations intervention in the name of human rights was unlikely since American and Soviet interests seldom aligned. In the last half of the twentieth century, what we now refer to as the human rights regime assumed a leading role in shaping human rights issues. The global human rights regime that has come into being is a loose institutional framework of international groups, international treaties and declarations, nongovernmental organizations, social movements, and discourse focused on the protection and expansion of human rights throughout the world. The regime has come to play an influential role in international affairs.

The curtain rose formally on human rights in 1948 when the countries of the world, the members of the new United Nations, issued the United Nations Universal Declaration of Human Rights (see Appendix). Eleanor Roosevelt chaired the committee that produced the document. The Preamble of the Declaration recognizes "the inherent dignity" and "the equal and inalienable rights of all members of the human family." The first article states, "All human beings are born free and equal in dignity and rights." The second continues, "Everyone is entitled to all the rights and freedoms set forth in this Declaration, without distinction of any kind, such as race, colour, sex, language, religion, political or other opinion, national or social origin, property, birth or other status."[21] Mary Robinson, the former UN High Commissioner for Human Rights, captured the essence of the document in an interview:

> The thirty articles of the Universal Declaration set out the rights we now call human rights—to life, liberty and security, to equality before the law, to nationality, to privacy, to freedom of movement, freedom to worship or not believe, to own property, freedom of association and assembly, to take part in government, to work and to rest, to an adequate standard of living, to education.[22]

Almost all countries have now ratified a later document, the International Bill of Rights, which consists of the Universal Declaration of Human Rights (1948), the International Covenant on Civil and Political Rights (1966), and the International Covenant on Economic, Social and Cultural Rights (1966). Although the process of international ratification makes these legal rights in international law, human rights constitute the foundation, which is distinctly moral in nature. The International Bill of Rights is part of an attempt to translate morality into effective legal rights.[23]

Law protects, of course, only when most members of a community comply with the law's demands and when an enforcement authority exists to take action when violations occur. With the creation of the United Nations, new possibilities emerged. As most states now at least recognize, "Since its foundation, the United Nations has removed increasing numbers of important issues concerning collective and individual human rights away from the realm of domestic concern and intervention."[24] In the 1990s, beginning with the strong international response to Iraq's invasion of neighboring Kuwait and the ejection of Iraqi forces during the First Gulf War, the United Nations and the international community began to provide some of that enforcement capability. The NATO intervention in Kosovo and a host of peacekeeping actions around the world, even though many met with limited success, all involved the protection of human rights to some degree.

Human rights today surpass in moral authority legal and political rights that exist only as a result of transient legislative fiat. Whatever justification for the authority of rights that one proposes—religious, philosophical, secular—advocates claim that "human rights . . . solidify and institutionalize the normative aspirations of all mankind."[25] Those who believe, as Amy Gutman does, that "human rights are important instruments for protecting human beings against cruelty, oppression, and degradation," find them useful and applicable everywhere, in all societies, whatever the imputed sources of the rights may be.[26] Gutman maintains that a universal rights regime should be compatible with moral pluralism, which is to say that there are multiple acceptable moral arguments for claiming that we can and should support human rights. In her words, a practical human rights regime must be compatible "with a plurality of comprehensive belief systems."[27] Since that claim is fully in accord with commitment to the Constitution and to the professional military ethic, we will not explore the issue of justification further. As a society, we are firmly committed to human rights, and groups within our society advocate different grounds for such rights. Too often, the fact of such differences becomes the basis of questioning the need to honor human rights at all, but there is no logical reason to insist that there can be only one acceptable argument supporting the claim that all should respect rights. If we can agree on that point, the next step in our exploration of the role of rights will take us to the relationship between human rights and the principles of sovereignty.

Sovereignty

We live in an international community of sovereign states, all members of the United Nations. The United Nations Charter specifically prohibits intervention in the domestic affairs of member states, as these provisions of Article 2 make clear:

All Members shall refrain in their international relations from the threat or use of force against the territorial integrity or political independence of any state, or in any other manner inconsistent with the Purposes of the United Nations.

Nothing contained in the present Charter shall authorize the United Nations to intervene in matters which are essentially within the domestic jurisdiction of any state or shall require the

Members to submit such matters to settlement under the present Charter; but this principle shall not prejudice the application of enforcement measures under Chapter VII.

Despite this strong support for state autonomy, as Michael Ignatieff notes, "The catastrophe of European war and genocide gave impetus to the ideal of moral intervention beyond national borders."[28] In recent years, on a number of occasions the United Nations has acted to stop systematic, widespread violations of human rights within member states. Although the United Nations seldom deploys military forces without the consent of the parties in conflict, the Security Council asserted its authority under Chapter VII of the United Nations Charter frequently enough in recent years to make it clear that sovereignty is no longer an impregnable legal barrier. Under Chapter VII, when threats to peace yield to no other means, the Security Council "may take such action by air, sea, or land forces as may be necessary to maintain or restore international peace and security. Such action may include demonstrations, blockade, and other operations by air, sea, or land forces of Members of the United Nations" (Article 42). In taking action, the United Nations has sometimes infringed on the sovereignty claimed by particular governments, just as the Former Republic of Yugoslavia claimed that NATO nations violated its sovereignty in 1999 when NATO intervened in Kosovo to stop "ethnic cleansing." The Russian support of the Serbs prevented Security Council action in Yugoslavia, but the United Nations intervened in Iraq in 1991 after Saddam Hussein's forces invaded Kuwait; in Somalia in 1993 (following the United States' intercession) to prevent widespread starvation; in Bosnia in 1996 to attempt to stop ethnic cleansing; and in East Timor in 1999 to stop extensive killing and injury. These and other military interventions in the name of human rights have led to concerns that the human rights regime has provided the basis for actually undermining state sovereignty in ways that threaten international stability and security.

If the United Nations, a regional organization, or even an individual government can justify employing military force within another country to ensure that the citizens of that country are protected against rights violations by their own government, the argument goes, then international stability disintegrates and the rule of law has no force. The United States has long resisted the authority of any outside agency being empowered to intervene in domestic affairs in America or to become involved in the adjudication of domestic rights of American citizens.[29] Part of that view, which at first appears to suggest a double standard in light of American interventions in other countries, results from a belief that the United States provides a democratic government in which the will of the people legitimizes rights practices. Further in this reasoning, governments exist to provide security and to protect rights. If states have no protection against superior force, chaos reigns and peace has no hope. Those who hold this view argue for the self-determination of peoples. The fact that self-determination does not produce utopia does not justify casting aside the principle of sovereignty that has made progress and the security of societies possible.

The issues involved in this discussion appear prominently in the Nuremberg Charter, as David Luban has observed.[30] Article 6(a) of the Charter declares the classical doctrine of sovereignty in making aggressive war—the violation of sovereignty—a crime. That provision prohibits all violations of sovereignty, under all circumstances, so long as a state does not launch a war. Thus, a government could viciously abuse its citizens and violate their fundamental rights and nonetheless expect to be free from interference from the international community. At the same time, Article 6(c) outlaws crimes against humanity, even when they are committed against a state's own citizens. Luban points out that Article 7 of the Charter supplements this provision:

"The official position of defendants, whether as Heads of State or responsible officials in Government departments, shall not be considered as freeing them from responsibility or mitigating punishment." By making even sovereigns legally liable for their deeds, Article 7 denies that the sovereign is the sole source of law in his state; it thus denies the doctrine of sovereignty itself.[31]

Article 8 rejects the superior-orders defense. Although it is clear that Germany's actions in initiating unprovoked wars during the World War II period prompted Article 6(a), and that its brutal actions against minority groups prompted Articles 6(c), 7, and 8, it is also clear that a problem exists if we take the articles at face value. Article

6(a) indicates that states have no justification for violating the sovereignty of other states; the other articles mentioned indicate that sovereignty is *not* protection against intervention by other states. A charitable reading suggests that the Charter tells us that sovereignty can be violated *only* when large-scale crimes against humanity occur, but another response is to say that the implication of Article 6(a), that sovereignty is essentially absolute, is simply no longer the case. That principle, anchored by the 1648 Peace of Westphalia, holds that the sovereign is the ultimate source of law for his or her nation. In the Westphalian concept, "sovereign states exercise both internal supremacy over all other authorities within a given territory, and external independence of all outside authorities."[32] Given that status, one sovereign could not intervene in the internal affairs of another state with justification. One state has no jurisdiction within the confines of another. By the same doctrine, a sovereign is above the law and cannot be held personally responsible for actions as the sovereign. For centuries, a monarch or state leader could not be punished for *acts of state* since no higher source of law existed.[33] Articles 6(c), 7, and 8 demolished that long-standing doctrine, established the basis for bringing heads of state and those who followed criminal orders before the Tribunal, and paved the way for the human rights regime that was to follow. The Nuremberg Charter and the Tribunal's subsequent decisions made clear that human rights take precedence over sovereignty. After forty years of wavering on the issue, the United Nations undertook missions in the 1990s, thereby confirming that precedence in practice.

As further support, we can say that respect for the sovereign status of governments cannot be absolute if we accept that the rights of the state derive from the rights of its members. There must be a balance between the protection of human rights and state sovereignty. When states over time systematically fail to respect the fundamental human rights of their citizens by violating those rights, and fail to provide any remedy within their political and legal systems, the governments lose moral authority and legitimacy. At that point, a state can no longer claim the rights of sovereignty that would otherwise derive from the rights of its citizens. The state can no longer claim that sovereignty provides a moral and legal constraint on humanitarian intervention by other states or organizations. State sovereignty has thus become an instrumental value related to human rights. Michael Walzer agrees with this view when he says that "a state (or government) established against the will of its own people, ruling violently, may well forfeit its right to defend itself even against a foreign invasion."[34] The prohibition against infringing sovereignty thus has a high threshold, but a threshold does exist—and the protection of the rights of the citizens of the state provides the means to measure its height. Since intervention puts life at risk—both the lives of combatants and the lives of civilians—only violations by the government that cause extensive death and suffering among the citizens of the state (or an inability of the government to prevent such violations) can justify intervention. Following intervention, the involvement of external authority in the institutional governance within a state is sometimes necessary to protect human rights and to limit threats to international stability. The situation in Kosovo after the capitulation of Serbian authorities provides a recent example. The United Nations continues to play a key role in the governance of Kosovo, thereby stabilizing the political situation in the former Yugoslavia. Such gradations of sovereignty make clear that "no sovereignty" and "complete sovereignty" are not the only options.[35]

The fact is that in the contemporary world states are constrained internally and externally by rules and requirements originating in treaties and agreements that move the locus of authority to places other than the state government. To use mathematical terms, sovereignty has become a variable rather than an absolute value. The European Union (EU) provides the most obvious example of this fact concerning state authority today, but all states now face constraints on the exercise of sovereign authority. Members of the EU do not have exclusive authority over a variety of internal institutional actions, ranging from economic decisions about managing currency issues to political decisions about allowing access across the state's borders. Members of the European Union have agreed to a dispersal of sovereign authority to agencies outside the state, ostensibly in return for the benefits of membership in a multistate federation. One strong motivation for federation is arguably that of enhancing the environment for the protection of human rights.

At this point, one may well ask, "Why is this subject of particular concern to members of the military profession? Why is the human rights regime a moral issue in military decision making?" Increasingly in recent years, military officers have led deployments generated by concerns about human rights violations. If they are to perform their missions effectively, they will make decisions about protecting human rights. In such situations, they will need to understand the limitations imposed on acceptable courses of action by human rights considerations. This same aspect of contemporary military operations determined many tactical and strategic decisions in the Second Gulf War in 2003. Ethical considerations played a major role in the decision making of both military and civilian leaders in creating the war plan for Operation Iraqi Freedom. Human rights provide a direct way to explain the nature of those considerations. All coalition commanders instructed their soldiers in the treatment of civilians and the need to respect noncombatants in tactical situations. The strategic plan proceeded in increments in an attempt to secure the capitulation of the Iraqi regime with the least destruction and suffering for the people of Iraq. Unquestionably, such measures were not altruistic. Coalition leaders recognized that perceptions in Islamic countries and among Muslims around the world would have political repercussions. Concern about those perceptions played a large role in giving prominence to human rights, as did concern with maintaining the support of the American people. Considering the vocal antiwar sentiment throughout the United States, the Bush administration undoubtedly recognized that any avoidable devastation would have generated intense domestic political pressure to change course. Whatever actual motivations influenced decision making, these issues were major concerns because of the widespread acceptance of human rights perspectives.

We should also step back from recent events and recognize that human rights affect military professionals in another way. The laws of war that have influenced the professional military ethic and that guide the actions of combatants were shaped by concerns about human rights. The bulk of the law-of-war texts appears in the Geneva Conventions and other treaties written after World War II. To put in perspective the relationships between the laws of war (sometimes referred to as international humanitarian law) and human rights, we will need to examine the just war tradition—the source of foundational considerations in framing the laws of war.

Just War

Constraints on the conduct of war have a very long history that extends beyond Western culture. One historian notes that armies in ancient China conducted warfare according to "chivalric canons" and that a body of rules found in the Hindu *Book of Manu* regulated conflicts in India during the same period.[36] The subject of ethics in war also appears in the *Bhagavad Gita*, another ancient Hindu sacred text whose origins may reach back to 500 BC. In Western society, limitations on the initiation of war trace their origins to the "just war" concept developed in Christian ethics, though the instances of limitations on armed conflict through custom can be found in the history of ancient Greece and the early Jewish tribes as well as in the practices of the Roman Empire. St. Ambrose (339–397 AD) and St. Augustine (354–430 AD) are well-known early proponents of the view that participation in war can be justified.[37] St. Augustine provided the first well-known argument justifying and supporting the use of arms by Christians to protect the state. Early Church doctrine championed peace and nonviolence, but the newly Christianized Roman Empire, under attack by barbarians and heathens, found a pacifist stance untenable. Eight centuries after Augustine promulgated just war criteria, St. Thomas Aquinas elaborated on this doctrine, specifying three conditions that justify war:[38]

1. War must be waged under the command of sovereign authority.
2. A just cause is required. Those attacked must be at fault.
3. Those initiating just war must have rightful intentions, which is to say they must intend to promote the good.

The just war provisions developed over the centuries help clarify when war is a morally appropriate option for states, but just war theory, with many variations, remains widely debated. Since World War II, the terms "just" and "unjust" have frequently been replaced by the terms "defensive" and "aggressive." The most severe critics of just war theory are radical pacifists who reject all use of force in response to violence.[39] Other critics of the theory base their criticism on moral arguments as well.[40]

In addition to the concept of just war, which concerned *when* war was justified *(jus ad bellum)*, a body of custom developed in

Western society concerning *how* war was to be conducted once it was initiated *(jus in bello)*. Theological concerns structured the justification for initiating war, but limiting the *means* of fighting had a more conventional status. The guidelines largely developed through customary practices. The customs and usages of war that came into being, though often honored in the breach, were widely recognized and accepted. One can persuasively argue that the rationale for the development and observance of the laws and customs of war was prudential—an attempt to minimize the costs of war. No early proponents talked of human rights. Trade, human and material resources, and other economic considerations were certainly major factors in the development of mutually accepted restraints. Many customs endured because of strong common self-interest among opponents in maintaining limitations on the conduct of war. Instances in which combatants did *not* observe restraints illustrate the point. The Crusades provide one such example, amply recorded during the medieval period. European nations did not consider the customs of war applicable to the religious wars against the "infidels," in part because the adversaries shared no common interests. Slaughter and cruelty were pervasive.

The Dutch jurist Hugo Grotius (1583–1645), often referred to as the "father of international law," established the structure of the laws and customs of war that constrained aggressive and defensive national action for two centuries. He began the process of secularizing the just war tradition, focusing it on the preservation of state sovereignty. Along with such seminal figures as Francisco de Vitoria (1485–1546), Baltasar Ayala (1548–1584), and Francisco Suarez (1548–1617), Grotius provided the philosophical and legal basis upon which the provisions of the just war tradition came to be accepted *as* law (albeit customary law) applying to all nations. Not until the later nineteenth century, however, were the laws of war codified in writing. We will address that process and subsequent developments in the next chapter. Despite the lack of codification, however, the just war tradition presents a degree of uniformity over the centuries that remains today. The attention paid to the just war tradition during the Cold War led to its recognition as a moral theory, especially since writers such as Paul Ramsey, Michael Walzer, and James Turner Johnson have made its criteria evaluative tools in judging the conduct of soldiers and state leaders.

The provisions of just war theory fall into the two categories noted previously: *jus ad bellum* (the initiation of war) principles and *jus in bello* principles (the conduct of war). Just war theorists insist that all six of the *jus ad bellum* criteria must be met before the use of military force against another state can be justified.

JUS AD BELLUM

1. *Just cause.* Only certain reasons can justify war. In the latter half of the twentieth century, the acceptable reasons narrowed to versions of self-defense (one's own or an ally's), though United Nations actions in the 1990s have raised questions about international authority. The legitimacy of intervention in the affairs of another state to prevent genocide or widespread atrocities has been accepted by most states and has been recognized by treaty.[41]
2. *Right intention.* This criterion prohibits undertaking war for reasons of national aggrandizement; only the defeat of aggression and the prevention of genocide are clearly acceptable intentions in going to war. The reason for using force must be pursuit of the just cause.
3. *Legitimate authority.* Recognized and appropriate governmental authority must declare the war. The individuals and institutions with such authority are usually designated formally in the governmental procedures of a country (i.e., the head of state and/or the national legislative body have authority to declare war). Since the establishment of the United Nations, the UN Security Council has also had the authority to initiate military operations under the provisions of the UN Charter (signed by all sovereign member states).
4. *Reasonable hope of success.* In view of the extensive damage caused by war, using military force is not acceptable if a nation does not have a reasonable hope of success. This principle requires an objective evaluation of the likely consequences of going to war.
5. *Proportionality.* The projected results of fighting the war must outweigh the expected costs of engaging in war.
6. *Reasonable exhaustion of peaceful remedies.* This provision is often referred to as "last resort." Most just war theory proponents now require states to attempt all "reasonable means" to avoid war.

Reasonably evaluating projected results requires clear identification of the purpose of the war.

1. *Proportionality.* This principle applies on the micro level in the conduct of military operations. The amount of force applied must be proportional to the specific objective sought. The standard example rejects the use of a B-52 bomber strike to eliminate an enemy sniper. The means would not be proportional to the objective.
2. *Discrimination.* Combatants are never to target noncombatants directly. (Though the criteria for identifying noncombatants have never been fully satisfactory, the principle provides a means of limiting the violence of war.) Discrimination also refers to sparing religious and cultural sites protected under the laws of war.

The first three just war criteria relate directly to the issue of sovereignty, the concept that links our interest in human rights and our interest in the just war tradition. Just cause places a stringent limitation on the reasons that one state can cite for the justified infringement of the rights (its political sovereignty and territorial integrity) of another state.[42] Right intention identifies a further restriction in requiring that the motivation for infringement must in fact be the pursuit of a just cause. Limiting the authority for the use of force against another state solely to formally established governmental leaders (those wielding sovereign authority) further protects sovereignty by making military intervention a national decision taken at the highest level.

The other three *jus ad bellum* criteria indirectly relate to sovereignty in that they, too, push the bar high with respect to initiating war. By limiting the circumstances under which war is justified, they provide further protection for the sovereign status of every state. These brief observations make it obvious that one of the central functions of the just war tradition is the preservation of the system of states founded on the principle of sovereignty. When we get to the laws of war in the next chapter, we will address the role of the *jus in bello* principles, especially with respect to human rights.

The just war tradition existed long before the discussion of human rights began, but it evolved notably in the era following World War II. That experience, which involved the death and suffering of millions of noncombatants, trampled human dignity and offended the conscience of mankind.[43] The just war criteria have subsequently incorporated concern for human rights by making massive violations of such rights a just cause for the use of military force against an offending state. In that sense, human rights are compatible with just war constraints. More broadly, if sovereignty has as its purpose the protection of the fundamental rights of a people, then the protection of sovereignty provided by just war theory in turn protects human rights. The all-powerful sovereign of Hobbes's political theory has departed the scene. Support for sovereignty today reflects commitment to the principle of self-determination, which is a commitment to liberty. In principle, the authority of the sovereign in contemporary affairs derives from the rights of the people of the state. To infringe sovereignty is to infringe the rights of the citizenry. Even repressive governments implicitly honor that principle when their propaganda agencies invoke such principles to justify their domestic and foreign policies. Since both sovereignty and just war theory today incorporate human rights, the first three concepts are not simply compatible, they can in fact be mutually reinforcing. Violations of sovereignty violate individual human rights and thus become a clear object of moral as well as legal condemnation. Individual human rights provide the moral authority for the provisions of just war theory.

Rights issues accordingly have come to play a significant role in applying just war provisions. Sociologist Martin Shaw argues that human rights awareness and the military dominance of the United States have brought into sharp focus the danger that war imposes on individuals—combatants and noncombatants alike.[44] Fairly or not, America's dominance made combat errors involving civilians the target of criticism around the globe. From the Gulf War of 1991 through the invasion of Iraq in 2003, America itself became more casualty conscious and risk averse. The television pictures that vividly present specific events on the battlefield to viewers around the world have made the danger and suffering of war personal to distant audiences. Television impressions have immediate political impact. The feasibility of war in political terms has become in part a function of expected casualties among U.S. forces committed to combat and international perceptions of noncombatant suffering—collateral damage. In 1991 the images of slaughter and carnage on the road used by the retreating Iraqi forces appeared to affect the decision making of the Bush administration. In the Afghanistan war of 2001 only one American combatant died from enemy action, a result of careful planning by military leaders, and all commanders took steps to avoid civilian casualties. As in Kosovo in 1999, members of the American military employed tactics that minimized risk. The prominent sociologist Charles Moskos exaggerated, but he highlighted the new American attitude toward "force protection" when he said, "Being a taxi driver is more dangerous than being a member of the military since Vietnam."[45] Soldiers who fought their way from Kuwait to Baghdad in the liberation of Iraq would probably beg to differ with that characterization of their role, for fighting was fierce on many occasions, but the total of U.S. deaths in Iraq before the fall of the Hussein regime was low in terms of wars prior to 1990. Of the 129 who died before the "end of the major combat operations," only 66 fell in ground combat. The risk to American soldiers was statistically comparable to that faced by policemen in the course of a year,[46] though the guerrilla-style attacks against Coalition forces during the post-war occupation caused somewhat higher casualties. The numbers reflect a variety of changes, such as much improved weapons and equipment, but concern with casualties is now undoubtedly much greater than in any previous period of American conflict. Shaw points out that the number of enemy casualties and noncombatant casualties in recent American military engagements generally, while very small in comparison to the major wars of the twentieth century, are quite large in comparison to friendly casualties. He claims that political concern about managing public attitudes toward war has been the principal reason for risk aversion, but I would argue that heightened respect for human rights plays a role as well.

Sensitivity about casualties is a reflection of the human-rights era concern about respect for individuals. In this period of American military dominance, such concern clearly extends to enemy noncombatants—though avoidance of friendly casualties sometimes appears to have top priority—and has led to great emphasis on the use of precision weapons. After the death of some four hundred civilians in the Amirya bombing in Baghdad during the First Gulf War in 1991, coalition forces terminated air strikes against Baghdad. The use of precision weapons has made noncombatant deaths on that scale during war unacceptable, thus affecting the *jus in bello* calculation of proportionality and the application of the principle of discrimination. Although such expectations may be unrealistic, they are firmly in place. If war cannot be prosecuted without incurring extensive civilian casualties, the war is unjust under *jus in bello* principles as now applied. The Second Gulf War saw stringent efforts to minimize civilian casualties, especially in the extensive use of precision-guided weapons that few countries other than the United States can afford.

Human rights have thus had a major impact the conduct of war. One can debate a host of related issues, to include whether the concern about friendly casualties erodes the "warrior ethic" and whether heeding such concern immorally transfers risks from soldiers to noncombatants, but one cannot argue that the language of human rights today dominates discussion of the application of just war theory.

Human rights also provide the most direct means of applying American social values to the military profession. We use human rights to identify behavior that is inappropriate or unacceptable in terms of the values of American society. Such considerations thus become part of the environment within which the military functions; military officers must grapple with human rights concerns in adhering to the military ethic.

Chapter Six

The Moral Character of the Laws of War

The Laws of War and Fundamental Values

Are there moral principles that provide a foundation for the laws of war? I believe there are, and that the American professional military ethic necessarily incorporates them when it incorporates the provisions of the laws of war into the ethical guidance for military professionals. These moral principles relate directly to the concept of human rights, the subject of discussion in the last chapter.

Regarding armed conflict in general, the states that comprise international society consider all combatants bound by the laws of war.[1] Individuals who violate the laws are subject to prosecution in either national or international courts.[2] The American military, however, has a closer relationship with those laws, as we discussed in Chapter 4. From a legal point of view, the existing laws of war in treaties and conventions to which the United States is a party expressly bind members of the American armed forces. Under the U.S. Constitution, treaty provisions have a legal force equal to Congressional legislation.[3] And where no relevant treaty provisions exist in cases involving interstate interests, U.S. courts apply as appropriate the customary law of nations. For instance, a 1974 Department of Defense Directive states that "the armed forces of the United States will comply with the law of war in the conduct of military operations and related activities in armed conflict, however such conflicts are characterized."[4] Each of the military services goes further and issues its own implementing regulations.

One of the principal tenets of the American professional military ethic is unswerving adherence to duty, as we have noted. Requiring adherence to the laws of war as part of the duties of Americans in uniform brings to bear the moral principles that underlie those laws, which members of the American armed forces have a duty to apply whenever appropriate. Since no set of rules or laws can provide specific guidance for every eventuality, the "spirit of the law" is the deciding factor in those cases in which the letter of the law is not specific or not applicable. That is merely to say that we must apply the principles that support the laws of war to reach a justifiable decision when the laws themselves do not determine appropriate actions. Accordingly, the principles that underlie the laws of war are particularly important for the consistent solution of new and unexpected problems not specifically covered by existing provisions. Applying moral principles is part of the professional process of "applying knowledge and skills case by case" that we reviewed in Chapter 2.

To understand the American professional military ethic, we must attempt to achieve a clear understanding of those moral principles. Besides being necessary for some decisions, purposeful revision of the laws of war should come from such insight. With respect to our examination of the American professional military ethic, logical consistency will require that the moral principles underlying the laws of war be compatible with the moral principles derived from the fundamental values of American society, which play a major role in shaping the professional military ethic. To recognize that the American professional military ethic incorporates the laws of war provides only a starting point in examining the effect of integrating the moral perspective of the laws of war into the moral structure of the professional military ethic.

In order to clarify the relationship between the American professional military ethic and the laws of war, we must determine both the moral character of the laws of war and the fundamental values of American society that directly affect the American professional military ethic. Specifically, we must examine two areas. First, we must consider the nature of the laws of war and the relationship that exists between that body of law, if it is such, and particular moral principles. Second, we will identify the particular set of "American values" that are central and enduring—those that would, over time, exert a continuous, shaping influence on the development of the American professional military ethic. We will turn to the second issue in the next chapter and thus focus here only on the characteristics of the laws of war.

Some legal scholars declare that "international law" cannot be considered law at all in any strict sense, which is a preliminary consideration of some importance. Since human welfare is at issue, moral authority provides the ultimate foundation for all law. If international law were no more than a form of circumstantially limited international agreement, its influence on the coherence of the professional military ethic would be much less significant. The only moral obligation involved in adhering to the laws of war then would be that resulting from the officer's commitment to the Constitution and to the professional military ethic. If the laws of war are ultimately based upon moral principles, however, then the officer is also morally committed to adherence to those principles, and it becomes necessary, in considering the coherence of the professional military ethic, to determine what those principles are. Most of the discussion in this chapter focuses on that investigation.

The larger significance of these issues is the degree to which they help provide an answer to the question as to whether the moral principles underlying the laws of war conflict with or complement the fundamental values of American society. If those sets of values are not at least compatible, American military professionals could find themselves faced with paralyzing moral dilemmas in performing professional duties. The issue of compatibility is our primary concern in this chapter.

Historical Development of the Laws of War

In a long historical view, with the understanding that armed hostilities must reach some level of significance to the society as a whole in order to be categorized as war, we can partially accept the sense of Clausewitz's general characterization: "War . . . is an act of violence intended to compel our opponent to fulfill our will."[5] In the modern era, when the flames of conflict have burned brighter and spread more widely than ever before, the condition of war has become a complex technical status because of numerous treaties and the development of international law. What constitutes a state of war is not firmly or exhaustively codified by a universally recognized set of criteria, but international law has established that war is a "legal condition in which the [claimed] rights of a state are or may be prosecuted by force."[6] Although it could include actions that we normally do not consider war, that definition does extend to the "war on terrorism." However, the definition provided by the U.S. Army's *The Law of Land Warfare*, which states that "war may be defined as a legal condition of armed hostility between states,"[7] does not, since it limits the participants to states. In both definitions, to include the concept of legality serves to emphasize that war is a state of affairs governed by specified constraints—the laws of war.

The extent to which the laws of war apply to the war on terrorism that the United States initiated after the World Trade Center attacks of 11 September 2001 remains controversial. Identifying and attacking shadowy terrorist figures of a nonstate organization like al-Qaida bears little resemblance to the conventional combat addressed by the laws of war. In the aftermath of the catastrophic attack on New York and the blow to the Pentagon, many who called for "war" also called for a ruthless, "gloves-off" response that would sweep aside legal and political obstacles. Because the laws of war were established for a much different form of conflict, we need to reflect on the principles and values that frame the laws and how they apply. Once we have done so, we will find that no moral justification exists for the claim that "anything goes" in the war against terrorists.

Limiting how wars can be fought is hardly a new development, as our examination of the just war tradition in the last chapter made clear. The codified laws of war now observed, however, are distinctly modern. This fact effectively counters an observation offered in criticism of the claim that the laws of war have a moral basis. If we consider the rationale for the restraints imposed by the customs of warfare in the distant past, beginning with the Greeks and examining practices from Roman times through the Middle Ages, we will indeed find little evidence of mercy or concern for human welfare. We do find considerable expediency and self-interest, which is sometimes taken as sufficient evidence for establishing the nonmoral nature of the customs and laws of war. To conclude, however, that the current laws of war are accordingly based on nonmoral considerations would be to mistake the motivations of those who promulgated and adhered to the customs and laws, both in the ancient past and in this century, for the substance of the laws of war. Those motivations do not necessarily reflect the nature of the laws themselves.

Our codified laws of war can be traced to underlying moral principles, though nonmoral considerations are not to be ignored.

Interestingly, one of the cornerstones of the codified laws of war
was emplaced in the United States. As one authoritative study of the
laws of war notes:

> The starting-point for the codification of the rules of war on land
> is the "Instructions for the Government of Armies of the United
> States in the Field" drawn up by Dr. Francis Lieber and revised by
> a board of officers of the United States Army at the instance of
> President Lincoln and issued from the office of the Adjutant-
> General to the Army as General Order No. 100, of 1863.[8]

The Lieber Code largely corresponded to the laws and customs of
war as they existed at the time. The code was innovative in that it was
the first example of a detailed manual for combatants concerning the
conduct of war that attempted to codify customary law and standards
applying to all nations. In Telford Taylor's view, "[The Lieber Code]
remained for half a century the official Army pronouncement on the
subject, furnished much of the material for the Hague Conventions of
1899 and 1907, and today still commands attention as the germinal
document for codification of the laws of land warfare."[9]

Soon to be joined with the rules presented in the Lieber Code
were the results of the efforts of J. Henry Dunant, founder of the
International Committee of the Red Cross (ICRC). Dunant, a Swiss
banker visiting northern Italy on business in 1859, found himself on
the battlefield at Solferino, where the fighting left over 40,000 casualties. The suffering he observed among those abandoned on the battlefield overwhelmed him. The war between the Austrian Empire
and the forces of France and Sardinia lasted only from April to July,
but the extent of suffering so impressed Dunant that he launched a
one-man crusade against war and organized an international conference in 1864 in an attempt to mitigate the suffering of combatants
should war occur. The beginnings of the modern international effort
to establish formal laws of war grew from that conference, which
produced the first Geneva Convention. The major components of the
subsequent development of the codified laws of war are depicted in
Figure 6.1.[10]

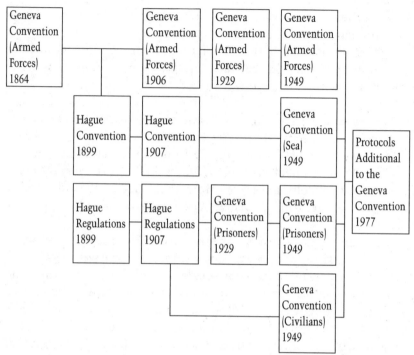

Figure 6.1 Development of the Codified Laws of War

The Existing Laws of War

The laws of war are a part of the body of law referred to as international law. Despite the lack of an established enforcement agency, international law has considerable weight. Morris Greenspan reflects current consensus when he says, "Today, most legal opinion throughout the world recognizes that international law is true law. Indeed, it would be difficult to hold otherwise since the world as a whole calls it law, regards it as law, accepts it as law, and expects it to be obeyed as law, even though the means of enforcing it are defective."[11] In fact, it seems clear in view of the Nuremberg Trials and the course of warfare since World War II that sanctions do exist for the laws of war, which form a part of international law. The International Criminal Tribunal for the Former Yugoslavia and the International Criminal Tribunal for Rwanda provide specific evidence. The sanctions consist of unilateral or multilateral retaliatory force and punishment, criminal prosecution, and the force of world opinion. Punishment of war crimes is required of all signatories under the Geneva Conventions, and any state having custody of the offender can exercise jurisdiction.[12] The sanctions may not be uniformly effective, but they do in fact exist.[13]

An eminent jurist, Bert A. Röling, who served on the International Military Tribunal of the Far East, notes a common distinction made in terms of the Geneva and Hague Conventions:

> Distinction is often made between the "law of Geneva" and "the law of the Hague," the law of Geneva giving rules for the protection and assistance to the victims of war, the law of the Hague giving rules for the prevention of people becoming victims. Stimulated by the appeal made by Henry Dunant, the Red Cross formed in Europe; its primary interest concerned the victims of war. But the conventions adopted at the Second Peace Conference of the Hague, convened on the initiative of the Russian czar, in which many rules of warfare were codified, contained also rules for the protection of victims. A third impulse to the development of the laws of war originated in the human rights development. The General Assembly of the United Nations adopted several resolutions on "human rights in armed conflict."[14]

We can be even more specific with respect to the distinction: "The Law of The Hague comprises the St. Petersburg Declaration of 1868, the Hague Conventions of 1899 and 1907, the Geneva CBW Protocol of 1925, and the Hague Convention of 1954"[15] (for the protection of cultural property in the event of armed conflict). The Law of The Hague largely concerns permissible means of fighting; the law of Geneva concerns treatment of the victims of war.

Before we consider the issue of the moral principles manifested in the laws of war, which is our central concern in this chapter, we need to identify the sources of the laws. The treaties and conventions to which various states have formally agreed constitute the most precise source of the laws of war. "This may be termed the statute law of nations; the law specifically enacted and reduced to signed documentary form. Particularly important are those treaties which have a great number of nations as parties . . . since their general acceptance demonstrates the generality of the principles which they contain."[16]

The most obvious source is the "customs and usages of war" that have developed and been recognized in the course of history as legally binding, comparable in nature to Anglo-Saxon common law. The legal profession and the courts have found both sources of law to be legal, binding, and practicable in application. Treaties create legal obligations for the specified parties but sometimes become so widely recognized and accepted that their provisions come to be considered "customary." That is the basis for the Nuremberg statement in 1946 that "by 1939 the rules of land warfare laid down in the 1907 Hague Convention had been recognized by all civilized nations, and were regarded as being declaratory of the laws and customs of war."[17] The Nuremberg Tribunal observed elsewhere that

> The law of war is to be found not only in treaties, but in the customs and practice of states which gradually obtained universal recognition, and from the general principles of justice applied by jurists and practiced by military courts. This law is not static, but by continual adaptation follows the needs of a changing world. Indeed, in many cases treaties do no more than express and define for more accurate reference the principles of law already existing.[18]

In addition to treaties and the customs and usages of war, we can identify two other sources of international law and its subset the laws of war.[19] The judgments of both national and international courts (such as the Permanent Court of International Justice at The Hague) and ad hoc international tribunals (such as the Nuremberg Tribunal, the Yugoslavia tribunal, and the Rwanda tribunal) have established principles and precedents that contribute to the laws of war. Lastly, courts have recognized that those general principles common to all national legal systems also apply in the international arena. The charges in the Nuremberg Trials included wording reflecting this view: "The acts and conduct of the defendants . . . constitute violations of the general principles of criminal law as derived from the criminal law of all civilized nations."[20]

In addition to the Hague and Geneva Conventions depicted in Figure 6.1, various multinational treaties and United Nations actions have contributed to the limitations in warfare. Two of the most important of these are the Geneva Gas Protocol of 1925 and the

Genocide Convention established by the United Nations in 1948. Most major nations ratified the Gas Protocol, though the United States did not do so until 1974. The United States ratified the 1993 Chemical Weapons Convention in 1997, though only after intense debate in the Senate. The 1997 Ottawa Convention banning the use of land mines promises to provide a significant limitation on the suffering that continues long after wars conclude. Land mines left in place after a war claim many civilian victims. Though over 130 nations have signed the mine treaty, the United States, Russia, China, Iraq, Libya, Cuba, and Pakistan, among others, have not. At this point, states that have not ratified the treaty are not bound by it, but in time the provisions of the treaty will become customary—and thus binding on all combatants.

At present, because of the number of treaties and conventions codified in the past hundred years, the laws of war are largely in writing. Of those, the four Geneva Conventions of 1949, consisting of over five hundred articles, constitute a large part of the codified law. Those Conventions almost exclusively concern the protection of war victims, such as prisoners of war and civilians in occupied territory. The Geneva Conventions have very little to say about the waging of war in terms of acceptable tactics and weaponry. The signatories intended the Conventions to supplement the laws of war in view of the experiences of World War II. The 1949 Conventions were ratified or acceded to by over 140 states, though some have attached exceptions ("reservations") to their accessions.[21]

The laws of war continue to evolve as the nature of war changes. In order to address issues that arose from the conduct of the war in Vietnam and other conflicts, the International Red Cross called for nations to send representatives to Geneva for conferences from 1974 to 1977. From those efforts emerged the Protocols to the Geneva Conventions of 12 August 1949. In 1977 sixty-two states signed the two documents, Protocol I and Protocol II, but the ratification process has been slow. The United States sees Protocol I as unacceptable because of its ambiguity and because its provisions would extend protection to terrorists at the expense of noncombatants. After the 9/11 attack, those provisions have little support in the United States. The U.S. Senate has not ratified either of the protocols.[22]

The ensuing references to specific portions of the laws of war provide a sense of their substance and content. In preceding paragraphs, as a beginning for our search for the moral principles that underlie the laws of war, I sketched the history and development of the laws. With an understanding of their factual character, we will be in a position to consider their moral character. The following excerpts are not intended to be comprehensive; they merely convey a sense of the substance of the existing codified laws of war.

The Beginning of War

The Contracting Powers recognize that hostilities between themselves must not commence without previous and explicit warning, in the form either of a reasoned declaration of war or of an ultimatum with conditional declaration of war.[23]

Article 2 of each of the 1949 Geneva Conventions adds to this provision of the Hague Convention and notes that the 1949 Conventions apply to "all cases of declared war or of any other armed conflict . . . even if the state of war is not recognized by one of the parties," and also to instances of partial or total occupation. The laws of war thus come into play in all international armed conflict under the current laws of war, whether a formal state of war is declared or not.

When war is declared, each party to the conflict should name a "protecting power" that will help safeguard the interests of the warring party, primarily by serving as a medium of communication between the belligerents. The responsibilities of the protecting powers are set forth in detail in the Geneva Conventions of 1949. These imply a major responsibility, in addition to communication, in that the protecting power is to be allowed to observe the conditions in which prisoners of war are held, particularly in response to complaints from the warring power whose interests it is safeguarding. This aspect of the laws of war has not come into play since World War II because no country has made a formal declaration of war since, despite major armed conflicts such as the Korean War, the war in Vietnam, the Gulf Wars, and the defeat of the Taliban in Afghanistan.

Discussion of the initiation of warfare has moved far beyond a focus on the codified laws, turning instead to moral and prudential analyses founded on just war theory. The United Nations perspective accepts as justified only those wars that are defensive in nature or those initiated for humanitarian purposes with the support of the international community. The United States' defeat of Saddam Hussein in Iraq has brought that paradigm into question. The administration of President George W. Bush explicitly adopted a policy of pre-emptive war[24] and then implemented the policy in attacking Iraq. The aftermath of the Second Gulf War has revealed the difficulty of establishing the boundary between pre-emptive war (initiated in response to a perceived immediate, grave threat to national security) and preventive war (initiated in response to a *potential* threat to national interests). The Second Gulf War also revealed the murky role of intelligence data in revealing and concealing the reality of enemy intentions and capabilities.

The Waging of War

Technological development has overtaken some of the provisions of the Hague Conventions, such as the prohibition against destroying submarine cables connecting an occupied territory with a neutral territory (Article 54, Hague Regulations, 1907). Reference today to satellite communications would be more appropriate. In a less direct sense, some of the general limitations established in the Hague Regulations (annexed to the Hague Conventions) have also been overtaken by changes in weapons systems. The requirement for "the besieged to indicate the presence of such cultural, medical, historical buildings or places by distinctive and visible signs, which shall be notified to the enemy beforehand" (Article 27, Hague Regulations, 1907)—the purpose of which is to enable the besieging force to meet the requirement that such buildings are not the objects of assault or bombardment—no longer provides much protection. The physical identification serves little purpose in a combat situation in which ground-to-ground missiles with ranges in excess of seventy-five miles are routinely employed, or in which supersonic bombers flying at 45,000 feet drop bombs on targets throughout a belligerent's home territory. The status and protection of noncombatant shipping spelled out in treaties agreed upon before the introduction of submarine warfare have also been overtaken by changes in the means of waging war at sea.

The incompleteness of the laws of war that results from the

changing means of conducting warfare is particularly evident with respect to air warfare and aerial bombardment. Technological advances have been so rapid and so dramatic that the slow process of achieving consensus through usage has not kept pace. The same is even more obviously true of nuclear weapons, which are not even implicitly recognized in the existing laws of war, unless one decides to include resolutions of the United Nations General Assembly as contributing to the corpus of existing law.[25] The great imbalance of power created among potential belligerents as a result of exploding technological "progress" in weapons systems tends to make national self-interest the dominant consideration in international discussions of limitations on war. That imbalance has precluded agreement concerning the ways air and nuclear warfare are to be restrained and regulated by law.

We can, however, discern the intent of the limitations in the conventions established at the turn of the last century, despite the sections that are hopelessly outmoded. Further, the conventions have provided the substance of the laws of war, as indicated in the Nuremberg Tribunal conclusion cited before, on which war crimes convictions have been based.

One of the most controversial yet influential provisions of the Hague Conventions is Article 22 of the Hague Regulations: "The right of belligerents to adopt means of injuring the enemy is not unlimited."[26] Article 23 continues by specifying that combatants are "especially forbidden"

  a. To employ poison or poisoned weapons;
  b. To kill or wound treacherously individuals belonging to the hostile nations or army;
  c. To kill or wound an enemy who, having laid down his arms, or having no longer means of defense, has surrendered at discretion;
  d. To declare that no quarter will be given;
  e. To employ arms, projectiles, or material calculated to cause unnecessary suffering.

That these restrictions have been frequently violated is indisputable, but in at least some cases the violations have resulted in postwar criminal convictions. Prudent adversaries in conflict must consider the conventions, even if, after such considerations, they decide to violate them. The objections to the American conduct of the war in Vietnam resulted in part from perceived violations of Article 23 and other laws of war; public opinion, national and international, was largely responsible for the withdrawal of the United States from Vietnam. While what constitutes "unnecessary suffering" is not a matter of consensus, the topic is seriously discussed and is apparently a consideration of some importance in state policy deliberation and weapons development. Such points notwithstanding, considerable ambiguity exists. The U.S. Army's manual, *The Law of Land Warfare*, interprets Article 23e of the Hague Regulations in this manner:

What weapons cause "unnecessary suffering" can only be determined in light of the practice of States in refraining from the use of a given weapon because it is believed to have that effect. The prohibition certainly does not extend to the use of explosives contained in artillery projectiles, mines, rockets, or hand grenades. Usage has, however, established the illegality of the use of lances with barbed heads, irregular-shaped bullets, and projectiles filled with glass, the use of any substance on bullets that would tend unnecessarily to inflame a wound inflicted by them, and the scoring of the surface or the filing off of the ends of the hard cases of bullets.

The use of explosive "atomic weapons," whether by air, sea, or land forces, cannot as such be regarded as violative of international law in the absence of any customary rule of international law or international convention restricting their employment.[27]

The existing laws of war appear to be regrettably incomplete in terms of providing guidance for the use of modern weapons. Interpretations or extrapolations such as those provided by the army manual attempt to bridge some of the most obvious gaps, though coherence becomes a problem, particularly with regard to nuclear weapons.[28]

In the 1970s, as I described previously, the ICRC launched a strong drive to prepare the Protocols Additional to the Geneva Conventions of 1949. The 1949 Conventions focus on the humanitarian treatment of service personnel and civilians in enemy hands and do not address the actual conduct of military operations. The ICRC project had the goal of updating the laws of war, not only with respect to broader application to all armed conflicts, but also with respect to modern developments in weaponry. Four international diplomatic conferences were held (one each year from 1974 to 1977) that produced the two Protocols. Though the agreements have not yet achieved the full status of accepted laws,[29] it is interesting to note nonetheless that Protocol I addresses both the conduct of hostilities and the treatment of war victims, indicating that a merger of the "Law of The Hague" and the "Law of Geneva" seems to be in process. While the adoption process is still incomplete, the Protocols represent the first comprehensive attempt since the Hague Conventions to limit the tactics and weapons permissible in war. Concern about the plight of war victims in World War II prompted the Geneva Conventions of 1949. The complexities of the Vietnam War, in which Americans pitted advanced weaponry against guerrillas and the forces of an underdeveloped nation, largely prompted the conferences that produced the Protocols.

We can trace certain constraints on the means of waging war to concepts presented by Immanuel Kant in the eighteenth century. One of those appears in the Lieber Code, in Article 16, which placed limitations on the extent to which military necessity could be used to justify measures taken against the enemy in warfare, saying, "It [military necessity] admits of deception, but disclaims acts of perfidy; and, in general, military necessity does not include any act of hostility which makes the return to peace unnecessarily difficult."[30] The use of the term "unnecessarily difficult" leaves this claim open to varying interpretations. If an act is justified by military necessity (i.e., it is necessary to subduing and defeating the enemy in some sense), how is such an act to be evaluated—moral considerations aside—in terms of making the return to peace "unnecessarily" difficult? Despite such difficulties, Dr. Lieber repeated the sense of one of the articles that Kant presented in his essay, "Perpetual Peace." Article 6 of that essay, which presented the provisions Kant thought necessary to the achievement of international peace, states that "[n]o state at war with another shall permit such acts of hostility as would make mutual confidence impossible during a future time of peace. Such acts would include the employment of assassins (*percussores*) or poisoners (*venefici*), breach of agreements, the instigation of treason (*perduello*) within the enemy state, etc."[31]

This concept has resulted in a variety of specific rules, such as, "it is improper to feign surrender so as to secure an advantage" or to notify enemy forces that agreement to end hostilities has been reached when such is not the case.[32] Similarly, a flag of truce "must not be used to obtain time to effect a retreat or secure reinforcements."[33] Such rules fall under the principle that, outside "measures for mystifying or misleading the enemy against which the enemy ought to protect himself . . . absolute good faith with the enemy must be observed as a rule of conduct."[34] The U.S. Army manual, the source of the preceding quotations, explains the basis for this principle: "Treacherous or perfidious conduct in war is forbidden because it destroys that basis for a restoration of peace short of the complete annihilation of one belligerent by another."[35] The echo of Kant's article proposed in the eighteenth century rings clearly.

The Treatment of Prisoners

Articles 4 through 20 of the Hague Regulations of 1907 concern prisoners of war, declaring that they "must be humanely treated." The text addresses details as disparate as mail processing and the exercise of religion. In the Geneva Conventions of 1929 and 1949 (see Figure 6.1), these provisions were considerably expanded. Article 13 of the 1949 Conventions includes the requirement that "prisoners of war must at all times be protected, particularly against acts of violence or intimidation and against insults or public curiosity." Article 14 deserves quotation in full to give the sense of the degree to which prisoners are to be accorded respect as persons under the current laws of war:

- Prisoners of war are entitled in all circumstances to respect for their persons and their honor.
- Women shall be treated with all the regard due to their sex and shall in all cases benefit by treatment as favourable as that granted to men.
- Prisoners of war shall retain the full civil capacity which they enjoyed at the time of their capture. The detaining Power may not restrict the exercise, either within or without its own ter-

ritory, of the rights such capacity confers except in so far as the captivity requires.[36]

The 1949 Geneva Conventions, which complement the 1907 Hague Regulations but replace the 1929 Geneva Conventions (Article 134, 135, Geneva Convention—POW, 1949), cover almost all aspects of the operation of capturing, maintaining, and releasing prisoners of war, involving quarters, food, and medical attention, personal property, correspondence, labor and rates of pay, records, wills, repatriation procedures, and a variety of other details. This formal international consensus, containing 143 articles and 5 annexes, also carefully specifies who qualifies as a prisoner of war (Article 4).

In addition, Article 3 of the 1949 Conventions specifies treatment of prisoners and other noncombatants even in "armed conflict not of an international character." Absolutely prohibited are the following:

- Violence to life and person, in particular murder of all kinds, mutilation, cruel treatment and torture.
- Taking of hostages.
- Outrages upon personal dignity, in particular, humiliating and degrading treatment.
- The passing of sentences and the carrying out of executions without previous judgment pronounced by a regularly constituted court, affording all the judicial guarantees which are recognized as indispensable by civilized peoples.

In the American-led war on terrorism, the status of the Geneva provisions concerning prisoners has been ambiguous. Although the United States claims to have treated soldiers captured in Afghanistan humanely, they were not categorized as prisoners of war. The Taliban and al-Qaida captives have been confined on the Cuban coast in the U.S. base at Guantanamo. The U.S. government has stated that the potential terrorists will be kept in prison so long as they pose a threat to Americans.

War Crimes

The Law of Land Warfare states that "every violation of the law of war is a war crime," applicable to any person or persons, military or civilian.[37] War crimes clearly include the "grave breaches" noted in Article 50 of the 1949 Geneva Conventions (e.g., "willful killing" of persons protected by the Conventions, "torture or inhumane treatment," "extensive destruction and appropriation of property . . . carried out unlawfully and wantonly"). The U.S. Army manual also provides the following representative list of war crimes:[38]

- Making use of poisoned or otherwise forbidden arms or ammunition.
- Treacherous request for quarter.
- Maltreatment of dead bodies.
- Firing on localities which are undefended and without military significance.
- Abuse of or firing on the flag of truce.
- Misuse of the Red Cross emblem.
- Use of civilian clothing by troops to conceal their military character during battle.
- Improper use of privileged buildings for military purposes.
- Poisoning of wells or streams.
- Pillage or purposeless destruction.
- Compelling prisoners of war to perform prohibited labor.
- Killing without trial spies or other persons who have committed hostile acts.
- Compelling civilians to perform prohibited labor.
- Violation of surrender terms.

This brief discussion of the history, nature, and content of the laws of war provides the basis for consideration of our major concern—the moral character of the laws of war.

Underlying Moral Principles

We commonly acknowledge that moral principles underlie and constrain the activity of members of professions such as medicine and law. Whether the same can be said of the military profession is another question, and one likely to provoke debate. Because American military professionals are committed to a particular set of values as part of their professional status, the question in their case becomes one of identifying the values and principles. But any military group, I will argue, that is committed to adhering to the laws of war is also committed to the two underlying humanitarian principles:

1. Individual persons deserve respect as such. (HP1)
2. Human suffering ought to be minimized. (HP2)

These two principles differ in terms of schemes of justification: the first does not look to the consequences of deeds but concerns itself with human rights, while the second invokes utilitarian considerations and does depend upon consideration of the results of contemplated actions. I contend that HP1 has priority over HP2 in the formulation of the laws of war.

Our brief examination of the content of the laws of war revealed the humanitarian concern that pervades the requirements and limitations established in their provisions. The "Martens Clause"[39] found in the preamble to both the 1899 and 1907 Hague Conventions indicates the spirit in which those two sets of constraints on warfare were promulgated:

> Until a more complete code of the laws of war can be issued, the High Contracting Parties think it expedient to declare that in cases not included in the Regulations adopted by them, populations and belligerents remain under the protection and the rule of the principles of the laws of nations, as they result from the usages established between civilized nations, from the laws of humanity, and the requirements of the public conscience.[40]

The U.S. Air Force manual concerning the conduct of armed conflict under the laws of war refers specifically to "the principle of humanity, which forbids the infliction of suffering, injury or destruction not actually necessary for the accomplishment of legitimate military purposes."[41] A subsequent passage states that "[t]he principle of humanity also confirms the basic immunity of civilian populations and civilians from being objects of attack during armed conflict."[42]

Through the Martens clause, the Hague Conventions are founded upon the "laws of humanity and the requirements of public conscience." As the Air Force manual further points out, the Geneva Conventions in turn "safeguard such fundamental rights as freedom from torture or cruel and inhuman punishment; freedom from arbitrary exile; freedom from arbitrarily imposed punishment; and right to legal remedy for any abuse; right to minimum standards of respect for human rights at all times; and right to health, family sanctity and non-abuse."[43]

Those attending the Diplomatic Conference of 1949, which produced the four Geneva Conventions, affirmed that their work was "inspired solely by humanitarian aims."[44] The law of Geneva specifically concerns four primary areas under the heading humane treatment for "protected persons":

1. Care of the wounded, sick, and shipwrecked
2. Treatment of prisoners of war
3. Immunity of noncombatants
4. Treatment of the population of occupied territory

Indeed, all of the prohibitions and requirements in the Conventions can be directly related to the protection of the rights of an individual persons.

The Geneva Conventions thus specify measures required by the concept of human rights, which manifest the concept of respect for persons. Respect for persons entails the ideas of equality of consideration and human dignity. Individual persons cannot be treated with respect unless they are considered equally as persons (though that consideration obviously does not further entail equal treatment). To give preferential treatment denies the individual discriminated against the full status of a person—a rational being who is capable of independent choice and thus deserving of respect from other rational beings solely on the basis of that status. Human dignity is inherent in such a concept. In terms of modern ethical theory (and practice), the preferred means of establishing a framework for assessing the actions required in order to respect the status of an individual person is the delineation of fundamental human rights.

The principal thrust of the Geneva Conventions of 1949 is the attempt to specify the legal rights of noncombatants. The primary categories of noncombatants are (loosely) those disabled from fighting and those not directly participating in combat. Honoring their rights as required by the Conventions is a moral and legal obligation for all signatories.

An examination of the Hague Conventions, which specifically concern the way to wage war, shows them logically consistent with the second humanitarian principle (HP2). Article 23e, which prohibits the employment of weapons or material calculated to cause unnecessary suffering, and the Hague Regulations, which concern the protection of prisoners of war and civilians, were framed with the intent of ameliorating the evils of war.[45] The articles prohibiting treacherous or perfidious actions were devised to achieve the same end by avoiding the prolongation of war, which would probably occur if such actions were taken. Unless some minimal standards of conduct are mutually recognized, there will be no basis for settlement of the conflict other than complete victory and unconditional surrender. Almost every provision of the Hague Convention can be seen as a direct means of minimizing human suffering, even though the motivation for establishing the conventions of war codified at The Hague may have been largely prudential.

Observance of the Law of The Hague will cause less human suffering in most cases than would be caused by its nonobservance. That the Law of The Hague manifests the first humanitarian principle (HP1), however, is not as clear. Whether a soldier shoots and kills an enemy with a standard .45 caliber round or whether he shoots and kills an enemy with a .45 caliber round with a notched bullet appears to have little to do with respecting his status as a person. Such a constraint, however, clearly does have to do with minimizing human suffering.

While there are few instances of provisions of the laws of war that are obviously attributable to one and only one of the two humanitarian principles, it also appears that HP1 and HP2 are nonetheless distinctly different principles that can conceivably come into conflict. A classical combat situation presenting problems of moral choice is one in which enemy soldiers are taken prisoner by a small force carrying out a critical mission behind enemy lines. By examining this type of situation carefully with respect to the two humanitarian principles, we can clarify the moral nature of the laws of war.

Consider the often-discussed prisoner case filled out as follows.

The success of the small force in carrying out its mission will allow the seizure of a major transportation center without a significant battle, which would affect a sizeable civilian population. If the battle does not occur, many combatant and noncombatant casualties as well as extensive destruction of civilian property will be avoided. The force carrying out the mission, however, captures several wounded enemy soldiers. The mission is such that accomplishment is not possible if the force keeps its prisoners in custody. The likelihood of discovery precludes leaving them behind, tied up, or otherwise constrained. If the commander releases the prisoners, the force will almost certainly be compromised and unable to fulfill the mission. Under the circumstances, the commander of the force must decide whether to kill the prisoners and whether he can justify such execution.

We are particularly concerned not with his decision, but with the laws of war that apply to such a situation. In the discussion that follows, we will apply the two humanitarian principles directly to situations involving choice among specific alternative actions. With respect to the laws of war as they exist, however, these two principles provide the basis for *formulating* the laws. Only in situations for which there is no applicable law or in situations in which the justifiability of a particular law is in question would it be appropriate to apply the principles directly in determining appropriate courses of action. We should also recognize that there can be a conflict between HP1 and HP2 if we apply the humanitarian principles themselves in attempting to decide what to do in a given situation. In our hypothetical example, consideration of the question under HP2 indicates that the answer is "kill the prisoners," for in the short term this action will cause considerably less suffering than not killing them. Unless we assume some condition such that the warring party to which the capturing force belongs would inevitably lose the war and that capturing the transportation center would only prolong the war with the result of increased suffering, the logical action under HP2 is to execute the prisoners and carry on with the mission.

One might object by saying that allowing the execution of prisoners will in the long run be counterproductive—that suffering will thereby be increased by heightening determination not to surrender and by encouraging battles and wars of annihilation. But if the prisoners are executed only in highly exceptional circumstances such as those presented in this hypothetical case, the objection in terms of long-term effects is not persuasive.

Under HP1, however, the decision to execute the prisoners cannot be justified. If the leader of the capturing force is to respect his prisoners as individual persons, he cannot eliminate them solely as a means of expediting his mission, which he would be doing if he executed them. The prisoners, under HP1, have a basic right not to be treated cruelly or inhumanely. Both descriptions apply to summary execution.

The two humanitarian principles appear to call for opposite courses of action in the prisoner example—a situation that indicates that different laws would be produced if one or the other of the principles were considered alone in framing laws concerning the treatment of prisoners. Similar situations can arise if the two principles are applied directly. Some of the most obvious involve deliberate attacks on groups of civilians, use of weapons considered inhumane, and resettlement of civilians in occupied territories. We can hypothesize situations in which one course of action appears to be the logical choice if we desire to minimize suffering, while a different course of action is preferable if we are to respect individual persons as such. Our concern with the prisoner example and others like it, however, is that of first determining what the actual laws of war require and then identifying which of the two foundational moral principles underlies the existing law. The answers to two questions will thus clarify the issue. First, what do the laws of war permit or prohibit? Second, from what moral principle is the applicable law of war derived?

With respect to our prisoner example, we can find clear evidence in specific national regulations that derive from the codified laws of war. Although the American manual *The Law of Land Warfare*, written in 1956, does not specifically prohibit killing prisoners under any circumstances, the wording suggests that intention: "A commander may not put his prisoners to death because their presence retards his movements or diminishes his power of resistance. . . . It is likewise unlawful for a commander to kill his prisoners on grounds of self-preservation, even in the case of airborne or commando operations."[46]

The U.S. Air Force pamphlet *International Law—The Conduct of Armed Conflict and Air Operations* reflects the same position in referring to Articles 12–16 of the 1949 Geneva Convention Relative to the Treatment of Prisoners of War, but in more unequivocal terms: "These provisions prohibit killing or mistreatment of PWs whatever the military reasons. . . ."[47] The laws of war, as construed by the United States, thus prohibit the killing of prisoners. This interpretation of the laws of war appears warranted, and all Geneva signatories claim to share it. Accordingly, the laws of war that apply in the case of captured prisoners are derived from HP1 rather than HP2, for by applying HP2 directly, we found that killing prisoners of war could be justified in some circumstances. We must conclude, then, that HP1 has priority over HP2 in framing the laws of war in this instance.

In fact, such appears to be the case in all situations in which specific rights recognized in the laws of war are involved. In the three additional circumstances suggested above (attacks on civilians, use of inhumane weapons, and resettlement), the applicable laws of war are based upon recognition of the rights of persons and thus derive from HP1. The most reasonable conclusion, then, is that with respect to formulating laws of war in general, HP1 has priority over HP2, and "military necessity" is thereby limited as a justification for action.[48]

Our discussion shows that the laws of war govern practice under moral principles; accordingly, the legal rights established in the laws of war should reflect moral rights. Such rights derive from HP1, which generates the concept of rights in the context of the laws of war. Since the laws of war do prohibit the killing of prisoners, a prohibition consistent with HP1, one could again conclude that the two humanitarian principles, HP1 and HP2, have a priority relationship in which HP2 is subordinate to HP1. As other examples of potential conflict between the principles indicate, it appears that HP1 will have priority in all cases involving recognized rights. The laws of war specifically recognize that prisoners of war have a right to be treated humanely and with respect as persons, which must certainly include the right not to be murdered. Therefore, the right of the prisoners not to be killed would have to be satisfied before the criterion of minimizing suffering is applied. Once we satisfy the nonconsequentialist principle, if more than one alternative law remains under consideration, we then turn to HP2 for further discrimination among possible laws.[49]

In sum, the two humanitarian principles that separately or jointly provide the moral basis for determining specific rules of conduct also define the moral character of the laws of war. The principle that individual persons should be respected as such can, however, conflict with the principle that human suffering ought to be minimized. When that occurs, it appears there is a plausible argument for holding that the first principle, HP1, has priority. If HP1 provided the basis for justified participation in war, then HP1 is more fundamental than HP2. And if that is the case, only when the first is satisfied will the second principle be applied.

Because the laws of war are incomplete, and will probably remain so, establishing these principles and their relationship is important. Situations to which existing laws of war cannot be directly applied can then be analyzed in terms of the underlying principles, making the resolution of problems more consistent and more appropriate. The "war on terrorism" appears to be just such a situation. Many of the specific laws of war will not apply to the fight against international terrorists, but HP1 and HP2, which reflect our fundamental social values, certainly do. Applying them will generate moral constraints consistent with both the laws of war and the essential values of American society. Lastly, though some commentators such as Richard B. Brandt consider a form of utilitarian theory to be the appropriate interpretation of the moral basis of the laws of war,[50] and would even argue that HP1 should be adopted for utilitarian reasons,[51] we have seen that HP2, which in itself can be considered a limited utilitarian principle, is more appropriately viewed as subordinate to HP1. HP1, in turn, is most plausibly seen as non-consequentialist and thus not a utilitarian guideline.

The last step in our discussion of the laws of war becomes a simple one. If HP1 and HP2 reflect the moral character of the laws of war, then we can compare the two principles to the values of American society in our examination of the American professional military ethic. Our initial discussion of the values manifested in the Constitution, in which I claimed that rights and liberties are at the center of any such analysis, can be offered as evidence that incorporating the principles underlying the laws of war may not present a problem in coherence. Our present discussion should also indicate the professional requirement for all members of the military to understand the limitations on action imposed by the existing laws of war. The more responsibility a member of the military has, the more stringent becomes the requirement to be fully informed concerning the provisions of those treaties and conventions concerning the conduct of war recognized by virtue of the Constitution's Article VI, Clause 2, which declares those agreements to be the "supreme law of the land."

Stating the role of the laws of war in the American professional military ethic is easier than determining what should be done in specific cases, as the prisoner example shows, so perhaps we should turn to another hypothetical situation to clarify the way the laws of war shape permissible alternatives.

Case Study: The Pilot

Situation

Major Blue is a career air force officer. The unit to which he is assigned as a command pilot is based in a small country from which B-52 support is provided for American and allied forces fighting in another nation of the region. American ground units have been committed in that country to help repel an invasion from an adjacent state. The conflict, in which the United States is deeply involved though no state of war has been declared, has thus far been confined to the territory of the invaded state. The avowed purpose of American involvement is that of preventing the conquest of the invaded state and of restoring the territorial status quo that existed before the invasion.

Major Blue's unit has just received the mission of bombing the capital city of the invading nation, and he has serious doubts about whether the mission is one that he can carry out. Specifically, the mission is as follows:

1. Destroy communications facilities located in a compound of government buildings in the center of the city.
2. Destroy an airfield on the west edge of the capital city that is the major reception point for war materiel supplied by nations supporting the invader's efforts.
3. Destroy a large warehouse section adjacent to the airfield but extending into the city where large amounts of war supplies are stocked, most important of which are anti-tank and surface-to-air missiles.

The heavy air bombardment ordered is expected to cripple the enemy's ability to resupply combat forces. It is also expected to be a severe psychological blow, for this will be the first air attack on a populated area in the invading nation. American air power has previously been restricted to direct support of the allied ground forces. The American strategy since joining the conflict has been to halt the invasion and to make the war too costly for the invading state to continue.

Major Blue believes American participation in the war is justified. The intervention of American forces, at the request of the invaded state and with the approval of the United Nations, was approved by Congress and is largely supported by the American public. Without the intervention of the United States, the invading nation would have overwhelmed the defending forces. In defeating the pro-Western state, the invading nation would also have gained control of waterways through which critical supplies of oil are shipped to the United States and other Western nations. American interests were clearly involved. From Major Blue's point of view, the intervention of American forces is both understandable and justified. The invasion has been halted, and the invading force has suffered serious losses that the invading state cannot replace.

The only feasible way to accomplish the mission with the B-52's is to run a bombing pattern through the airfield, the storage area, and the government compound. Air defense weapons around the capital are not considered a serious threat to the B-52's, but they could be deadly against aircraft at lower altitudes. The densely populated capital city will suffer heavily as a result of the raid. Extensive civilian casualties are inevitable. Fires and secondary explosions will undoubtedly cause widespread damage.

Major Blue has tried to suppress nagging doubts that arose when he was briefed on the warning order received by the unit, but he is troubled by the certainty that the civilian death toll will be extremely high. Such a result is not only apparently envisioned by higher headquarters but actively sought. In particular, Major Blue finds it difficult in this case to sort out the distinction between aiming at a legitimate target while running the risk of heavy collateral damage and aiming at nonmilitary targets in order to achieve the military purpose. Though he has such doubts, he is not at all sure what he should do.

Discussion

Major Blue may well ask himself whether the order is legal. He is bound by the professional military ethic and by regulations to adhere to the laws of war. Air Force publications state that "[t]he law of armed conflict applies to an international armed conflict regardless of whether a declared 'war' exists. This rule, necessitated by the law's humanitarian purpose and disuse of the legal status of war in international conflicts, is confirmed by international agreement and consensus."[52] If the order is in some way illegal, Major Blue is obligated to oppose or disobey the order. The codified laws of war do not address clearly the subject of air warfare—except for archaic restrictions in the Hague Declaration that apply to the use of balloons—but the subject has received widespread consideration. Article 25 of the Hague Regulations (1907) states that, "The attack or bombardment, *by whatever means*, of towns, villages, dwellings, or buildings which are undefended is prohibited." The emphasis on "by whatever means" was included to ensure that aerial bombardment as well as other means would be limited by the article.[53] The American military, in seeking to clarify this provision, has declared that "[t]here is no prohibition of general application against bombardment from the air of combatant troops, defended places, or other legitimate military objectives."[54] The capital city is guarded by a dense system of air defense weapons, and a number of army units are stationed there as well. Under the generally accepted sense of the term, the city can be considered "defended." Attacks on military targets in such cities thus appear justifiable in terms of the laws of war so long as "loss of life and damage to property" are not "out of proportion to the military advantage to be gained."[55] If the advantage sought is the inability of the invading state to continue the war, considerable loss of life can perhaps be justified.

One particular convention, *Rules of Air Warfare* (1923), applies directly to this situation. The United States, however, never ratified the convention. Nonetheless, the United States participated in the conference that produced the convention, and, to a great extent, the rules are looked upon as corresponding to the customary laws of war in this area. Article 24(2) states that aerial bombardment

is legitimate only when directed exclusively at the following objectives: military forces; military establishments or depots;

factories constituting important and well-known centres engaged in the manufacture of arms, ammunition, or distinctively military supplies; lines of communication or transportation used for military purposes.[56]

One could argue that the communications facilities are an important part of the line of communication and that the airfield is part of the line of transportation for military equipment. Article 24(3) of the *Rules of Air Warfare*, however, seems to clear up such questions:

The bombardment of cities, towns, villages, dwellings, or buildings not in the immediate neighbourhood of the operations of land forces is prohibited. In cases where the objectives specified in paragraph (2) are so situated, that they cannot be bombarded without the indiscriminate bombardment of the civilian population, the aircraft must abstain from bombardment.[57]

If this rule were accepted as part of the laws of war, the issue under discussion would be quickly settled. Unfortunately, in view of actions in World War II and subsequent conflicts, one may conclude that Article 23(3) of the *Rules of Air Warfare* has *not* become part of the "customary" rules of war insofar as the prohibition against bombardment of civilian targets not in the immediate neighborhood of ground operations is concerned. Nonetheless, indiscriminate bombing of the civilian population is generally accepted as a prohibited act under the laws of war in any situation.

Further, the Hague Regulations require that "[t]he officer in command of an attacking force must, before commencing a bombardment, except in cases of assault, do all in his power to warn the authorities."[58] This article is generally interpreted by the American military to refer only to places in which there is a civilian population,[59] but this is the case in our situation. Accordingly, the bombing mission as presented here appears impermissible under the laws of war unless warning is given to the invading nation that such an attack is to be made.[60]

If such a warning has not been given, it appears to be Major Blue's responsibility to bring this to the attention of his superiors. If the mission is not modified so as to render civilian casualties much less likely or if warning is not given, Major Blue is morally constrained by the professional military ethic to consider the mission order illegal and to refuse to obey. This conclusion is harshly demanding in terms of Major Blue's conduct, but it follows from the circumstances and the professional military ethic. If the mission were legal under the laws of war even though civilian casualties were likely to be inordinately high in Major Blue's view, what action should he take—as a professional soldier? If appeals to his superiors were unsuccessful, what *ought* Major Blue to do under the professional military ethic?

First, we recognize that as a professional military officer, Major Blue has the responsibility to determine not only whether the order is legal but also whether it is morally acceptable. His first step in making that determination is to apply the professional military ethic. Major Blue must evaluate both objective and subjective factors in deciding whether it would be acceptable or unacceptable to carry out his mission under the professional military ethic. Subjective factors include the intent and motivation of the agent, which are objective factors concerning the factual circumstances. If Major Blue carries out his mission with the motive of performing his duty in the most competent fashion of which he is capable, he can be confident that his action is justified from a subjective standpoint, for motive and intention are primary subjective elements. If he carries out his mission with the motive of avoiding conflict and the intention of furthering his career, his action may not be objectively wrong from a professional standpoint, but it is inadequate and unworthy in terms of the ideal standards of the professional military ethic.

Objective factors will be decisive in this situation as it stands. The action itself, aerial bombardment, is not immoral considered in isolation. Bombing as an instrument of war is acceptable, but how the military forces carry out the bombing is a separate question. If in fact the technique selected is appropriately termed indiscriminate insofar as military and civilian casualties are concerned, the laws of war appear to prohibit the action.

Our discussion earlier in this chapter revealed that the laws of war limit the operation of the principle of military necessity. In the same fashion, the principle of proportionality identifies morally permissible actions—until specific provisions of the laws of war come into play. Then the range of permissible actions is limited by the existing law, even if the principle of proportionality would allow a

wider range. Though ending the war in short order may well be considered an extremely valuable consequence of action, it will still be
an inadequate justification for violating the laws of war. If a potent
but short-lived biological agent were available that could decimate
the entire enemy nation and bring the war to a rapid conclusion, it
would still be morally and legally unacceptable to use it. Such use
would conflict with the moral principles underlying the laws of
war as well as violate the commitment of the United States not to
employ such weapons. Indiscriminate bombing also violates those
moral principles. It disregards the fundamental American values of
equal consideration and respect for persons as individuals. In disre-
garding those values, the action of indiscriminate bombing violates
the foundations of the professional military ethic. Accordingly, the
action cannot be justified under the duty principle. It is morally unacceptable under the professional military ethic.

Indiscriminate bombing can also be described as knowingly aiming at nonmilitary targets for military purposes, which would be a
violation of HP1 and again unacceptable under the professional military ethic, which incorporates that principle. What number of probable civilian casualties is unacceptable is also relevant to the objective
evaluation. Bombs without guidance systems are clearly indiscriminate instruments of war. Precision-guided weapons are discriminate
only if targeting information is detailed. Once released from an aircraft, they can make no distinction between the military target and
uninvolved civilians who may be in the target area through no fault
of their own. The *use* of such weapons is the critical factor, for they
may be used discriminately or indiscriminately. One civilian casualty does not render the use of a B-52 strike necessarily indiscriminate; 50,000 casualties obviously would make it highly probable that
the label was appropriate. Somewhere in between is a level at which
the professional officer must draw a line. In any particular situation, a host of specific features will indicate where such a line is reasonably to be drawn, but identifying that point is a professional
responsibility.

We seldom attain certainty in moral judgment in the complex
situations that need the structure of moral evaluation sketched here.
When a subordinate is certain that the moral judgment of a superior
is wrong from a professional point of view, he or she is professionally
obligated to take action. However, if the subordinate is uncertain of

the correctness of his or her views in a situation in which professional judgments conflict—assuming no gross error is obvious and factual elements generating the respective judgments are recognized by the responsible commander—the judgment of the commander obviously takes precedence for the professional officer functioning under the professional military ethic. In such a situation, duty clearly requires obedience.

The difficulty of moral evaluation does not end here, of course. After analyzing the situation with respect to legal requirements and in terms of the professional military ethic, Major Blue still faces a third level of evaluation that involves his own beliefs. Persons of strong character are the ultimate resource for any military organization, and persons of strong character are by definition persons of integrity—individuals whose actions are consistent with their beliefs. Major Blue must finally determine whether the actions he is ordered to take are consistent with his central moral beliefs. If he finds that the actions are clearly unacceptable, even if he can rationalize them under the professional military ethic, as a person of integrity he must have the moral courage to take a stand. Many years ago in Southeast Asia, I knew men in uniform who took a stand for moral reasons, and while I did not agree with them, I still respect them for doing so.

Discussion in this chapter has concerned the way in which incorporation of the laws of war generates limitations on the conduct of members of the American military in combat. The equation is not a simple one. We now turn to an even more complex subject: the relationship between fundamental American values and the professional military ethic.

Chapter Seven

The Values of American Society

The Moral Framework for the Professional Military Ethic

Our discussion of the laws of war shows that they manifest humanitarian principles and, accordingly, certain values: human dignity, intrinsic human worth, and freedom from suffering. The American military, in adhering to the laws of war and in accepting the laws of war as legally and morally binding, implicitly accepts these principles and values as well. Together they form part of the moral framework within which the American military functions, and thus we must consider them in examining the moral coherence of the American professional military ethic. The other major aspect of the moral framework consists of the fundamental values of American society, the subject to which we now turn. Within that set of ideals, distinctively moral values concern us in our examination of the role of American values in shaping and applying the American professional military ethic.

In Chapter 4, I suggested that the Constitution serves as the documentary statement of our national values and that the interpretations of the Constitution, most formally through the rulings of the Supreme Court, serve to reconfirm its status as a bearer of national consensus concerning values. In this chapter, I will turn to various sources that not only argue for that conclusion but also support my earlier contention that we can identify these fundamental national values reflected in the Constitution: freedom, equality, individualism, and democracy. The meanings of those abstract terms require explanation as well.

Our discussion will provide the content necessary to apply the proposition that if professional ethics are to be justified by the values of the generating society, they must be consistent with those values. If we can identify the fundamental values of American society, we can apply this proposition, and we can then come to a conclusion about the coherence of the three major influences that I claim to shape any professional military ethic: the exigencies of the activity, the laws of war, and the values of society.

American Values and the Professional Military Ethic

Any discussion of social or national values, unfortunately, will necessarily suffer from oversimplification. The attempt to attribute a specific set of values to a nation as large and diverse as the United States may well arouse skepticism. Any limited set will ignore internal oppositions and contrasts that are major factors in the life of a pluralistic society. For example, to accept equality in some sense as a fundamental value of American society without extensive discussion is to gloss over the fact that America began as a slave-holding society and is still characterized by strong racist attitudes and ethnic prejudices. In 1954, seventeen states still had laws making racial segregation mandatory. We can find exceptions to any generalization involving a population that includes as many widely varying subgroups as we find in the United States. At the beginning of this new century, the American population reflects virtually all of the world's ethnic communities.[1] Many of them preserve their ancestral cultures, adding to the diversity that is now the central characteristic of American society. So long as the values we identify, however, are plausibly verifiable and do not exclude important aspects of American culture that bear upon the nature and content of the American professional military ethic, our conclusions will have a reasonable claim to validity. And even though agreeing upon enduring American values may prove problematic, I argue that anyone intending to justify or fundamentally criticize the professional military ethic must attempt to identify, understand, and apply that value set.

While it does seem intuitively plausible that "the concept of culture implies that there is a typical constellation of . . . orientations that form the basis for the behavior of most Americans,"[2] most of us

would need more evidence to be convinced. Conflict between generations is often attributed to "changing values," which calls into question the assumption that accurate statements can be made about
enduring national or social character. Among those who study the
subject, however, many support the claim that characteristic, identifiable social values do exist for distinct national entities. David
Hume's essay "Of National Character" suggests not only that distinctive characteristics can be expected but moreover that such are
inevitable:

> The human mind is of a very imitative nature; nor is it possible
> for any set of men to converse often together, without acquiring
> a similitude of manners, and communicating to each other their
> vices as well as virtues. The propensity to company and society
> is strong in all rational creatures; and the same disposition,
> which gives us this propensity, makes us enter deeply into each
> other's sentiments, and cause like passions and inclinations to
> run, as it were, by contagion, through the whole club or knot of
> companions.[3]

One might argue that eighteenth century Europe can hardly be
compared to the world of the twenty-first century, but in the highly
developed nations, information distribution and exchange is in fact
incomparably wider than in Hume's day, rendering his thesis even
more plausible rather than less.

One can argue not only that there is a national character in
America but also that it changes in glacial fashion:

> If an index of political culture is the content of public statements
> about America's values, norms, and beliefs, it seems reasonable
> to conclude that they have not changed significantly during the
> history of the nation. Presidents are still giving voice to essen-
> tially the same themes that were expounded by the writers of the
> Declaration of Independence and the Constitution. . . . Indeed,
> several very profound students of America's intellectual and
> cultural development have emphasized the absence of major
> change at this level. Louis Hertz, Daniel Boorstein, Henry Steele
> Commager, Ralph Barton Perry, and Robert McCloskey, all have

claimed the American tradition to be essentially seamless and continuous.[4]

The same point echoes in the work of many sociologists who note that in the midst of change there are nonetheless "common elements in all periods, and a definite and recognizable continuity in the course of development of the society. Some of the basic values and conceptions of the nature of man held at the birth of the Republic are still widespread and viable."[5] One respected researcher, Seymour Lipset, observes that "the value system is perhaps the most enduring part of what we think of as a society, or a social system."[6] Influential commentators such as Francis Fukuyama, Lawrence Harrison, Samuel Huntington, and Robert Putnam all argue that cultural traditions and values are remarkably enduring.[7]

Whereas standards of conduct vary noticeably over time and in various parts of society at the same time, the values upon which such norms are based seem to be much more constant. Those values produce and shape enduring social institutions. The fashions and temporary preoccupations of society certainly affect practice and behavior for a period, but the structures of social institutions are shaped by social values that persist. We can reasonably conclude that, over time, the values that are pervasive, predominant, and persisting will most deeply affect institutional ethics. This conclusion applies forcefully to professional ethics (such as the American professional military ethic) that derive from functional requirements and social values.

Considerable research indicates both that certain values endure in society and that empirical studies can reveal such values. I think of values simply in terms of criteria for choice, which is consistent with the more elaborate conceptions of sociologists.[8] Social scientists study typical modes of choosing. The considerations that preoccupy people in their daily activities are indicators of values. Conduct declared good or bad, in conjunction with operative social sanctions, reveals the existence and nature of values in society. These and similar observations support the contention that the values of society can be empirically established and identified. Repeated studies over a long period of time—many decades—would be necessary to generate conclusive data, but we can supplement recent studies with wider observations about American institutions.

My concern in examining the influence of the values of society on the American professional military ethic is obviously to identify a system of valuation, or the enduring elements of such a system, that is applicable to military activity and whose ascription to American society is verifiable and largely uncontroversial. The subset of national values that we must identify are moral values, those that have an interpersonal focus or that concern good and bad character. The moral values of society will exercise the major influence on the content of particular ethical codes within that society, and of those, what I have termed fundamental moral values will be most important. Without question, within the body of American values as a whole there will be real and potential conflicts, particularly between moral values and nonmoral values. In terms of consistency and justification, however, the fundamental moral values are directly relevant to our project.

The American Value System

For most of the nineteenth century, the majority of Americans were small landowners, and the family farm formed the basis of American life. This fact of social organization appears to have strengthened the individualism implicit in John Locke's philosophy, which in turn greatly influenced political thought in America during the Revolutionary Period. Gerald Critoph sees this as a dominant aspect in the development of the American value system:

Some of the major American democratic beliefs resulted from the experiences of the majority of Americans in agrarian settings during the formative years of the republic. For instance, the strong, abiding conviction that a free individual's identity should be held sacred and that his dignity and integrity should not be violated was a belief that came out of situations in which an individual had to confront the forces of nature just about on his own.[9]

Critoph's general observation refers to several of the values that seem to be included in almost all analyses of the American value system: democracy, freedom, individual integrity and dignity, equality in terms of rights, struggle or competition, and achievement. The last two, of course, are not clearly moral values. The others deserve and require considerable elaboration if we are to address the issue of coherence confidently.

Freedom

Freedom is the watchword of democracy. The two concepts are so much a part of the American national fabric that it is difficult to stand back far enough to gain perspective on the issues. The thirteen colonies fought for freedom from British repression; the protection of freedom was the overriding consideration in creating the Constitution; and throughout our national history, the facts of particular cases aside for the moment, we have maintained that freedom and the preservation of democracy are the only causes justifying the use of our armed forces. I use freedom as synonymous with liberty, though I recognize that liberty suggests freedom within the constraints and support of a political system. It is this qualified sense of freedom to which I refer. Ralph Barton Perry maintains that although usually described as a "form of government," democracy is a social system and may properly be called an ideology, one in which the two fundamental values are freedom and equality.[10] The freedom that Perry identifies is "the principle of maximum freedom which is consistent with a similar freedom for all."[11] Freedom thus informs social institutions and in turn is "a product of organization—of the moral and legal institutions, which define areas of freedom, and guarantee them in the name of rights."[12] Thus freedom and liberty are interchangeable terms in my discussion. Just as democracy and freedom seem to be conceptually bonded in an inseparable way in the American tradition, so too are freedom and rights. In our democratic society, rights are the insurance of freedom.

The sociologist Robin Williams also sees freedom as one of our most widespread and persistent values, though he sees it as part of a pattern—a centuries-long process through which the restraints of feudal Europe were broken. In his view, colonial America was part of a larger sea change in Western attitudes, and in America,

the historical process left its mark in a culturally standardized way of thought and evaluation—a tendency to think of rights rather than duties, a suspicion of established (especially personal) authority, a distrust of central government, a deep aversion to acceptance of obviously coercive restraint through visible social organization.[13]

The peculiarly American sense of freedom presents no objection, Williams explains, to a situation in which the forces of competition and the marketplace result in a certain income or a certain role for an individual, whereas any form of overt social coercion would be profoundly objectionable. "To be tied to a given locality by diffuse cultural pressure and lack of economic opportunity is regarded as a quite different kind of constraint from such controls as a police order or a governmental regulation."[14] Such an environment provides a foundation for a kind of economic meritocracy, with which we are all familiar. Those who obtain wealth, short of using disreputable means, are respected for being wealthy, and we consider them free to use their wealth as they see fit. This conception is in turn closely tied to a particular view of the value of equality.

Equality

Equality can come in many forms. We immediately recognize the sense of equality that emerges in the Constitution, where we can find specific references to equal protection of the laws and equal participation in the political process in terms of both voting and seeking political office.[15] The wider traditional American view is anchored in the Revolutionary period, when equality meant emancipation from a system of status.[16] The American sense of equality focuses on opportunity in that each person can make his or her own place in society and achieve whatever innate potential allows. Equality of opportunity as opposed, say, to equality of distribution means that equality of income or wealth is not expected or even desired. One reaps the benefit of opportunity in proportion to capacity and effort.

While not at all the same as equality of distribution, equality of opportunity—long the slogan of the "melting pot of the world"—does require society's support in the form of equality of education, social security, apportionment of the tax burden, and equality before the law, among other measures. Obviously, we can debate the degree to which the United States has achieved the ideal of equality of opportunity, but Americans sincerely support that value as an ideal. And while "inequality of natural endowment is undeniable and ineradicable, and whenever the conditions of life are equalized, men will profit unequally by these conditions," in our society such conditions are indeed considered "not only unavoidable but desirable."[17] Robin Williams explains the concept as a particular form of fair competition:

> The tautology that inequality is not resented unless considered to be undeserved takes on an important meaning, however, as soon as we are able to specify what "undeserved" means. By and large in the United States, it has meant *categorical* privileges (rewards not earned by effort and achievement) within the basic institutional rules for fair competition. Here is the core of the "American tradition" of equality. The dominant cultural value is not an undifferentiated and undiscriminating equalitarianism, but rather a two-sided emphasis upon basic social rights and upon equality of opportunity.[18]

This particular conception of equality is consistent with the value of individualism, with which the value of equality has a relationship of mutual dependence.

Individualism

The worth and primary importance of the individual (as opposed to the group, the community, the nation) in American culture undoubtedly results from a complex set of factors. Among them has to be the religious tradition in which every person has an immortal soul and thus has value in God's sight, even though religious beliefs no longer play the role they did in early American history. Freedom in America is freedom for the individual to live as he or she sees fit. Much of our law and many government institutions focus on the individual. Whereas some societies, particularly authoritarian ones, have emphasized the welfare of the collectivity over the welfare of the individual, American institutions tend to protect personal freedom and autonomy. Our discussion of the Bill of Rights in Chapter 4 emphasized the institutional bias toward the individual.

We can trace the intellectual individualism that has so profoundly affected American tradition to major figures in Western thought such as Thomas Hobbes and John Locke. In their differing views of social contract theory, in which men create and submit to governments as a means of furthering their individual interests, the autonomous, independent individual is the central figure. John Locke stated the claim clearly:

> Men being . . . by Nature, all free, equal, and independent, no one can be put out of this Estate, and subjected to the Political Power of another, without his own Consent. The only way whereby any one divests himself of his Natural Liberty, and puts on the bonds of Civil Society is by agreeing with other Men to joyn and unite into a Community, for their comfortable, safe, and peaceful living one amongst another.[19]

The focus on the individual in American culture produced the consistent emphasis on competition and personal achievement so evident in our history.

Democracy

The intrinsic worth of individual persons contributes notably to the values of both democracy and equality. As Williams suggests, the American concept of democracy rests upon an "implicit belief in natural law as opposed to personal rule, and the moral autonomy of the individual."[20] The idea that certain natural rights are inalienable is critical in a system in which we believe both (1) that the majority rules and (2) that each person is to be treated as an "end in himself" and is thus considered equal to any other in so far as his status as a person is concerned. Democracy in America is a complex theme that can be described either as constituted by or as subsuming other values such as freedom, individualism, and equality. To the extent that it incorporates those values, we might best call it democratic constitutionalism. A constitutional system provides protection for the individual against the potential tyranny of the majority. Democracy also implies a positive characterization of the nature of man (e.g., the people as a whole *can* govern themselves satisfactorily) and a belief in the possibility of progress. The concept of democratic constitutionalism in this country is also invested with moral value, an aspect of our national values captured by Perry:

The adherent of democracy rejects skeptical relativism and claims truth. He refuses to concede that democracy is just one among conflicting ideologies, each of which is good for its own devotees. He claims it is the optimum form of social organization, endorsed by advancing enlightenment and acceptable even to present opponents in proportion as their ignorance, inexperience, or willful perversity is overcome. . . .[21]

Because democracy, filled out by the values of freedom, equality, and individualism, has become an ideology, we tend to judge all other countries by our democratic standards. Nationalism and emphasis on patriotism have been the result, though that perspective was shaken by the deep divisions created by the events in Indochina in the 1960s and 1970s. Temporarily at least, the assault on terrorism following 9/11 fully revived the public's passion for America. At the same time, the domestic antiwar sentiment generated by the Second Gulf War in 2003 made it clear that such passion was not purely nationalism. In many instances elsewhere in the world, nationalism has become an ideology that focuses the supreme loyalty of the people on the nation-state.[22] Acceptance of nationalism as a social value usually includes ideological commitment in which the particular nation-state is recognized as the ideal form of political organization. The existence of the state then assumes moral value in itself. While that is true of the United States to some extent, our national-patriotic orientation seems to conceive of patriotism "as loyalty to national institutions and symbols because and in so far as they represent values that are the primary objects of allegiance."[23] That characteristic in the past has saved us from a dogmatic form of nationalism that can be a severe threat to peace. Nonetheless, American nationalism, based upon the fundamental moral values we have discussed, is linked to the idea that "the American way" is a shining moral light that should lead to a morally superior existence. This quality of the nationalistic attitude reflects our general cultural tendency to see the world in moral terms, and because Americans believe democracy to be the most enlightened and humane form of government, democracy as a value tends to clothe itself in nationalistic colors.[24]

Part of the moral orientation of American culture has found expression in a persistent tendency toward humanitarianism, which will relate to my comparison of American values and the laws of war. Williams cites strong evidence for such a tendency:

> [Americans persistently demonstrate] a quick, impulsive sympathy for people who are in distress "by no fault of their own"; in anger at the overbearing individual, group, or nation; in pride in America as a haven for the downtrodden and oppressed. The proverbial generosity of American people toward other societies facing mass disaster . . . has elements of exaggeration and myth; but it does index a real and persistent theme. . . .[25]

Sociologists readily admit that the subject of "social values" is of such complexity that research to date has been insufficient to support definitive conclusions. The relationships among values are not static, which unquestionably admits of the possibility of conflict even if fundamental value changes occur slowly. Nonetheless, there do appear to be characteristic patterns of valuation that are generated by the culture of a given society. Also encouraging is the fact that there seems to be considerable agreement concerning the values that could be termed fundamental. Freedom, equality, democracy, and individualism are included in most serious examinations of American society. Extensive sociological studies involving surveys and questionnaires by Milton Rokeach, Norman Feather, and others support the contention that these concepts form the basis for a national value system whose substance can be established empirically.[26]

Democratic equalitarianism was proclaimed as a national ideal in the basic documents of the American Revolution and has remained as such to the present day, though its manifestation has changed as we have become a technically advanced information society. The Declaration of Independence, our statement of national identity, proclaims the universal rights of man. It constitutes the basic documentary manifestation of our natural law tradition. "We hold these truths to be self-evident; that all men are created equal, that they are endowed by their Creator with certain unalienable rights, that among these are life, liberty, and the pursuit of happiness."

This brief sampling of studies and informed opinion supports my contentions about the values generally recognized as "fundamental" in American society. From a nation of Atlantic coast farmers and fishermen, southern planters, and western cattlemen, we have become a giant corporation that is in turn becoming an information-processing society. Still, the principles of individual responsibility and effort, achievement and success, and freedom of choice in a democratic system of equality appear to constitute the major underpinning of the American value system. The United States is a polity founded upon, and self-defined in, terms of these values and derivative principles, which are held to be universally true of all human beings.

Comparing the Laws of War and American Values

We can now compare the moral principles underlying the laws of war with American values in order to determine whether these two sets are conflicting, complementary, or indifferent with respect to each other. Such a comparison is in order since these are two of the primary influences on the provisions of the American professional military ethic.

In the previous chapter I referred to the Air Force manual to emphasize the humanitarian aspect of the laws of war. The same quotation also reveals the extent to which the Department of Defense recognizes the 1949 Geneva Conventions as concerned with the concept of freedom. The conventions, according to the manual,

> safeguard such fundamental rights as freedom from torture or cruel and inhuman punishment; freedom from arbitrary exile; freedom from arbitrarily imposed punishment; and right to legal remedy for any abuse; right to minimum standards of respect for human rights at all times; and right to health, family sanctity and nonabuse.[27]

The Department of Defense obviously interprets freedom in terms of rights, which is the traditional tendency in America. In an abstract sense, *literal* freedom is the capacity to choose without external constraint. In the world we know, the concept exists only as an ideal. The exercise of certain limited, specified freedoms, however, is generally a recognized human value, and in the United States it is firmly held. The listing of certain basic freedoms in the Geneva Conventions reflects the commitment of the formulating body to freedom as a value; I have previously described this commitment as implicit in the application of the wider moral principle that individual persons are to be respected as such (HP1). HP1 and the specification of derivative rights are fully consistent with the sense of freedom I identified as a fundamental American value. Personal freedom of choice is the foundation of moral responsibility, which makes freedom a moral value in the spheres of both the laws of war and American values. On this point, the laws of war and American values do not conflict.

Part of the concept of individualism in the canon of American values is the idea that each person is self-determining. Individuals are thus directly responsible for their actions. This view is closely allied with the concept of moral responsibility and the idea of freedom (or the exercise of freedom) as a value. Respecting individual persons requires restricting the exercise of one's own freedom so as not to infringe upon the capability of others to exercise a degree of their freedom equal to that reserved to oneself. This requirement defines morally unacceptable infringements of the exercise of free choice by individual persons. Any such infringement demeans the status of other persons as morally responsible agents.

In the context of our discussion, violations of the individual's right to exercise free choice in the sphere of the laws of war constitute unjustified applications of physical force, where justification is limited to those actions by a national entity necessary for the equal protection of the ability of its citizens to exercise basic rights. In the sphere of national values, such infringements are the unjustified (in the same sense) applications of physical or psychological force through government agencies or social institutions as well as through personal relationships. Thus, the values of freedom and individualism found in American society and reflected in the laws of war appear to be in accord.

The sense of equality that HP1 embodies is that of a natural equality and, derivatively, equality before the law: all persons are to be treated and judged under the same standards. If government or social institutions fail to provide such treatment under due process, they fail to respect the dignity of individuals. The discussion of the American value of equality focused on equality of opportunity, but we base that concept on the idea that all persons are created equal in being entitled to certain basic social rights that are summarized in the right to "life, liberty, and the pursuit of happiness." Thus, both the laws of war and American values incorporate and demand respect for fundamental rights. On the basis of these observations, we can conclude that the specific rights presented in the 1949 Geneva Conventions are fully compatible with the American concept of equality.

Democracy is a theme of variable hue, but if it is an ideology, as Perry claims, whose fundamental values are freedom and equality, there will be no obvious conflicts between the concept of democracy as a value and the principles of the laws of war. To the extent that democracy is considered a morally superior system providing the justification for radical nationalism and interventionist policies, however, it could present a potential for conflict with the laws of war and the concept of defensive war. In most of the twentieth century, the collective nations of the world, in conventions and United Nations declarations, maintained that only defensive wars were morally and legally justifiable. In the 1990s and the early years of the twenty-first century, military intervention ostensibly in defense of human rights as well as the Bush doctrine of pre-emption have altered that formula somewhat. But to the extent that we include humanitarianism as an aspect of American values, we find those values and HP2 in accord. Both HP1 and HP2 thus appear to be fully compatible with the moral values of American culture.

Nationalism—closely allied for the United States with our fundamental beliefs because we value freedom, equality, individualism, and democracy so highly—constitutes one of the great threats to social stability and civilized existence. Radical nationalism does present the possibility of conflict with the principles underlying the laws of war. Many actions that would be otherwise morally unacceptable can be condoned if nationalism is granted priority over other values and moral considerations. In a radical or dogmatic form, nationalism can introduce inconsistency into the values of American society. We have generally avoided that problem in the past.

The incarceration of Japanese-Americans during World War II provides an unfortunate example of what can occur when dogmatic nationalism and national security concerns outweigh the rights of individuals. American citizens of Japanese ancestry were placed in concentration camps in the United States in 1942 because of an emotionally charged but vaguely conceived possibility that they represented a threat to national security. The action was taken under the authority of emergency war powers and was upheld by the Supreme

Court, but the rights of this group of law-abiding and apparently patriotic citizens clearly were not respected, and the legality of the action remains at best problematic. The choice faced by government officials appeared at the time to be between endangering the welfare of American citizens in general and violating the fundamental rights of a relatively small (and politically inconsequential) minority. That concern has emerged again in the war on terrorism. In numerous cases after 9/11, authorities in America held individuals for questioning for long periods and denied them any communication with family or legal advisors. Individuals captured in Afghanistan while fighting for al-Qaida and the Taliban presented a dangerous threat to Americans and received even harsher treatment. The 9/11 events made clear what a few fanatics can accomplish. Add weapons of mass destruction and security concerns become insistent. The captives transported to Guantanamo were part of a situation that again generated concern about security versus human rights. As enemy combatants, the Guantanamo prisoners were to be held until "hostilities" came to an end. That treatment conformed to accepted practice for hostilities between states. The difficulty in this instance arose because the war on terrorism is an open-ended campaign against non-state entities. It may well continue for many years. Some of the prisoners claimed they were not combatants but were swept up in the confusion of war. They were not allowed to provide evidence for their claims. The U.S. government denied that they had a right to legal process to try to establish their innocence.

The type of conflict that most frequently arises for the military is slightly less complicated but similar: the military professional must choose either to respect the rights of certain individuals or to achieve a particular objective that appears to be required by his commitment to serve society's interests. In addition, in any particular situation the interests of society as articulated by the state may not be in accord with the professional's private conception of the interests of society. Any resolution of such conflicts must specify the nature of the professional's commitment and must establish a priority among values. Since freedom is a fundamental American value as well as a value underlying the laws of war, the spotlight shifts from the laws of war to the realm of conflict among American values. For our present purposes, we need only observe that any conflict between the principles of the laws of war and the principles that are generated by American values undoubtedly exist for the American professional military ethic before the laws of war are considered. The controversy over the prisoners in Guantanamo makes that point clear. Difficult choices result from a conflict between the American commitment to freedom and respect for individual persons, on the one hand, and our right to defend ourselves and enhance our own security, on the other. To date the U.S. government has concluded that recognition of the human rights of enemy combatants does not require or justify placing American lives at risk.

Though our discussion has been brief, perhaps it is adequate to establish the following: (1) a set of values can be characterized as fundamental to American society as that society has developed, and (2) substantial agreement exists that freedom, equality, individualism, and democracy are basic moral values characteristic of American society as a whole. The Constitution manifests these values in its provisions. Commitment to "support and defend the Constitution" is thus also a commitment to the fundamental moral principles we have identified. Military professionals need to recognize the logic of that commitment and to understand its implications. While it is not the case that commitment by the military professional to the Constitution and the fundamental values identified here eliminates confusion in difficult choice situations (though it certainly helps), the analysis I have presented provides the basis for a strong argument that the American professional military ethic and the laws of war are consistent. If that is so, and if the fundamental American values are consistent with one another, the primary influences on the American professional military ethic appear to be morally coherent. Except for the possible dissonance created by the ethnocentricity of nationalism, which can be reinforced through a relation to the values of achievement and ideological democracy, the humanitarianism that informs the laws of war also operates in the American value system. HP1 and HP2 are consistent with the fundamental American moral values and thus with the principles to which military professionals are committed through their fealty to the Constitution.

One major consideration remains concerning our investigation of the American professional military ethic: the issue of role differentiation. If the three primary influences on the professional military ethic are consistent and compatible, as I have claimed, one can still reasonably question whether the role, which requires extreme departures from the moral behavior expected in normal social activities, is fully or partially differentiated. In Chapter 3, I suggested that the role of a military professional is partially differentiated. In the next chapter, I will present my reasoning for that conclusion. Doing so will also clarify priorities among the various factors that affect military decision making.

Chapter Eight

Justifying Military Decisions

Taking Stock

Before we launch into the subject of justification, it may be worthwhile to review the major considerations we have developed thus far. We have, among other things, examined the professional status of the career military officer, articulated the general principles that govern the moral conduct of members of the American military, considered the importance of human rights as a moral issue for military leaders, and come to some initial conclusions concerning the compatibility of the three major influences on the American professional military ethic. We found that under most proposed sets of defining characteristics for a profession, the career officer corps qualifies as one. Our examination also revealed that the role of the professional officer calls for a deep commitment to a particular function critically important to American society: maintaining the security of the United States under the authority of the Constitution. The oath of office makes those responsibilities clear. As we find in parallel fashion in the fields of medicine and law, the central function of the profession generates a fundamental value for members of the American military. The commitment of the military professional is on behalf of a client—American society. Within the state, the government is the state's executive agency and the military is one means the government employs to execute policy and pursue national objectives. The military is thus an institution within an institution, serving a larger cause than interests internal to the military itself.

That larger cause requires the use of armed force. All civilized societies in some form regulate the use of armed force, killing, and other forms of intentional violence. Without such regulation, society itself could not exist in any stable condition. None of us could realize the benefits of social existence if law and convention did not curb violence against others. The military and police forces are exempted under law and convention from the prohibition against violence except in self-defense. Both groups are considered justified in applying force—even to the extent of killing—when it is necessary to enforce the law in the case of the police, or to defend the state, in the case of the military. If the duty of the military, which consists generally of those actions necessary in maintaining the security of the state, includes killing other persons, our society considers such actions justified, as do most cultures. Particularly in American society, where the dominant social values are moral values, the actions of the military are considered to have a fundamental moral justification. This assumes, of course, that the actions are properly part of the effort to preserve the state and are part of a defensive rather than an aggressive policy or program. It is this moral justification that makes the American professional military ethic of singular interest. The nature of that justification has to do with the ends served by the military and the state it protects.

Accordingly, as we have discussed, the military pursues a moral purpose that a professional code governing conduct supports. The code facilitates the accomplishment of the professional function. Within the context of a given society, the moral purpose justifies the profession, and, in most cases, the professional function allegedly justifies the code. For the American military, we have established that the professional ethic is a noncodified traditional ethic that is perpetuated through the process of professional socialization. The professional military ethic is primarily the result of the influence of three major factors: the exigencies of the profession, the values of the society served, and the laws of war. We have seen that the moral principles underlying the laws of war are compatible with the fundamental values of American society, which eliminates one potential source of incoherence.

I presented this claim at the beginning of our discussion: the role of the American military professional is a morally coherent, partially differentiated role that is rationally justifiable within the context of American society. I have thus far limited my argument for coherence to showing that we can reasonably contend that the fundamental values of American society and the laws of war are compatible. The next step in examining the American professional military ethic is that of considering the partially differentiated status of the military role. Can we confidently hold that it is justifiable from a moral point of view?

I believe it is, given the following qualification: certain boundary conditions limit those elements of the professional military ethic that find their primary source in the requirements of the profession. The boundary conditions limit military necessity and provide the moral coherence that might otherwise be questionable. I noted earlier that in most cases the professional function for any professional group justifies the code that governs the activity. That is not true, however, of the American military. In the context of American society, it is not the case that a justifiable professional military ethic is one determined by functional requirements alone.

The three principles that are most obviously traceable to functional requirements are those of duty, truth telling, and professional competence. Admirable though such characteristics are, as elements of the professional military ethic they are justifiable only if certain boundary conditions hold. Those conditions ensure compatibility with the enduring moral values of American society. Without the conditions, the professional military ethic becomes a predominantly consequentialist ethic that is oriented to mission accomplishment. Such an ethic produces results that can conflict with our common moral intuitions and are inconsistent with fundamental American values, as we will discuss further in this chapter. Not all members of the American military profession fully understand or accept such boundaries, which is why the issue is an important one. The principles of truth telling and professional competence do not raise urgent moral questions, but the duty principle does. That, for the American military, is more than a functional requirement. Before we examine the duty principle itself, however, we need to set the stage by contrasting full and partial differentiation.

Differentiation of the Military Role

One way to reveal the differentiation status of the military role might be to consider the views of authoritative members of the profession. Examining the views of one such spokesman, General Maxwell D. Taylor, reveals an ambiguous perception of the military role. His position and the views of others suggest that the moral end served by the armed forces in American society must be a central consideration in arguing the justifiability of differentiation.

General Taylor, in considering how military professionals ought to make moral choices, suggests that the appropriate choice is that which would be made by the ideal professional officer, "one who can be relied upon to carry out all assigned tasks and missions and, in doing so, get the most from his available resources with minimum loss and waste. Such resources might include men, money, weapons, equipment, allies, time, space, geography, and weather."[1] General Taylor's approach to ethical choice prescribes no specific rules. Instead, it suggests that the decision made by an officer of requisite character in the role would be the right decision.

Some structuring principles appear, however, as General Taylor continues. For example, he refers to the function of the military professional, who is "a lineal descendant of the warrior who, in company with the king, the priest, and the judge, has performed throughout history a primal function essential to the survival and well-being of civilization."[2] General Taylor does not raise the concept of differentiation in his discussion, but he suggests that the officer's commitment to the security of the state is an overriding ethical consideration. If one accepts that the professional military function is "essential to the survival and well-being of civilization," such a suggestion is not surprising. The following quotations from General Taylor's essay indicate the degree to which he sees broad moral rules as subordinate to the dictates of professional requirements:

> [A]n officer has little choice but to assume the rightness of a governmental decision involving the country in war. Having made this assumption, he is honor-bound to carry out all legal orders and do his best to bring the war to a prompt and successful conclusion.[3]

> Our model, recognizing that obedience to orders is one of the highest military virtues, one without which armies are worse than useless, will be instinctively inclined to obey any legal order.

As for his attitude toward the voice of conscience as a guide to military behavior, he has serious doubts as to its reliability.[4]

What General Taylor means by "conscience" in this passage is unclear. Elsewhere he provides a variety of possibilities, such as a "God-given moral sense," "the voice of conventional morality," and "self-interest in a pious guise." The last suggestion is probably ironic, for there is a distinct difference between evaluations of what one morally ought to do and what will be of greatest personal benefit. People often rationalize and fabricate moral reasons for what they desire to do, but few seriously contend the two actions are one and the same. Despite the status of ethical theory sometimes granted to ethical egoism, few claim that that which is moral is that which an individual believes to be in his or her best interest.

General Taylor's other suggestions might well be considered possible labels for "ordinary morality," or the moral norms that apply to members of society in general. If so, General Taylor appears to be advocating a rejection of considerations of ordinary morality in favor of higher or overriding principles that derive from the professional function—that is, he appears to be advocating a fully differentiated ethic. Moreover, he seems to suggest that the functional requirements of the profession are the only appropriate basis for moral evaluation from a professional point of view. These conclusions concerning General Taylor's intent remain purely speculative, of course, and may not be accurate. He may be advocating only a partially differentiated role, one in which professional considerations are given additional weight in relation to the prescriptions of general moral criteria rather than being the *sole* basis of evaluation. But from his essay, it is not clear which position he would support. That ambivalence exemplifies the difficult problem of decision criteria that military decision makers face in a world of swiftly moving and dimly perceived events, when choices must be made, if only by default, and lives and perhaps national fortunes hang in the balance.

To encounter such a lack of clarity or a statement of a position implying full differentiation is not unusual in discussions of this subject. We find sufficient variation and ambiguity among members of the profession to discourage reliance upon any particular statement by an "authoritative" member of the profession and to indicate the need for further study. I suggested earlier that the military role in American society is partially differentiated, but an advocate of full differentiation could argue that even though the fundamental values of American society have indeed shaped the professional military ethic, once produced, the ethic itself is the sole source of moral guidance appropriate for military professionals as professionals. Some might hold an even more extreme view, claiming that "a true soldier" will be guided solely by functional requirements.

In any military organization that intensively trains its members to be deeply committed to mission accomplishment and concentrates on developing the mental and physical toughness of its fighting force, more than a few of its members will conclude that winning is everything. And isn't that what we as a society appear to ask of our military? Don't we, in the final analysis, expect them to win, however tough the fight, no matter what it takes? The answer, of course, is no, we do not expect that, but between our national preoccupation with winning and the nature of much of our military training, one should not be surprised to find that many civilians as well as members of the military have received and accepted the message that military necessity rules when national survival is at stake. That issue has become even more prominent in the war on terrorism, in which the enemy desires not our defeat but our destruction. In that situation, it is but a short step to believing that we must do whatever is necessary to win when we go to war. When one is fighting to preserve freedom and all that is good in human life, can anything *short* of total, unrestrained effort be justified?

Full differentiation would certainly simplify the task of making decisions concerning actions that affect others. No variety of moral perspectives is then involved; no complex utilitarian evaluation is necessary. One merely applies the rules for the fully differentiated role (though doing so may be controversial and demanding in itself). Then adherence to the special norms of the profession becomes justifiable regardless of the moral content of specific circumstances (in terms of general moral criteria). Still, to claim that actions are to be justified solely in terms of the professional ethic or functional requirements is to take an extreme position. To determine whether such claims provide an ultimate "ought," we have to look *through* the specific actions to the moral ends served.

To examine the moral ends served by a professional activity in American society, we can proceed quickly by considering rights. Alan Goldman points out that "rights express interests important enough to be protected against additions of lesser interests across persons."[5] If this view is characteristic of a society, it follows that its members will treat rights, or at least some rights, as absolute in relation to utilities, though rights themselves may be ordered—indeed they must be—in resolving conflicts among rights. Such seems to be the case in American society. We maintain that protection of individual rights, however abused in practice and obscured by social complexity, is fundamental to a free, democratic society. Such a society can realize the dignity and integrity of the individual only if it defends the corollary principle of equal consideration of interests. Although that principle does not entail equal *treatment*, the interests of each individual should receive equal consideration, from which it follows that within recognized and accepted parameters, equality of opportunity should be preserved. If the interests of certain individuals or groups are preferred as a result of society's public institutions for reasons that are not morally relevant, the integrity of the individual is necessarily violated. And in a society that holds the integrity and autonomy of the individual as a foundational value, such violation will normally be both unjust and immoral.

How does this apply to our immediate concern? The moral end of the military, which serves the direct purpose of maintaining the security of the state, lies in the protection of rights that derive from the foundational moral values. These are the human rights we have discussed at length. Only through such a moral end can ultimate moral justification for the military be sought. In the United States, the protection of rights is the moral end, and the rights concerned are those that the state exists to provide. Thus, we find ourselves once more at the Constitution and the values it manifests. At a minimum those values include freedom, equality, democracy, and individualism.

The situation that results sometimes appears contradictory. To protect and preserve the values from which fundamental rights derive, it sometimes seems necessary to override the fundamental rights of certain persons or a particular group. But if the professional ethic governing such actions is to be morally coherent in terms of such values, it must at least be consistent in terms of those values.

Explaining coherence requires a more searching examination of the issue of full versus partial differentiation.

The Case for Full Differentiation

The primary function of the American military is the systematic application of force. The military employs force to maintain the security of the state in the interests of the moral ends, as I have discussed. In considering the question of justifying differentiation, we can profitably ask whether the military professional can achieve the moral ends of the profession, and thus fulfill the social responsibility of the professional officer, without the status of full differentiation. We will first consider whether special norms are indeed necessary, and then how we should categorize those norms. Answers to questions in these areas may indicate how the authority of military professionals should be limited.

Throughout our early history, our geographic location largely assured our military security. The oceans were major considerations in any strategic analysis; formulation of the nation's foreign policy could begin with the assumption of secure borders. Twentieth-century warfare and modern technology fundamentally altered the strategic picture, however, and the functional imperatives of military security now require capable, standing armed forces. "Fortress America," guarded by the Atlantic and the Pacific, no longer exists. That became abundantly clear after the events of 11 September 2001, and our realization of America's vulnerability to weapons of mass destruction.

In contributing to military security, the armed forces do provide what is apparently an essential service, and the performance of that service makes necessary specified relations with the rest of society. Such direction is necessary because the profession wields extensive influence over the welfare of the members of society, and moral guidelines help prevent the use of such influence to the detriment of the interests of society. For the armed forces, such direction is found to a large extent in the operation of the professional ethic.

The American professional military ethic is an amalgam of law, custom, and tradition, the content of which we considered in Chapter 4. In examining the justification for the ethic, however, we can consider some structural elements without regard to content. Legal statutes and codes provide detailed guidance for judges, for example, but we can consider the question of whether judges should scrupulously adhere to the law without examining the detailed content of the statutes and codes that govern judicial actions. Comparison of the situation of the judiciary as a profession to that of the military may provide some clarification of the issues involved. For the military, the principle of maintaining national security may be analogous in function to the principle of the rule of law for the judiciary. Maintaining national security is the raison d'être for the armed forces, just as maintaining the rule of law is such for judges. National security interests would then dictate the structure within which military decisions are made, just as the law establishes the structure for adjudication.

The apparently ultimate priority of national security interests brings into play the principle of necessity. Controversy has erupted in the past because of the priority given to state self-preservation and the protection of critical national security interests. In Chapter 7, I mentioned the inexcusable treatment of Japanese-Americans in World War II. Military decision makers have been caught in difficulties similar to those of the government officials who decided to put the *Nisei* in camps in 1941 and those who left the Guantanamo prisoners in limbo. On the level of issues rather than personalities, the relief of General Douglas MacArthur during the Korean Conflict exemplifies such a controversy. General MacArthur's convictions concerning the actions necessary to pursue vital national interests brought him into conflict with his civilian superiors. The principle of subordination of the military to civilian authority was seemingly opposed to the obligation to pursue what he saw as the most effective course of action in successfully terminating the conflict. As a result of his views, General MacArthur, despite being America's best known and arguably most highly respected soldier, was relieved from command of forces in the field. President Truman's action upheld and strongly reinforced the principle of civilian control.[6]

Necessity at the highest level of national affairs is seldom the direct concern of the military professional; that responsibility lies with the national leadership. Insofar as international law is concerned, the principle of necessity provides justification only in those cases in which the breaches of international law are committed in response to acts unlawful in character.[7] Insofar as moral justification is concerned, actions taken in the name of necessity are taken on the authority of the state. In such cases, justification of the actions must be in terms of the fundamental values of the society concerned or the moral reasoning will indeed be incoherent. If the society is to be consistent, ultimate justification is clearly not a function of national security interests alone; it is, rather, a function of the value system of the society. Ultimate justification must be moral, not legal or merely expedient. If it is consistent, such reasoning will provide rational justification for moral choices. Considerations appropriate for the civilian leadership of the state apply to the military leadership as well.

With these points in mind, we can pursue the issue of full differentiation and our comparison with the situation of judges. Do military professionals require special norms in carrying out their function as judges apparently do? We have established that such special norms are in effect. The authorization for killing and destruction provide the central case. The authority to infringe individual liberty and the right of free speech exists in virtually all military institutions. To withdraw such authorizations and the authority to employ force when called for in national defense would be to render the military ineffective at best. If these authorizations represent a group of special norms, as they apparently do, we can ask whether the set to which they belong establishes a fully or a partially differentiated role. Parallels with the judiciary are suggestive.

Justice and equal status before the law are moral ends served directly by the functioning of the judiciary. The decisions of a judge materially affect the law and establish a precedent (in the Anglo-Saxon legal tradition) that has a formalized effect on subsequent judicial proceedings. This fact renders any degree of arbitrary judgment detrimental to the system. Judges must always remember as well that all decisions are subject to human fallibility. To interpose personal moral judgments in situations in which all facts can never be known and in which the effects of such interpositions can never be accurately calculated would be to undermine the predictability and stability essential to the very functioning of the institution of law. All legal systems provide sanctions, but they operate on the basis of voluntary compliance with the law. If the vast majority of citizens do not voluntarily follow the law, the legal system could dissolve in

chaos. A major factor in such compliance is the expectation of predictability and stability.

These factors support the position that holds that the role of
judges is and should be fully differentiated, which is to say that they
should adjudicate solely in accordance with the law, without regard to their own or other moral evaluations. They should do so in
the name of the higher moral ends served by the institution of law,
thereby ensuring that a conclusion is based upon the functional requirements of their professional role. They are constrained to apply
the law regardless of their personal views, and actions under such
constraint are deemed morally justifiable even if such actions in specific cases lead to results for the individuals directly concerned that
are much less than optimal from a moral point of view. While we
may not agree with this view concerning a judge's role (and I have
doubts), it is a strong argument.

To what extent can we make a similar argument for the military? If one assumes that the actions of the American military under
consideration are taken in the context of a just war, then one might
argue that the actions required by military necessity are appropriate
actions taken to further national security. We have established that it
is not the case that *any* action can be justified by the principle of
military necessity, but it appears that any action permissible under
the laws of war that is also militarily necessary is indeed justifiable.
One could claim that for a military professional to refuse to carry out
such an action on moral grounds would be to betray the moral ends
that the military is seeking to achieve through preserving national
security.

One could then propose that the reliability achieved through
discipline and obedience to orders is an essential characteristic of
effective military operations. If the requirements of legal missions
were subject to the moral views of individual officers, it might not be
possible to achieve meaningful levels of reliability and predictability,
which are as significant for the military as for the judiciary. Without
reliability and predictability under the rule of law, the institution of
law itself would not survive. Similarly, without the stability obtained through discipline and obedience to orders, one could argue
that the military institution could not function and that national
security could become subject to the will of other states or a particular group within the state. If discipline and obedience to orders are

necessary for an effective military force, and if that force is necessary in order to preserve the value system of society, then it would seem that duty should override personal moral judgments. To refuse to obey orders because certain actions are morally unacceptable or undesirable would set a precedent that could undermine military effectiveness in general.

Given such considerations, it does seem that the special norms of the profession take precedence over moral considerations that would apply to a general member of society. (Though I will argue *against* this view shortly, I want to present it fully before discussing my objections to it.) Professional soldiers can take actions, such as deliberately expending the lives of persons under their command in combat operations, which would be morally impermissible outside the professional role. The authority and the obligation for the pursuit of duty derive directly from the responsibility for the military security of the state. Thus, it appears that special norms are necessary to the performance of the functions of a military professional. If the duties of the soldier, assuming they do not involve illegal activity, are not only justifiable but morally obligatory, then it is wrong for the professional to substitute personal moral views or the conduct morally prescribed for a civilian in place of the dictates of the professional norms. The conclusion of this line of argument is that military professionals are constrained in applying their moral beliefs (just as judges are constrained in applying the rule of law).

Yet another restriction indicates the military role is differentiated, perhaps even to the extent of full differentiation. In discussing the role of the judiciary, Goldman argues that an individual in the role of "member of society" is under no moral constraint with respect to the law.[8] Indeed, he claims that citizens in general should maintain a critical attitude toward the law. "Not only is one not obligated to give the fact of law extra independent weight in moral calculations, but it is not morally permitted to do so."[9] This is the case because "it is healthy for society to have the moral sense of citizens act as a check to the legislative power to command conformity with laws that may not always have moral ends."[10]

The soldier's situation seems clearly different—as does that of the judge—with respect to the pertinent laws, which are here the laws of war. Because of their role, members of the military have a moral obligation to act in accordance with the laws of war. The

American professional military ethic incorporates the laws of war, which we have noted as being legally binding under the Constitution and the regulations of the services. Members of society in general, as noncombatants, cannot legally participate in combat operations under the laws of war.[11] Because the laws of war constitute part of the American professional military ethic (as noted in Chapter 4), we might consider this as further evidence of full differentiation.

The argument for full differentiation for the military professional can thus be made on the basis of at least four factors: the moral ends for which the professional institution exists; the necessity for discipline and obedience if the functions of the military are to be carried out effectively; the operation of military necessity that overrides all localized moral considerations; and the moral obligation to adhere to the laws of war without substitution of independent moral judgment.

The Case Against Full Differentiation

Analysis of each of the four factors that appear to support full differentiation, however, shows that they provide an inadequate basis for such a conclusion. Justice and equal status before the law are moral ends served directly by the functioning of the judiciary. The military appears to differ significantly in that the military directly serves national interests by executing government policy. Such policies and interests, narrowly conceived, may or may not be in accord with the moral ends cited previously. If recent history teaches no other lesson, it makes clear that national interests and national purpose, measured in terms of government action, range the moral spectrum. Only if the actions of a national government *are* in accord with the enduring, broadly conceived moral ends of society can the military function (in a society in which civil authority determines overall military objectives) be said to have "ultimate" moral justification. Consequentially, we do not find such justification solely within the function of the military, as seems possible in the case of the judiciary. Comparison of the effects of the military function with the moral ends of society is necessary.

Even after we recognize such a relationship, however, without obedience and discipline the military cannot function effectively.

The implication is that the duty principle is absolute in some sense. Frequently, in arguing what actions are appropriate in particular cases, military officers appear to assume that full differentiation is necessary if warfare is to be waged successfully. Similarly, one could suggest that consistent behavior in a fully differentiated role must be based upon functional exigencies alone. The situation of the military professional is closer, therefore, to that of the lawyer than the judge in this regard. We can examine the differentiation status of the advocate role to see how this is the case. The role of the lawyer provides some useful insight into the question of the differentiation status of the military.

The American Bar Association *Code of Professional Responsibility* requires a lawyer to pursue a client's interests without exception within the limits of the law.[12] This is the "received view" that has dominated since Lord Brougham, the crusading nineteenth-century jurist, established the principle. The traditional interpretation of the principle of full advocacy implies a fully differentiated role similar to that of the judiciary. It is not clear that such a view is unwarranted.

The operation of the principle of full advocacy in our adversary system of law reflects one of the fundamental values of American society that we discussed earlier: "[P]rotection of individual dignity and autonomy, even at the expense of collective public welfare, is pervasive in our legal system, as that institution reflects our deeper rights based moral framework."[13] To accept full advocacy solely on this basis, however, would be premature. To do so would be to affirm full role differentiation in that those actions required by service to a client that were impermissible under general moral criteria, would nonetheless be justifiable and obligatory for lawyers. Several considerations suggest that the principle of full advocacy should be modified by dictates of ordinary morality.[14]

Normally, the wrong of punishing the innocent outweighs the wrong of failing to provide maximum protection to the public in general. However, when a lawyer knows on the basis of factual evidence—not the interpretation of evidence, where we are all fallible—that the client is guilty, or when the harm to innocent persons that will result from full advocacy would make a mockery of the pursuit of justice, general moral principles may properly rule out some actions apparently justified by the code under the principle of full advocacy. In this view,

> lawyers are not . . . justified in using all those tactics to secure acquittal, including presentation of false testimony, harmfully aggressive cross examination, or impeachment of testimony of truthful witnesses, that they might be justified in using to prevent conviction of an innocent client.[15]

If this is so, the role of the lawyer is partially rather than fully differentiated.

Strong arguments support both sides of this question in the realm of criminal law, but in the context of corporate law, the principle of full advocacy no longer applies in the same sense. As a functioning part of the corporate entity, the corporation lawyer is no longer a disinterested advocate. To a significant extent, he or she is representing personal interests. In addition, as corporations influence the law itself through their legal divisions in lobbying activities, the adequacy of the restriction to actions within the law becomes questionable.[16] Much of the legal activity on behalf of corporations is not conducted in an adversarial context. The purpose of the principle of full advocacy, which assumes vigorous and informed pursuit of opposing interests by both sides, will often be morally inappropriate. Those whose interests are in jeopardy (the public) are not represented when lawyers lobby to weaken regulations controlling the safe manufacture of drugs. In such a case, which is outside the criminal justice system, it is even more obvious that moral considerations other than the professional code itself apply if we are to see responsible decisions.

Another argument bearing on the justification of the principle of full advocacy involves the equitable distribution of legal expertise. If justice is to be served, all parties should have equal access to the services of a lawyer. Setting aside the question of the varying ability of clients to afford legal services, equal access will presumably be the best basis for deciding cases on their merits and thus doing so justly. In the case of judges, the legal system is dependent upon members of the bench applying the law as it exists. One could claim that the same principle applies to lawyers, since an unequal distribution of legal services will result unless lawyers provide every advantage to a client allowed under the law. While inequality of legal competence among lawyers may be an intractable fact, deprivation of adequate legal counsel through the moral discrimination of lawyers can at least be avoided, under this argument, by compliance with the principle of full advocacy. Without it, clients that lawyers disliked or disapproved of would not receive adequate representation. The operation of the principle thus provides the fairest distribution of legal resources.

This position, however, is not convincing. Lawyers function as individuals rather than as undifferentiated parts of an institutional monolith. If a client feels his lawyer will not serve his or her interests adequately, he or she can seek another. Such is hardly the case with a judge. Thus, if a lawyer informs a client that she will limit her actions to those that meet certain moral considerations, and the client feels the lawyer, as a result, will not serve his interests as he desires, the client can seek legal representation elsewhere. Because legal assistance will still be available even though lawyers do apply general moral criteria to professional decisions, this consideration does not support the argument that the professional function requires full differentiation. One might object that *all* lawyers might refuse their services, but if that were the case, surely it would be overwhelming prima facie evidence (considering the variety of moral perspective among lawyers) that support of the client's objectives cannot be justified in any coherent rationale. We can conclude from this argument that the lawyer's ethical code should not prevent them from denying their services to a client when they feel that pursuit of a prospective client's objectives would be patently unjust or immoral.

Further, if lawyers employ the tactics permissible under the full advocacy principle as traditionally interpreted, which not only permits but requires undertaking legal but immoral actions that further the interests of the client, it appears that the issue of deciding cases on merit is subordinated—in which case the fundamental purpose of achieving justice is not fulfilled. One could argue that it is the court as a whole that has the responsibility of deciding the merits of a case, and that lawyers best contribute to this by presenting the most effective argument possible for their clients. However, Goldman argues this is difficult to maintain when one recognizes that extreme legal tactics, which are not only permissible but required under a full differentiation view, serve in many cases to obscure the truth through deception, concealment, and clearly immoral actions.

The reasons for qualifying the principle of full advocacy are strong. There are other arguments against the moral acceptability of full advocacy, and some similar arguments for modifying the principle of confidentiality for lawyers. The conclusion strongly suggested by such arguments is that although the legal profession sometimes appears to assume a fully differentiated role, analysis reveals that only a partially differentiated role can be justified.

The point of Goldman's argument is not that there are some actions allowable under the professional ethic that, from a moral point of view, no lawyer should perform. The point is that functional requirements alone do not require full differentiation in the lawyer's role. There is room within the necessities of functional considerations for adherence to moral standards not included in the codified ethic of the legal profession itself. Goldman argues that lawyers should not be required to follow the ethic literally and specifically in all cases. To do so, in his view, leads to results contrary to the values commonly held to justify the ethic of the legal profession—the values of American society. His quarrel is thus with the way the legal ethic is currently applied. My concern is not with whether he is right about legal ethics, but with the pattern of analysis that he employs.

In a sense analogous to the situation of lawyers as analyzed by Goldman, a military professional's refusal to carry out certain activities on moral grounds, while undoubtedly having traumatic career effects, would normally result in responsibility being shifted to another individual (since the military is a vertically organized institution with an explicit hierarchy of command). Only in the most unusual situations would such refusal have a crippling effect on the military function, and the question of full differentiation cannot be settled on the basis of extraordinary and unlikely scenarios.

In another consideration suggested by the status of lawyers, we can see that actions by the armed forces on behalf of their client can be quite harmful to individuals, both citizens and noncitizens. If full differentiation is not functionally necessary in a clearly demonstrable way, and if it may in addition work to the detriment of achieving the moral end served by the profession, claiming such a status appears quite dubious when the moral end is protection of individual integrity and autonomy.

As I noted earlier, the decisions of a judge materially affect the law and establish a precedent that has a formalized effect on subsequent judicial proceedings. No such formalized effect results from the military professional considering moral factors other than the professional military ethic alone. Goldman also argues that the fallibility of human judgment makes it necessary for judges to follow the rule of law exclusively. To interpose their personal moral judgment would be to render the administration of law unpredictable and to some extent arbitrary. Under such conditions, the institution of law would no longer be capable of promoting justice and stability.

Fallibility works in reverse in the military situation, however, because of the separation of military function and moral end. All decisions are subject to human fallibility. If individual officers err in applying their moral judgment, the organizational hierarchy ensures that the military function can continue, but if there is no corrective within the chain of command—that is, if the total obedience of full differentiation ruled—grave moral errors could be endlessly and disastrously propagated. Total obedience would render correction of any fallacious judgment impossible. The interests and moral ends of society could themselves be critically endangered from within by one wrong high-level decision. Precisely because of human fallibility, the moral judgment of each individual military officer must act as a check on the military system if the rights of members of American society are ultimately to receive protection.

The third of the four factors that appear to support full differentiation involves necessity. If the operation of military necessity were held to override all other considerations, as it was in the German doctrine of *Kriegsraison geht vor Kriegsmanier*,[17] the moral ends served by maintaining the military security of the United States could themselves be endangered. The principle of proportionality, accepted as a *jus in bello* principle in any moral evaluation of actions in war, requires that the means employed in warfare be proportional to the military ends or objectives involved. Unqualified application of such a principle, however, becomes a utilitarian calculation. If the military end or objective is given an extremely high value (unlimited, perhaps, if the stakes are national survival), then essentially any means can be justified. Even if limited by the laws of war, such a principle makes concern about persons, to include the moral rights of individuals, subordinate to utilities. Such a result clearly subverts the fundamental values of American society that the military exists to serve. As Goldman said of lawyers, the defense of moral autonomy and the rights of the individual cannot extend to systematic invasion of the proper domain of individual sovereignty. The emphasis here should be on "systematic." To say that military necessity necessarily overrides other moral factors is to establish such a systematic invasion in the functioning of the military. Accordingly, the principle of military necessity must itself be subject to the moral judgment of the military leader. In many situations in which decisions are necessary, the military professional alone is in a position to make the required judgment.

The fourth feature suggesting full differentiation is also questionable. The obligation to adhere to the laws of war is clear, but the laws of war are fundamentally a means of moral enforcement—a means of implementing certain moral principles. Whereas compliance with the laws of war is indeed a duty for members of the military, all such laws are subject to review under the moral criteria that are now recognized. If the law in a particular situation does not serve the moral purposes of the law, a basis exists for applying independent moral judgment or the criteria of "ordinary morality." Military professionals are well prepared to apply such judgment because of their extensive formal education and experience. As they attain positions of greater responsibility and their decisions have ramifications that are more extensive, their education and experience progress accordingly.

The case against full differentiation for the role of the military professional is at least as persuasive as the case against full differentiation for lawyers. Nonetheless, the moral aspects of the professional's role call for him or her to give special weight to the norms of the profession. At least three categories of actions show this to be true, and they are distinguished with respect to the persons whose moral rights are overridden. One category covers those involved in personal relationships with the professional; moral obligations to both family and friends that would normally be ultimate reasons for action are subordinated to the demands of duty. A second category involves the status of members of the armed forces with respect to civil rights. Rights such as those of free speech and personal liberty that would require recognition and deference from a general moral perspective are in certain situations subordinated by military authorities on the basis of the requirements of the professional military ethic. Such subordination normally falls under the operation of the duty principle. The third category concerns various classes of persons outside the parent society—most particularly, hostile combatants and citizens of the state with which the United States is at war. Members of hostile armed forces in war are subject to attack even though they present no immediate or direct threat to the offensive force. The uniformed members of a quartermaster unit that repairs tents are legitimate targets of attack, for example, even though the use of lethal force against such a target would obviously be morally unacceptable outside the role of a combatant in the circumstances of war. "Scorched earth" methods ordered by a retreating military commander that call for the destruction of private property also involve this third category of actions. No one outside the military role in comparable circumstances could justifiably override the property rights of citizens in such a manner. Role conduct under professional norms thus differs from the conduct permissible under the general values and moral standards of American society (and Western society).

To summarize, the military professional, in the preparation for and conduct of war, appropriately takes actions that would not be morally permissible outside the role. The function of the military would not be possible otherwise. Because of their special responsibility to society, however, military professionals must consider and weigh the significance of their actions in terms of the general moral principles that derive from the basic values of society. While fundamental American values have shaped the professional military ethic, the content of the American professional military ethic as discussed in Chapter 4 does not deal directly with the broad value concepts of freedom and equality that are so central to the American value system. And of course no code of principles attempts to eliminate the use of judgment by those governed by it. If professionals subordinate individual moral rights, the rationally consistent justification must ultimately be in terms of the fundamental values of society. If the foundational values of self-determination and individual personality appear to be subverted by specific alternatives, officers must weigh their special obligations as professionals and their functional requirements against the violation of individual moral rights. This constitutes what I have presented as partial differentiation. Thus, in a partially differentiated role, and in applying an ethical code that reflects such partial differentiation, two sets of somewhat differing moral rules must be applied to choices among morally significant actions. This partial differentiation differs from that of the lawyer in that the limitations on conduct are ultimately determined not by functional requirements but by moral principles independent of the professional function. If military professionals are to make consistent decisions involving moral issues, what must be settled is the relationship between the two sets of moral considerations: the professional military ethic and the fundamental values of society.

Fulfilling the responsibilities of a partially differentiated role can obviously be quite difficult. Succinct, absolute norms simplify the moral universe. In a role in which such simplification shifts toward consequences cumulatively considered "best" and unattainable through even well-intentioned judgment, full differentiation can perhaps be justified in teleological terms. But in the case of the military professional, simplifications would create an unacceptable threat to the very values the American military exists to protect. Further, full differentiation is not clearly essential to the function of the military professional, whereas partial role differentiation is. If the military is to exist as a profession, it must have, in applying force, the moral authority to take those actions necessary to defend American society against threats to its continued existence. The responsibility to wield such authority appropriately places a severe demand upon the judgment of officers in their function as the defenders of a free society—and that is precisely why the role of the military careerist should be that of a full-fledged military professional insofar as commitment and competence are concerned.

We can compare the relationship between the boundary conditions and the professional military ethic to the relationship between the rules of a particular kind of athletic contest and the norms of society. The participants in the contest have an objective: establishing the conditions under which one contestant is declared the winner. The rules of the game focus on the appropriate means of accomplishing that end. However, the rules must themselves be consistent with the norms of society, for in our peculiar contest, the winner is to exemplify the normative standards of society. If those standards and the means of achieving victory were inconsistent, the significance of the contest would be lost. In such a case, the norms of society are not formally part of the rules, but they are integral to the contest in that they have shaped the nature of such rules and they also establish limits on what the rules can require.

In a similar sense, the values of American society are not part of the professional military ethic, but they establish limitations within which the prescriptions of the professional military ethic necessarily fall (if they are to be consistent). If all values of American society were actually part of the professional military ethic, it would indeed be fully differentiated in a simplistic sense (one would follow *only* the professional military ethic in making moral choices), and our only concerns would be articulating the professional military ethic and maintaining internal consistency. That, however, is not the nature of our model, which differentiates roles within the context of a particular society with respect to conduct permissible under the moral standards and values of the society. To the limiting relationship between the professional military ethic and the values of American society, we can apply the term "boundary condition." The boundary condition relationship is particularly significant with respect to the duty principle.

The Duty Principle

Without some further clarification, the broad principles of the American professional military ethic in Chapter 4 could conflict with each other. They could also dictate actions that appear inconsistent with fundamental American values. Both results would tend toward moral incoherence and logical inconsistency, and the latter result would make it difficult to argue that the professional military ethic is rationally justifiable in the context of American society. Certain conditions for applying the principles—what I have referred to as boundary conditions—are necessary to avoid such consequences.

The principles of the uncodified professional military ethic are subject to these boundary conditions. As articulated in this discussion, the principles state that professional soldiers:

1. Accept service to country as their primary duty and defense of the Constitution of the United States as their calling. *They subordinate their personal interests to the requirements of their professional functions.*

2. Conduct themselves at all times as persons of honor whose integrity, loyalty, and courage are exemplary. *Such qualities are essential on the battlefield if a military organization is to function effectively.*

3. Develop and maintain the highest possible level of professional knowledge and skill. *To do less is to fail to meet their obligations to the men and women with whom they serve, to the profession, and to the country.*

4. Take full responsibility for their actions and orders.

5. Promote and safeguard, within the context of mission accomplishment, the welfare of their subordinates as persons, not merely as soldiers, sailors, or airmen.

6. Conform strictly to the principle that subordinates the military to civilian authority. *They do not involve themselves or their subordinates in domestic politics beyond the exercise of basic civil rights.*

7. Adhere to the laws of war and the regulations of their service in performing their professional functions.

Conflict among these principles is obviously possible, but the resolution of some of the apparent conflicts is not difficult insofar as the priority of the principles is concerned. If, for example, the requirements of a particular mission, itself reasonably conceived, are detrimental to the welfare of the individual soldier, the duty of mission accomplishment comes first. The most compelling requirements of duty are those actions necessary in the preservation and furtherance of the security of the state under the Constitution. In many actual instances, duty at lower echelons reduces to obedience to orders, for the relation of specific actions to the security of the state will not be clear. These are the situations that can become agonizing for individuals, but the relationship between the principles is not in question.

Equating duty with obedience to orders is a common but serious failing of the officer corps. Though duty prevails for the military professional, obedience to orders may be questionable when strong evidence exists that certain actions will *not* be in the interests of the security of the state. Such questioning is itself based upon the requirements of the duty principle, because duty for the American military professional is not simply a commitment to subordinate personal and other interests to those of national security. The commitment of the American military officer is to maintain a particular value structure within American society. When officers swear to support and defend the Constitution, they swear fealty to the principles and values it proclaims.[18] The duty principle, in the American professional military ethic, is thus considerably broader than it would be if it were determined by the functional requirements of military activity alone.[19]

Another type of situation sometimes considered problematic is when the duty to preserve the security of the state appears to conflict with the principle of subordination to civilian authority. The duty to preserve the state, however, is that of preserving the security of the state *under the Constitution*. And "under the Constitution" limits the military's responsibilities to those designated by civilian authority. So long as the civilian authorities act within the legal limits established by the Constitution and municipal law, there is no question concerning the relationship between these two principles. The duty of the military professional is to preserve (and thus inherently to accept) the authority of the civilian leadership as a fundamental aspect of the security of the state.

By briefly relating these principles to the principle of duty, I do not intend to minimize the complex problem of determining precisely what one's duty consists of in the shifting, dimly comprehended circumstances of actual situations. Even when the factual aspects of a situation are clear, moral choice may demand more moral courage than even a competent professional can muster, as our various case studies indicate.

Such encompassing terms provide insufficient guidance for some difficulties. Those that are of particular concern again center on the duty principle. Its role in the professional military ethic is central in the same manner that the principle of full advocacy is central in the legal code: if the principle derives from functional requirements alone, it becomes the basis for arguing for the status of full differentiation. In the case of lawyers, if the principle of full advocacy as stated in the *Code of Professional Responsibility* is accepted without qualification, it follows that the role is fully differentiated. In the case of military officers, if the duty principle as stated here is restricted to functional considerations alone, full differentiation appears to be indicated. The rationale for justification in both cases begins by claiming that full differentiation is necessary if the profession is to achieve its primary purpose. If we conclude, as we have, that full differentiation is neither necessary nor justifiable, the question is how we are to modify the duty principle. What are the boundary conditions that allow the duty principle to facilitate the professional function and yet do not permit using the principle to justify every alternative presented by military necessity and proportionality?[20]

Part of the answer emerged in Chapter 6. The laws of war, under the seventh provision of the professional military ethic, establish specific limitations. The laws of war, however, are both incomplete and changing. Their content is a result of a process of evolution and compromise. Quite simply, the laws of war alone do not render the professional military ethic consistent and coherent in application. In any particular case covered by the laws of war, however, members of the American military are constrained in their actions by the laws. In addition, the fundamental values of American society constrain the principle of duty. Three sets of boundary conditions for morally permissible conduct thus exist, with the functional requirements of military activity—military necessity if you will—being the most inclusive in terms of allowable actions. The laws of war, as a second set of boundary conditions, narrow the spectrum of allowable actions further, and the third set—the fundamental values of American society—will in most cases constrain permissible actions even more.

The type of case in which issues of morally permissible conduct are most evident is the kind of situation in which actions apparently necessary to accomplish assigned missions (such as those essential to the critical interests of American society) conflict with the rights of a person or group. The fundamental values of freedom, equality, democracy, and individual personality establish limitations on the actions that are morally permissible under the duty principle if that principle is to be justifiable in terms of those fundamental values.

A rather dramatic hypothetical case illustrates difficulty of choice between national interests and individual rights. In recent years, people have repeatedly discussed variations of the following situation, referred to as the "ticking bomb" scenario. A military unit captures a terrorist. Available evidence suggests the agent knows the location of an atomic weapon hidden in Washington, DC, a weapon known to be set to explode within a short time. The time is insufficient to warn the civilian authorities and convince them of the accuracy of the report, let alone to evacuate the capital. The security of the state appears to be seriously threatened. If the officer in charge believes the situation to be as described, is he or she justified in using all possible methods to make the captured agent reveal the location of the weapon? If such revelation could prevent the explosion of the bomb, is it legally and morally permissible to torture the prisoner? Is the officer justified in threatening and then performing the torture or execution of innocent persons important to the terrorist if that will persuade him to reveal the location?

The question of torture is hardly new. Weapons of mass destruction today simply make the stakes overwhelming. One could argue that the attempt to destroy a large segment of the population of Washington is a sufficient basis for claiming that the terrorist has forfeited the right to treatment as a person. For our purposes, however, we will assume that the prevailing norms of morality would apply to the terrorist, and that those norms prohibit torture. The United Nations Convention Against Torture and Other Cruel, Inhuman, or Degrading Treatment or Punishment clearly makes torture illegal under international law. Even though torture is thus illegal, we may still find ourselves unsure about what the officer in charge should do in these specific circumstances. The officer has a particular duty to preserve and further the security of the state. That duty goes beyond the moral obligation that any person would have to prevent significant harm to others if such prevention were in his or her power and could be achieved without harm to self or others. The professional officer has made a specific moral commitment and has a more extensive responsibility. In this hypothetical situation, if torturing the prisoner will prevent the explosion of the weapon, the result will be one in which fewer violations of fundamental moral rights will have occurred than if the action had not been taken. In addition, preventing the explosion will apparently enhance the security of the country.

Whereas an individual person might not be morally justified in torturing the agent, the officer in charge wields the authority of the state. He or she has the authority and responsibility to employ violence in protecting state interests. If we were to assume that the state will no longer exist if the weapon explodes (dubious though that assumption is), the issue of necessity comes into play. One might be tempted to say that the soldier then has the authority and the responsibility to take action that would not be appropriate for a general member of the society.

Though fundamental rights are those that cannot be overridden by the aggregation of lesser interests over a number of persons, the rights involved in this case are equally important. In question are the rights of both the agent and the people of Washington to life and to freedom from suffering purposely inflicted by others. Without question, fewer such rights will be violated if the agent is tortured and the population spared. If rights are in some sense commensurable, if we can compare them and assign weights to the elements compared, we can readily resolve the situation.

If one concludes that, within the context of American society, torture is justified in such a case (which is to say, at a minimum, that torture is morally permissible in certain circumstances), a principle appears to have been invoked. Despite the focus on rights, the principle is consequentialist and quite familiar: the results of the action justify the means employed, at least in extreme cases such as this. Although we are usually reluctant to concede the acceptability of the consequentialist or utilitarian position if the stakes are not high, our moral convictions often appear to undergo a transformation when national survival is at stake.[21]

Such a transformation, however, would render our moral position inconsistent. In the most obvious rationalization, nationalism appears to receive the highest priority among the values of American society. But our previous discussion suggests strongly that this should not be the case. As one eminent critic pointed out, "[A democratic society] is itself required to respect the individual's autonomy and liberty, and in general to treat him justly."[22] Otherwise, the society is no longer one characterized by the values we profess.

If the value of individual personality and consequent principles hold, numbers do not dictate a change in application. Thus, an argument based on human suffering will not provide justification either. If rights derive from the intrinsic worth of persons, then rights are not additive across persons. Equivalent rights of five people are not to be weighed more heavily than the same right of one person because of numbers alone. If it is morally wrong to sacrifice one person for another because of what it means to be a person, it must also be morally wrong to sacrifice one person against his or her will for fifty thousand others. To conclude otherwise is to resort to a form of consequentialist calculation. And while some might argue for just such reasoning, to do so would be to depart from the fundamental moral concepts professed by American society.[23]

One response to this argument is to say that theoretical discussion provides a kind of mental gymnastics but has little application to the reality of imminent death and immense suffering that the atomic bomb scenario represents. Many would point to the Israeli response to the threats to the security of the state as more realistic. The Israeli Defense Force also has a professional military ethic called *The Spirit of the IDF*, which has been codified and published. With respect to value conflicts, the code states that "the obligations to fulfill the mission and be victorious in war will be the compass guiding any effort to balance the system of values and basic principles of *The Spirit of the IDF*."[24] That statement appears to make the security of the state the trump card in situations that present moral dilemmas. Although the code specifies that "IDF soldiers will operate according to the IDF values and orders, while adhering to the laws of the state and norms of human dignity, and honoring the values of the State of Israel as a Jewish and democratic state,"[25] soldiers are to preserve the state in resolving conflicts that could arise between that goal and adherence to the "laws of the state and norms of human dignity." American service members do not receive that guidance. If the officer in charge in our terrorist scenario does take action to force the agent to provide information, we may well excuse his action to some degree, which is to say that we may find the actions he takes to be less blameworthy than they would be in other circumstances, but we will not be able to justify them in terms of the professional military ethic. We will not be able to say, without qualification, that torture of the terrorist or those involved with him was the morally right thing to do.

In essence, neither the American professional military ethic nor the American value system is consequentialist in nature. Within the context of American values, torture and other uses of persons solely as means are not morally permissible. The officer in our hypothetical case may decide to torture the prisoner, but he or she cannot claim moral justification in terms of the American value system. The actions may be morally excused to some degree, but they cannot be justified. Those who would claim that they can must argue a case that reduces to justifying the violation of individual rights on the basis of benefits to many. Although such arguments are familiar and often plausible in various guises, they are not sufficient in terms of the American value system, nor of any moral system in which the individual is recognized as having intrinsic worth and as possessing fundamental moral rights that can be overridden only on the basis of a principle such as that of greatest equal liberty.[26] We can also reach this conclusion in another manner. If professional exigencies alone are considered, the values of the military perspective indicate that whatever action is necessary to preserve the state or minimize injury to it should be taken. The value of nationalism in the military perspective certainly could be considered as a sufficient basis for an ultimate justifying reason. That this is not the case in the American professional military ethic is significant. The modification of the military perspective is the result of the value system of American society. In that system, as we discussed in Chapter 7, nationalism is instrumental in terms of moral ends rather than being an end in itself. Accordingly, considerations arising from the American value system limit morally permissible actions under the duty principle of the American professional military ethic. We concluded previously that one of the humanitarian principles underlying the laws of war, which states that individual persons are to be respected as such, was also operative under the American value system. This principle is an important element in the laws of war that protect human rights, including the right not to be tortured. The laws do not allow the mistreatment of any persons under military control, whether soldiers or civilians, spies or saboteurs, terrorists or murderers.

The same restrictions apply to the military in any professional function. In any armed conflict or state use of military force, the military is restricted by the laws of war and the principles underlying them. Torture is obviously not permissible under this consideration. Because the humanitarian principle can also be derived from the American value system, in parallel fashion torture is morally impermissible as a result of the boundary conditions for the application of the American professional military ethic.

One further comment may be in order since variations of the "ticking bomb" scenario are so popular—and perhaps so persuasive. Even if one were to adopt a consequentialist view, the effectiveness of torture is problematic at best, even after we determine what definition we are going to use to discriminate between aggressive interrogation and torture. The United Nations Convention defines torture as follows:

> For the purposes of this Convention, torture means any act by which severe pain or suffering, whether physical or mental, is intentionally inflicted on a person for such purposes as obtaining from him or a third person information or a confession, punishing him for an act he or a third person has committed or is suspected of having committed, or intimidating or coercing him or a third person, or for any reason based on discrimination of any kind, when such pain or suffering is inflicted by or at the instigation of or with the consent or acquiescence of a public official or other person acting in an official capacity.

Whether this definition includes measures such as sleep deprivation, the discomfort of environmental extremes (temperature, light, noise), and psychological disorientation—techniques reportedly used by the United States—remains a matter of debate, but torture in the conventional sense of agonizing physical injury historically yields unreliable results. Individuals respond quite differently to various forms of coercion, but terrorists and others committed to a cause, indeed willing to die for it, can be expected to withstand pain for some time. In addition, to be able to torture effectively, the torturer needs training and experience; that fact calls for a formal policy and program of torture. To have such capabilities available, a minimum set of institutional requirements appears necessary—and immediately gives pause.

INSTITUTIONAL REQUIREMENTS TO SUPPORT A POLICY OF
APPLYING TORTURE FOR INTELLIGENCE PURPOSES

1. Participation of medical practitioners before, during, and after the application of torture.
2. Biomedical and psychological research in the methods and effects of torture.
3. The training of torture interrogation units.
4. Coordination of torture agencies with the police and with the judiciary.

5. Incorporation of torture units within the military or government agencies, or both.

6. Justification to the public of the institutional use of trained torturers (concealment in a democratic society would most probably be unsuccessful, and attempts at concealment would lead to violations of domestic law).[27]

This array of institutional requirements suggests that the United States should not establish a formal policy of torture to be used in especially dangerous cases, which leaves us with the option of encouraging or allowing individuals to use their judgment about the use of torture in instances when they believe, rightly or wrongly, that the stakes are so high that any means to the end will be morally acceptable. As the preceding discussion indicates, a member of the military might so decide, but he or she could not rationalize the action in terms of the American professional military ethic.

Furthermore, the final boundary conditions are the set of fundamental American values. It provides the answer to the question, "What factors, after consideration of the professional military ethic itself, limit what can be done to achieve successful mission accomplishment?" Actions required under the duty principle are limited to those that are consistent with the American value system, meaning that actions taken under the professional military ethic are morally permissible only if they do not subvert or controvert the fundamental moral values of American society. Such a conclusion denies a consequentialist basis for the *moral* aspects of professional decisions. The professional military ethic functions under a moral teleology, but the purpose of the professional military ethic is to guide the efforts of the military to maintain the state under the Constitution. Therefore the purpose is to maintain a matrix of institutional values. To provide consistent guidance, the professional military ethic cannot extend approval to actions that conflict morally with that set of values.

As a result of the boundary conditions established by the American value system, authoritarianism—one of the functional tendencies of military activity—is also limited. The American professional military ethic traditionally has not accepted or condoned stereotypical obedience to orders, even though indoctrination and particular practices may sometimes suggest the opposite. Within the context of tactical actions on the battlefield, immediate and reflexive response to orders is indeed the objective of some military training because it makes a military unit more effective in the overwhelming confusion and stress of combat. Such training, however, does not abrogate the individual's responsibility to refuse to obey illegal orders.

Does that requirement place individual soldiers in situations that they may perceive as moral dilemmas—situations in which all choices involve violating some moral constraint? While that may be the case, the policy of insisting on an individual responsibility remains morally necessary. Situations do occur in which privates must act and in acting apparently choose between risk to themselves and their units, on the one hand, and risk to unarmed noncombatants on the other. Flag officers sometimes face the decision whether to issue orders that are not only necessary to make success in war possible but that also endanger the lives and welfare of civilian populations. Throughout the spectrum from individual soldier to theater commander, members of the military must choose and act knowing that life and death hang in the balance.

No set of rules can provide answers in every case. We can only seek to understand the applicable moral principles clearly, weigh our experience and our responsibilities, and determine which course of action is most defensible. Long after traumatic events like the bombing of Hiroshima and Nagasaki, despite years of analysis and debate, we are often unable to reach a moral consensus on those actions. In the sphere of combat, however, as death and disaster hammer the senses, time for reflection is seldom available: the person in uniform must choose a course of action. Because so much hangs in the balance so often, war is indeed the hardest place to maintain our humanity.

Chapter Nine

Making Choices: Case Studies

Purpose

As a form of commentary as well as practical application, I offer a set of case studies that require moral choices. Although I have grouped the case studies to reflect the level of responsibility of the decision maker, the notable feature of military operations today is that even junior leaders should be prepared to make decisions that may have far-reaching effects. The conclusions I draw are subject to debate. Nonetheless, I do want to maintain two points: (1) the process of moral analysis suggested here is appropriate for such cases, including "the hardest place," and, (2) for a military professional, moral decisions are unavoidable. American soldiers, sailors, and airmen cannot evade or reject moral responsibility.

In each of the discussions that follow, I examine the circumstances in terms of the American professional military ethic. Where necessary, I invoke the boundary conditions to clarify the conceptual issues and moral considerations involved in identifying a resolution justifiable in terms of the model of moral analysis I have discussed. When the morally preferable choice is not clear in a situation, one should examine the alternatives in terms of the boundary conditions that structure the American professional military ethic.

Junior Leaders

Case 1: The Peacekeeper

Situation. The 109th Infantry Division is conducting peacekeeping operations in Sindonia following a cease-fire between the oppo-

181

nents in a civil war. The two ethnic groups involved, the Sindonians and the Dreds, have continued vicious reprisals against each other, unable to get beyond the bitterness generated by widespread atrocities committed on both sides during the war. The Dreds are also notorious for a long tradition of smuggling, drug running, and "protection" operations that extract payments from commercial enterprises. Dred society remains centered on clan loyalties. The Sindonians, who dominated the government when the war began, are a minority in the country but are well armed and noted for their brutality in combating enemies.

Lieutenant Gold, platoon leader, has responsibility for Ceravica, a small city of 8,000. His mission is to maintain the peace by keeping the Sindonians and the Dreds from attacking each other, to support the reestablishment of the rule of law, and to disarm combatant groups in the city.

During the first two weeks in Ceravica, Lieutenant Gold finds that both local groups are disdainful of the UN mission and the U.S. forces assigned to carry it out. On three occasions, snipers have taken Lieutenant Gold's soldiers under fire. A group of men wielding clubs attacked one squad caught in a confined area. The rules of engagement forbid firing except when necessary to prevent loss of life and, given the emphasis on restraint, the squad leader chose not to fire his weapons. In the melee, two soldiers were injured. There is no local police force.

Lieutenant Gold's battalion commander and company commander visited him and told him that he had failed to take control of the situation. His battalion commander emphasized that the 109th is the law in the province and in Ceravica. Unless the 109th can establish stability, the local population will not be able to return to a normal way of life and the danger to American soldiers will be unacceptably high (force protection seems to be an overwhelming concern for the division). He notes that Gold is in a particularly demanding situation because of his distant location from other divisional elements and the fact that Ceravica is a hub for drug activity. He tells Gold that he must make clear to the local factions that the 109th will not tolerate opposition.

One evening two days later one of the UN interpreters with the platoon tells Lieutenant Gold that he just came from a bar where, apparently unrecognized by the patrons, he overheard a discussion in which a local Dred named Gradic revealed that the Dreds were going to assassinate a leading Sindonian figure as a means of intimidating the Sindonian population. Gradic also referred to an arms cache that the Dreds were going to use to eliminate the Americans when they reacted to the assassination, which would occur in conjunction with a noisy ambush. The interpreter further reported that Gradic said that a major drug shipment coming through Ceravica soon would provide the financing necessary to reestablish the dominance of the Dreds in the area once the Americans pulled back to regroup.

Lieutenant Gold goes immediately to the bar with a squad and apprehends Gradic. When he interrogates Gradic, the Dred tells him that the Americans will not live to see the sunrise. Gradic appears full of bluster but is clearly deeply apprehensive about his captors. Gold concludes that it is vital to find the arms cache and to learn what the plans are for attacking his platoon. Intercepting the drug shipment would also be a major step in retaining control of the area. He is further concerned that an assassination will cause an explosion of violence that will destroy the cease-fire locally if not more widely. He directs his platoon sergeant to obtain a rope and throw it over a beam in the room, and then Gold carefully and deliberately fashions a hangman's noose. He also sinks the tip of his bayonet knife into the top of a wooden table. Knowing that being stripped weakens any prisoner's self-confidence, he orders his men to remove all of Gradic's clothing and tie his hands behind his back. As Gradic stands shivering in the cold room, Lieutenant Gold directs the interpreter to tell Gradic that unless he provides information, the knife will ruin his day and the hangman's noose will end his evening.

Discussion. The action the Dreds apparently have planned threatens the lives of platoon members and the success of their mission. Further details about the threat would allow Lieutenant Gold to react more effectively in protecting his men and accomplishing his mission. If he can prevent an assassination, seize illicit weapons, and interdict a major drug shipment, he will have taken several important steps in protecting both his men and the community. A demonstration of strength and ruthlessness may deter future actions by the Dreds as well. Coercive interrogation could provide those desirable results. If Lieutenant Gold does not prevent an assassination, does not find the weapons cache, and does not interdict the drug shipment when he apparently has the means to do so, he may be criticized by his commander and others, including the Sindonians who may suffer if he fails. He has strong reasons to use coercive interrogation. Forcing information from the prisoner would appear to be in keeping with the provision of the professional military ethic that directs military professionals to "promote and safeguard, within the context of mission accomplishment, the welfare of their subordinates."

The professional military ethic also directs adherence to the laws of war and service regulations. Although a peacekeeping mission ideally will not involve combat, peacekeepers must be prepared to use force under established rules of engagement. American units are always required to observe the constraints of the laws of war in such missions; indeed, because of the focus of maintaining peace, protection of noncombatants has even higher visibility than in combat operations. Service regulations and the laws of war prohibit coercive interrogation—the use of physical and mental suffering to extort information from a prisoner. Lieutenant Gold thus faces a conflict between the prohibition of abuse of prisoners and detainees and his need for information that he believes will help him thwart actions by the Dreds.

When such a conflict occurs, turning to the next set of constraints on action can help clarify the moral considerations in a situation. Here the mission requirements appear to call for coercive interrogation. The professional military ethic does not provide clear guidance, in that it calls for both protecting subordinates and obeying laws and regulations. For many, the duty of service to country, the backbone of the professional military ethic, may not establish a priority for one course or the other. Duty requires adherence to law and regulations; it also requires mission accomplishment and protection of one's soldiers.

When we examined the laws of war in Chapter 6, we discussed two principles that underlie the legal provisions. The label frequently applied to those provisions—"international humanitarian law"—suggests that the humanitarian principles may be of help. HP1 states that "human beings should be respected as such," and HP2 states that "human suffering should be minimized." The question in this case is just what means are morally permissible to use in trying to obtain information that may minimize suffering. Torture might be rationalized as a way to minimize overall suffering—by preventing the assassination and curtailing illicit activity—at the cost of severe trauma for one person.

Since the specifics of the laws of war are already in play in the requirement to obey international humanitarian law, we can move to the last set of influences that have shaped the professional military ethic and accordingly have generated constraints for U.S. service members. The enduring core values of American society—freedom, equality, individualism, and democracy—all emphasize human dignity. Some confuse battle-hardened determination, a quality we seek in our fighting forces, with a willingness to abuse the helpless. True strength of character and commitment to the professional military ethic do not mix the two. That fact coupled with the requirement to obey the laws of war and service regulations point the way to resolving this situation. The considerations establish that coercive interrogation, or torture, is not permissible. Current national and international law both specifically prohibit torture.[1] In Lieutenant Gold's situation, he can no more justify torturing a detainee than he could justify police brutality against a prisoner in the United States.

In addition to this principled conclusion, practical considerations apply. The detainee Gradic may not in fact have information. He may have been lying about the planned actions for reasons of his own. Further, our reflections in Chapter 8 provide strong reasons to doubt the accuracy of information obtained through abuse. It is doubtful that Lieutenant Gold or any of his platoon members have any expertise in the application of psychological or physical pressure to extract information from an unwilling subject. Possible negative repercussions include damage to the reputation of U.S. soldiers, provocation for further violence against the platoon, and the undermining of the concept of justice and due process. Abuse of the prisoner would present the implicit claim that force rules. Upholding that claim may sometimes produce short-term results, but it does not appear to be the most effective way to establish long-term stability and peace in the region.

As an alternative, Lieutenant Gold can warn the Sindonians of the suspected plot. His soldiers are forewarned. He can seek other information about the drug shipment. The information Lieutenant Gold has already provides him with a distinct advantage in attempting to thwart the suspected plans of the Dreds. Gradic's arrest will not be a secret; if the Dreds suspect he might talk, they may choose to alter their plans in any event. At a minimum, even if Gradic were to provide truthful information, it might no longer be accurate. The argument for torture cannot be sustained.

Case 2: The Baby Ram[2]

Situation. In an Eastern European country racked by ethnic violence, U.S. Army units, part of a larger UN force, are attempting to prevent confrontations between two hostile ethnic groups. A program of ethnic cleansing led to a massive exodus of refugees who are now returning to their homes. Until the recent conflict, the two groups had lived in integrated towns and villages. A carefully orchestrated plan is in place for the gradual movement of small groups of the Andolosians back into their homes where they formerly lived side by side with the other ethnic group, the Zandals. The current mission of the U.S. Army force is to prevent the arrival of Andolosians ahead of the agreed upon schedule, especially the arrival of large, unruly groups that would spark violent confrontations. People on each side seek revenge for recent atrocities.

Captain Tan has set up four roadblocks at choke points on the road that refugees must take to return to a town that has been a flashpoint. His orders are to prevent any Andolosians from returning to the town until the following Monday. When Monday comes, he is to let only families or groups of three or fewer people through the roadblocks. They are to be spaced so that no large groups suddenly appear in the town. The Zandals suffered badly at the hands of the Andolosians during the conflict and even small incidents could spark rioting as the Andolosians return.

At his command post at the second roadblock Captain Tan receives a report that a large group of Andolosians has broken through the first roadblock. The lieutenant rendering the report states that three Andolosian men aggressively approached the roadblock carrying babies in front of them at chest height. When they reached the line of U.S. troops blocking the road, they strode forward thrusting the babies at the soldiers. The lieutenant reported that he let the Andolosians through rather than endanger the infants and that the rest of the people surged through the roadblock behind the "baby ram."

As he receives the report, Captain Tan sees a mass of people—thirty to forty—marching swiftly toward his second picket line. Several men in the vanguard are indeed carrying babies. It appears they plan to repeat their ramming tactic.

Discussion. Captain Tan's mission is to prevent the Andolosians from proceeding to the town. Blocking movement will prevent a fight between the Andolosians and the Zandals that would inflame passions in the region and result in injuries. Fighting and rioting appear inevitable if the two groups confront each other. While he is restricted from using deadly force except in self-defense, Captain Tan has instructed his soldiers that they are to be forceful denying any significant number of Andolosians access to the town.

The tactic of forcing a way through roadblocks trades on American reluctance to harm the innocent. In a peacekeeping mission that seeks to contain hostility and maintain a peaceful environment, the protection of noncombatants assumes particular importance. The cooperation of the populace is critical to peacekeeping operations, and such cooperation will not be achievable if harm comes to innocent people because of the actions of the peacekeepers. In this situation, Captain Tan faces an apparent dilemma: he can pursue his mission by ensuring that no Andolosian groups pass on the road, or he can act to avoid any immediate injury to Andolosian civilians. The fact that the Andolosian men are trying to exploit the American soldiers' reluctance to put babies at risk heightens the emotional impact of this situation.

The professional military ethic highlights duty, responsibility, and competence. Applying those values in this situation presents a challenge. Ideally, Captain Tan can satisfy all three. The dilemma may not exist—often, what appears to be a dilemma is instead a difficult situation that can be resolved. One means of responding to Captain Tan's circumstances would be to isolate the men with the babies. By acting quickly and decisively, it may be possible to open the line of soldiers suddenly, pull the baby teams through, and then

close the line to the rest of the crowd. Any tactic that presents significant risk to the infants violates the principles that undergird the laws
of war and the purpose of the rules of engagement (ROE).[3] Another
course of action would be to delay by having this line of soldiers
retreat as slowly as possible without placing the infants at risk and to
immediately begin placing a physical obstacle at the next roadblock,
one that renders ineffective the use of the babies as rams.

Three points emerge distinctly from this set of circumstances.
First, mission requirements become the anchor around which other
considerations coalesce. Second, decisions required of junior officers
are no less difficult than those faced by senior officers. The difference
is only a matter of scale. Junior officers still will need to resort to the
professional military ethic and other sources of moral guidance in
making military decisions. Third, situations that appear to present a
moral dilemma—a set of choices in which each possibility will result
in violating a moral rule or principle—frequently reveal an acceptable
alternative if the decision maker analyzes the circumstances carefully and imaginatively.

Case 3: Human Shields

Situation. Captain Ivory is an armored cavalry troop commander
performing an advanced guard mission for his squadron in combat.
He has moved rapidly to a crossroads village surrounded by rugged
hills. An enemy force entrenched on the village outskirts has taken
the troop vehicles under fire. As he maneuvers his Bradley fighting
vehicles in the limited space beside the road and brings his tanks
forward, he observes a group of people walking slowly to positions in
front of the enemy force. In the next fifteen minutes he learns that
the civilian population of the village has been marched across the
enemy's front. Since the local population is known to be sympathetic
to the cause of the coalition to which Captain Ivory's unit belongs, it
appears obvious that they have been forced to interpose themselves
between the enemy and the cavalry troop. Through his binoculars,
Captain Ivory can see children as well as mothers carrying infants.

The troop has orders to move rapidly to secure the crossroads.
An armor battalion is following behind in a narrow valley where it
is subject to air attack. The battalion commander wants to move
rapidly to avoid being caught in the confined area. He urges Captain

Ivory to push forward, assault the enemy positions, and clear the way. He has called for helicopter gunship support to assist.

Discussion. Captain Ivory needs to eliminate the obstacle the enemy force creates. He also recognizes a duty to protect the civilian population and minimize suffering on their part. This type of situation has become increasingly common in recent military operations. Accomplishing one requirement appears to conflict with the other. Captain Ivory's first response must be an attempt to identify a course of action that will satisfy both objectives. He may be able to bypass the enemy position. He may be able to maneuver to the enemy's rear and force the enemy soldiers to reposition. If aviation support is available, he may be able to airlift some of his soldiers into a position to attack the enemy with reduced danger to the civilians. Captain Ivory will consider various courses of action that could accomplish his mission, to include those that will put his soldiers at additional risk in the attempt to minimize civilian casualties. At times commanders will accept such risk to their subordinates if doing so does not place mission success in jeopardy.

In circumstances such as these, "nonlethal" weapons systems could be of use. Chemical weapons that temporarily inhibit the enemy's capability to fight would minimize civilian casualties.[4] Directed energy or acoustic weapons that accomplish the same purpose could be employed in a swift attack. While such capabilities are not yet available, they are under development.

If Captain Ivory reviews all alternatives, however, and finds none feasible, the basic question remains: does he attack conventionally, causing civilian casualties, or not? Realistically, Captain Ivory will respond to orders he receives, but either Captain Ivory or his commander will have to weigh the importance of accomplishing the immediate mission against the potential loss of civilian life. In the context of just war theory, the issue is one of proportionality on the tactical level. This situation is one in which the theory of double effect applies. The calculus of double effect is as follows:

1. The intended action must be a legitimate act of war.
2. The direct, intended result of the action must be morally acceptable.
3. The foreseeable, regrettable result of the action must be unin-

tended; it must not be the means of achieving the intended result.

4. The intended result must be sufficiently important to outweigh the unintended, morally regrettable result.

Though this reasoning process falls between an objective analysis and a subjective choice, it establishes a perspective that decision makers in combat should keep in mind if they adhere to the American professional military ethic. The professional military ethic reflects values that include respect for human dignity and concern for human suffering. The philosopher Michael Walzer adds a further condition to the doctrine of double effect that is now widely considered. He says that if the action that causes an evil effect is to be justifiable (in addition to the conditions noted above), the agent must also accept additional risk to himself,[5] a claim that I endorse.

The use of the troop weapons and supporting fire in attacking the enemy force is certainly a legitimate act of war, which fulfills the first condition of double effect. The intended result, killing or incapacitating the enemy soldiers, is indeed morally acceptable if one believes that war is justifiable. Civilian casualties that might result from attacking the enemy positions are undesirable from Captain Ivory's point of view, but they are not the *means* by which he will defeat the enemy force. They are indeed foreseeable, but they are not themselves intended. The question of proportionality will always be less clinical. Is the defeat of the enemy force in these circumstances sufficiently important to outweigh the loss of innocent life? The number of civilians involved will matter. The degree of risk to their units that Captain Ivory and his commander identify in relation to alternatives will matter. In this case, Captain Ivory may choose a plan of attack that incurs more risk to his soldiers than he would otherwise. In many cases, he would attempt to rout the enemy through overwhelming power from supporting artillery and air strikes. Because of the civilians on the battlefield, he may choose a mounted attack with carefully directed fire against enemy emplacements. In the end, however, he may choose to attack despite the risk to noncombatants. He will do so recognizing that his decision will be subject to moral and legal evaluation after the fact. The American military should expect that enemy forces in future conflicts will attempt to use our acceptance of moral constraints to their advantage on the battlefield.

Case 4: Cultural Judgment[6]

Situation. Captain Auburn is a Company Commander in the 10th Mountain Division (Light Infantry). The Division has deployed to the fledging Republic of Paldora in South America, where the Brazilian Civil War destroyed most businesses and industry. Its mission is to conduct "Nation Building Operations" and to assist the Paldorans in the maintenance and development of democratic institutions. Paldora is a new country that emerged after economic and political turmoil resulted in the disintegration of Brazil. Approximately the size of New England, it is large in area but has a small population. Much of the land is part of the Amazon rain forest.

Captain Auburn received the following mission briefing from Colonel Highpower:

This is a nation-building mission. We are here to assist the Paldorans in building and modernizing their country. In order to succeed, we have to increase the standard of living for the common Paldoran. This means everything from building schools to giving inoculations. Work through the local government officials in your area. We need to show that they are in charge and that we working with them. I don't want to give the people the impression that we are down here for any other reason than to help their own government.

One of the things you have to be particularly aware of is the fact that the Paldorans are a very mixed bunch. Part of the population consists of a well-to-do middle class that would fit into our culture with ease. Other parts of the country are less advanced. The highlands have a large population of people we might call superstitious peasants. The population of the rain forest consists of tribes who are not all that far removed from the primitive hunter-gatherer society. Whatever your sector is, it is important for you to get a feel for the customs and beliefs of the locals. Because of the size of the area and the differences in people and culture, you will have to use your best judgment in making decisions that will affect the overall success of the mission. I have the utmost confidence in your abilities.

The brigade intelligence officer provided the following report:

The tribe that populates your area of operations is the Tiní. Little was known about them prior to 1998. It is only in the past five years that they have been exposed to the outside world. Prior to that, they lived deep in the rain forest. In 1998, Brazil launched massive lumber projects in the heart of the Tiní lands that expanded contact with the Tiní people.

The tribe consists of about 4,000 (est.) men, women, and children. For the most part they are a peaceful society that has adapted quickly to the outside world. Although generally peaceful, they have a reputation for being implacable enemies when wronged. Neighboring tribes call their warriors the "ghosts that seek vengeance" because of their ability to move through the forest undetected.

The Tiní are a deeply religious people who place great value on ritual and tradition. Both their religion and society place an emphasis on promoting the welfare of the society over the individual. Many consider Tiní society a theocracy because the tribal chiefs function as civil, military, and spiritual leaders. Their power derives from their special relationship with the Gods. The world of the Tiní is in perpetual danger of destruction from the forces of Evil, led by the serpent god, Balzaar. The constant efforts and sacrifices of Leal (the great, good god) prevent final destruction of the world. Only those who follow in Leal's footsteps and sacrifice for the common good of society will reap the reward of reincarnation in a higher life form or eternal life with Leal in "Parva"—the Tiní paradise.

This "First Story of Leal" was recently recorded and translated. It explains some of the Tiní religious beliefs. In that story, Balzaar is attempting to destroy the world by drying up the earth's water. Having just finished his second battle against Balzaar, Leal has found a place to rest.

As the great god Leal lay hurt and bleeding from his battle with Balzaar, an old woman appeared with cool water and herbs to treat his wounds. As she finished, the Tochis (demon warriors) of Balzaar appeared and attacked. Although Leal ultimately defeated the demons, one of the Tochis chopped off the leg of the old woman. After the fight, Leal cared for the woman. As he was doing this, the serpent god himself appeared and attacked Leal. Weakened by his wounds, the great god was unable to defend himself and suffered wound after wound from Balzaar's fierce fangs and mighty *opé* (war axe). In one terrific blow the serpent king severed Leal's sword hand, leaving him defenseless. As the Evil one coiled for the strike that would destroy Leal, a young girl appeared. Without hesitation she threw herself at Balzaar in an attempt to protect Leal. Infuriated, Balzaar sank his fangs into her throat and then cut her apart with his *opé*. While the serpent king was distracted, Leal regained his sword and with a mighty swing cut off one of Balzaar's heads. Howling with rage and pain, the serpent king fled.

Leal then went to the hurt old woman and the body of the young girl. He touched some of his blood to the woman's leg and healed it, saying, "In helping me you have helped all of mankind. You shall be reborn a great and wise queen." He then approached the young girl's body and said, "You who have sacrificed all for mankind shall receive eternal bliss." He then raised her spirit up to paradise.

After three weeks in sector the company is making excellent progress. Captain Auburn's troops have already built a small clinic that is providing needed medical aid. He has also begun building a new school and a levee to protect crops from flood damage. Relations with the Tiní are good. They appear to be a friendly, generous people who appreciate the soldiers' efforts to help them. They have been assisting on all the projects. Many of the tribes have unofficially adopted members of the company and provide them with food.

As the first month draws to a close, Captain Auburn receives an invitation to the "Moon Ceremony." This ceremony signifies the triumph of Leal over Balzaar in their continual struggle. Many members of the company attend. Tribesmen pour into the area for the semi-annual ceremony. After a dinner feast, the actual ceremony occurs. Several warriors lead an elderly woman and young girl to an open area. Amid great ceremony, they reenact the fight of Leal and Balzaar. As the ceremony concludes two of the tribal leaders suddenly step out carrying *opés*. With practiced blows they kill and dismember the woman and child. Their act brings forth a wave of cheering and chanting from the assembled tribesmen.

Stunned by the sudden change of events, Captain Auburn asks the tribe's chief for an explanation. He states, "These two have gone to help Leal fight Balzaar. By their willing sacrifice, they ensure the continuation of the circle of life. Great honor and rewards shall they receive in their next life with Leal in eternal paradise."

As Captain Auburn leaves the ceremony, he can see the incidents have horrified and angered his soldiers. One of them gets into a scuffle with the executioners. Only quick intervention by the First Sergeant prevents it from getting out of hand.

During the night, the First Sergeant reports that the soldiers are in an ugly mood. The ceremony horrified them. The elderly woman had become a particular friend of some members of the company. Rumors are flying that the "Moon Ceremony" runs for three days, repeating the ritual of sacrifice each day; more people will die tomorrow. The next morning Captain Auburn confirms that the ceremony does run for three days. More sacrificial ceremonies are scheduled. On his rounds, he hears his men saying, "This is plain wrong," and "We have to stop it." Concerned, Captain Auburn radios higher for guidance, but nothing helpful comes.

As Captain Auburn reflects on his choices, he reviews the task force rules of engagement.

1. American troops have the right of self-defense at all times. The use of deadly force is authorized to protect the lives of our soldiers.
2. Deadly force is authorized to protect the lives of Paldoran Nationals.
3. Riot control agents and weapons can be used at the discretion of company commanders.
4. The use of force should be a last resort. When faced with hostile situations, soldiers and units should first issue verbal warnings, then use warning shots and physical force prior to using deadly force.

Discussion. Cultural differences complicate the situation Captain Auburn faces. The religion of the Tiní tells them they are doing what is right. Captain Auburn's beliefs and those of his soldiers condemn human sacrifice in any culture. The captain's orders make clear that he is to respect the Tiní's beliefs, but of course his commander did not know about the ritual of sacrifice when the commander passed on that guidance. The ROE under which the company operates center on force protection; they are of little help in these circumstances. The conflict in this situation is between the Tiní beliefs about the welfare of their tribe and the American values that consider human sacrifice morally unacceptable.

Captain Auburn must consider the likely results of the two major courses of action available to him. He can choose not to intervene in the Moon Ceremony, or he can decide to intervene in an attempt to prevent more Tiní deaths. If he chooses not to intervene, he will implicitly underwrite the Tiní practice and four more people will almost certainly die. Since it is an annual practice, however, U.S. influence may be able to prevent the ceremony next year. The Tiní appear to believe that the ritual is essential for the welfare of the tribe in the months to come. If he decides to intervene, he may destroy his ability to work with the tribe and help them. He should be able to postpone or prevent the deaths of the next two sets of ritual victims, but his actions, in the tribe's view, would place in jeopardy the welfare of the tribe in the coming year. If the Tiní beliefs are strong, the sacrifice will probably occur elsewhere, out of the control of Captain Auburn's men.

Captain Auburn may choose to discuss the issue with the Tiní leadership. He could explain the violation of the beliefs of his society and ask if there is any way to avoid the deaths of the tribe members who will participate in the upcoming ceremonies. In view of the conflict of beliefs, it may be possible to establish a compromise that will stop the killing. At a minimum, he can decline the invitation to attend the events of the next two days and explain his reasons in the hope that the Tiní will reconsider their plans for the ceremonies.

If the Tiní choose to proceed as planned, Captain Auburn should ensure that his soldiers are isolated from the event. They might be tempted to take action on their own. Interference with the tribe's practices could generate a violent response—an important factor for the commander to consider. If his talks with the Tiní leadership fail to stop the remainder of the sacrificial ceremony, it appears that interference would be counterproductive for both the tribe and for his force. He will continue to seek guidance from his higher headquarters, but he must also recognize that he may have to choose a course of action without that guidance. At this point, noninterference appears to be the most logical action. Captain Auburn recognizes that the Tiní have their own beliefs, their own governmental processes, and their own system of justice. If his only course of action that will stop the sacrifices requires the use of coercive force, potentially deadly force, he cannot justify that course of action within his own belief systems. If he concludes that the Tiní's ways should change for their own benefit, he will need to focus on ways to influence their future practice of sacrificial rituals.

Case 5: The Operations Officer

Situation. Captain Green is an infantry battalion operations officer serving with American forces fighting in the Vietnam War. His battalion has been fighting intense but brief battles with enemy units on the northern edge of the Mekong Delta. The unit is protecting the capital city of Saigon by blocking routes to the city from the southwest and attacking enemy units in the area.

The southern part of the battalion's area of operations has been declared a "free fire zone" under the rules of engagement, which means that all persons considered friendly to the Vietnamese government have been evacuated. Any persons remaining in the zone are to be considered enemy and can be fired on if it has been established that no friendly military activity is under way in the zone.

The method of operation employed by Captain Green's battalion is that of occupying patrol bases of company and platoon size to block any movement toward Saigon. Frequently, the battalion consolidates and conducts heliborne operations against enemy concentrations. The battalion is about to conduct such an assault. The infantry units are in the air aboard helicopters, and Captain Green, along with the battalion commander and other staff officers, is in a command and control helicopter above the landing zone (LZ) the battalion will use. Helicopter assaults are seldom conducted outside the range of supporting artillery, but this attack is an exception. Since it is outside supporting artillery range, the LZ is being fired upon by armed helicopters before the landing in order to eliminate or suppress potential enemy resistance, though no enemy forces have been observed in the vicinity. Following his established pattern for such operations, the battalion commander gives his orders to Captain Green, who then uses the helicopter's communications systems to coordinate execution.

The battalion commander has been intently observing a small village about 400 meters from the area in which the helicopters will land. He is uneasy about the risk involved should the VC (Viet Cong) offer significant resistance during the landing. The LZ and the village are just north of the free fire zone boundary, so the operation has been carefully coordinated with the Vietnamese district chief who controls this area. Any fires delivered in the district other than in situations requiring immediate return fire in self-defense must be approved by the district headquarters. The village causing the battalion commander concern has not been fired upon during the LZ preparation by the armed helicopters.

The battalion commander turns to Captain Green and asks if the village is outside the area cleared by the district headquarters for the LZ preparation. Captain Green replies that it seems to be right at the edge of the clear-to-fire area according to his map overlay. The battalion commander directs Captain Green to have the armed helicopters hit the village with rockets and machine gun fire as the landing begins. He suspects some automatic weapons may be emplaced in the village that could fire on the lift helicopters as they approach the LZ. Captain Green points out that they have seen women and children running to what appear to be earthen shelters in the village during the LZ preparation, but the battalion commander is firm: he wants the village taken under fire.

Captain Green is struck by indecision. He has no inclination to disobey his commander's order—quite the contrary. At the same time, he recognizes that firing on the village will almost certainly cause injuries among what appear to be noncombatants. Further, the rules of engagement in this area preclude firing into built-up areas without coordination and prior approval unless such action is immediately necessary in self-defense.

Discussion. Captain Green has a duty to obey his commander—a stringent duty essential to efficient military operations—but he also has a duty to disobey illegal orders. He must decide whether the order he has received is illegal. If there are enemy forces in the village that directly threaten the battalion, directing fire specifically against those forces is a legal act. If it is known that some noncombatants are in the immediate vicinity of the enemy positions, and the enemy fire immediately endangers one's own soldiers, returning fire is still permissible under the rules of engagement. Assuming that the intent is to save one's own unit, unintentional injury or loss of life among noncombatants caught in the crossfire is one of the tragedies of war. Responsibility for the injury to noncombatants rests primarily with the enemy force that failed to remove the noncombatants. While the noncombatant casualties would be deeply regrettable, the life-threatening situation and the mission would justify firing in defense. If no life-threatening situation exists, however, the order to fire upon the village is illegal as well as immoral.

Military necessity is sometimes cited in defense of acts that constitute willful killing of noncombatants, who qualify as "protected persons" under the Geneva Conventions. If firing on the village caused the injury or death of noncombatants, it would certainly appear to be willful and to fall under the prohibitions of the 1949 Geneva Conventions.[7] In this case, there appears to be no basis as yet for claiming military necessity.

Situation continued. Captain Green tells the battalion commander that they should seek approval from the district headquarters since no enemy elements are actually known to be there. The battalion commander decides to refrain for the time being. Moments later, however, one of the armed helicopter pilots reports that he has received automatic weapons fire from the village and requests permission to initiate suppressive fires. The battalion commander tells Captain Green to "take care of it." Captain Green again finds himself struck by indecision.

Discussion continued. Captain Green recognizes that firing on the village will almost certainly cause noncombatant casualties. He should also recognize that the situation is not immediately life-threatening. The helicopters can avoid flying over the village. Immediate suppressive fires are not obviously justifiable. Both the size of the enemy force and the number of noncombatants in the village are unknown. Captain Green also remembers that in any case, under the rules of engagement, built-up areas are not to be fired upon except in self-defense without approval from higher headquarters. The act of firing upon the village in these circumstances would be unauthorized and thus probably unjustifiable under the existing rules of engagement established by the American military command. Captain

Green also knows that the helicopter assault can be redirected to an alternate LZ. His logical course of action is to recommend to the battalion commander that the incoming lift helicopters be rerouted to an alternate LZ. To provide flexibility as the situation develops, he may also want to initiate a request to the district headquarters to fire upon the village.

Firing on the village in an attempt to eliminate the enemy threat—knowing that noncombatants would be as likely to be injured as the enemy—could be justified only if failure to do so would immediately endanger the lives or critical resources of American forces. That would be the case even if the technicality of obtaining the village chief's permission to fire had already been met. It would be true as well if noncombatants had been identified in a similar situation in the free-fire zone to the south.

The limitations that determine Captain Green's acceptable alternatives are both legal and moral. While the moral innocence of those identified as noncombatants is sometimes problematic, even the most basic respect for persons requires that the presumption of innocence be extended to those who appear to fall into the category of noncombatants. To do otherwise would clearly contravene the fundamental American values of freedom and individuality. Such contravention would mean that the application of the professional military ethic—if it were considered to condone or require an action that involved denial of the presumption of innocence—was not limited by the set of fundamental social values. A professional military ethic that is not so limited is not a justifiable professional military ethic in the context of the American society that our military serves.

Case 6: The Company Commander

Situation. Captain White commands an infantry company participating in an antiguerrilla campaign in a small Central American nation. American forces have been committed to combat to help maintain a tottering democratic government that is opposed by well-organized revolutionary forces supported by various states, primarily Cuba. The American forces provide security for sensitive areas in the country, thereby freeing the beleaguered government forces for offensive operations. Captain White's company patrols a sector through which small guerrilla raiding forces have moved for some time. The company is part of a network of units securing a large port and logistical center on the coast.

Each day, twenty-one company-sized units providing security receive a requirement to send out a certain number of patrols and ambushes into designated areas within their sectors of responsibility. In response to these orders, each company submits a plan showing patrol routes and ambush locations to their various battalion headquarters. These are in turn forwarded to the Logistic Support Center Command (LSCC).

The daily routine has gone on for nearly six weeks. Casualties in Captain White's company have been rather high, and most of them have occurred in Area B-7, a reference to a particular portion of the company's sector. The B-7 subsector is an elliptical area with the long axis running north and south, framed by two rivers created when a larger tributary splits into two channels at the north end. The two channels rejoin at the southern point, creating an island three-fourths of a mile wide and two miles long. In the center of the area is a village of perhaps one hundred people who work small plots of land in the vicinity. Each day Captain White receives a requirement to conduct one moving patrol and one ambush patrol within B-7. Time and again, as his units move into the area, they are themselves ambushed or encounter mines and booby traps. The men in Captain White's company have nicknamed Area B-7 "the Cemetery."

The area in which the company operates is a patchwork of dense jungle and open areas resulting from past efforts at cultivation. Within B-7, the ground is mostly level and open, but along the river banks, the growth is impenetrable. There are only two foot routes into B-7: small footbridges on the east and west sides. The approaches to the footbridges are continually booby trapped, and it is almost impossible to move into the Cemetery undiscovered.

Captain White's security responsibilities are such that he cannot leave a force in B-7 permanently. He is dubious about leaving them there in an isolated position anyway. Helicopter support is infrequent, making reinforcement by air unreliable. All airmobile assets other than medical evacuation are devoted to offensive operations. Captain White has told his commander of his difficulties and requested that the B-7 patrol requirements be dropped. He has used boats on the river in an attempt to find other entrances to B-7 but to no avail. He has talked to the headman in the B-7 village, but the villagers are struggling to remain neutral and want to avoid retribution by either side in the conflict, though they always manage to avoid booby trap locations. Captain White suspects that there are guerrillas among the villagers, but he knows that the command policy concerning civilians is extremely strict. The American command is determined to avoid the abuses that occurred on occasion in Vietnam.

Each day the patrols go into B-7, and almost each day one or more men are lost. The noncommissioned officers in the company have worked an informal policy in which each man, after making four patrols into B-7, is assigned to other missions until all men in the unit have made four trips to the Cemetery. The turnover rate has been such that few men have had to make more than the four patrols.

On the previous day Captain White accompanied one of the patrols into the Cemetery. A booby trap consisting of a small mortar shell surrounded by crockery killed two men and wounded a third. The device was located about fifty yards from the bridge across the river. Though the patrol's approach had been extremely cautious, with a search for booby traps and mines, the command-detonated shell was not discovered before it exploded.

Captain White is respected by his men, as are his officers and sergeants. They know that Captain White has gone into B-7 many times. Morale is extremely low, however, and the pressure of the daily patrols against an enemy seldom seen but constantly threatening is taking a severe psychological toll. Captain White recognizes that unless the pattern changes, his men may one day refuse to go into the Cemetery.

The requirement is one imposed by a distant headquarters that displays no sensitivity to "minor patrolling losses." Captain White's commander is an experienced career soldier whose primary concern is efficiency and mission accomplishment. He appears unwilling to make an issue of B-7 with higher headquarters. In Captain White's assessment, the B-7 requirement most probably stems from a staff officer's aversion to asymmetry in the dots on the map reviewed daily at LSCC headquarters. He has come to the conclusion that his men are casualties of bureaucracy and inertia more than enemy action. The previous day's losses have crystallized his growing misgivings. He feels that further casualties in an apparently senseless mission are intolerable.

A night of intense introspection has revealed several possible actions. The most radical of these is to refuse to send his men into the Cemetery again on routine patrols. Captain White recognizes that such a protest would result in his rapid replacement by another company commander who would, initially at least, continue the B-7 missions. He could report patrols but simply not send his men out. That possibility, however, is one that Captain White simply cannot accept. It conflicts with his fundamental view of himself as a professional officer and with the standards of performance that he applies to his conduct. In addition, for technical reasons—including regular infrared and "people sniffer" missions by intelligence elements— such an evasion would soon be detected.

Various alternative techniques of meeting the patrol requirements, such as infiltration and stay-behind patrols, have been tried and failed to solve the difficulty. Restrictions on the use of supporting fires make "firepower solutions" unacceptable. If required to go into B-7, Captain White would prefer to go in behind a wall of artillery fire, but that is not possible in this situation.

After Captain White examines all the potential solutions that he has identified, he believes that he faces a fundamental choice: either (1) refuse to obey orders, or (2) continue sending men to death and injury for no defensible purpose.

Discussion. In this situation, the professional military ethic requirement to perform assigned duties appears to run headlong into the requirement to safeguard the welfare of subordinates. In more general terms, duty performance appears to conflict with the humanitarian requirement to treat individual persons with respect as such. To continue sending men into a situation in which casualties appear inevitable, for no apparent end other than following orders, is clearly to use them solely as means. In fact, however, low-ranking members of the chain of command seldom know the larger purposes of generals and armies (when there are such purposes), and they are even less frequently in a position to evaluate the requirements and ramifications. Explanation of detailed policy and purpose to the lower operating levels would often mean insufficient responsiveness and the failure of those policies and purposes. That fact is the reason for the functional requirement for obedience in military activity. Such combat realities are one of the sources of the functional military values of discipline and loyalty. If war is undertaken for apparently just purposes, individuals at operating levels must perform legal orders if the just purposes are to be realized. The platoon leader ordered to make a frontal assault on an enemy position that obviously cannot be penetrated by such a force may well feel lives are being wasted, but he can seldom know whether such an action is not part of a larger series of planned events that will in combination be the wisest and most humane course of action available.

Captain White may be in such a position, but the relevant fact is that he believes he is not. He is sure that the hemorrhaging of his unit is pointless and thus intolerable. He perceives both a moral and a professional obligation to change the course of events. He does not feel it is morally acceptable to continue the patrolling of B-7 in the manner required by his orders.

His first step, regardless of what follows, is to inform his commander of his convictions in the matter. He has already expressed his concern, but now that his doubt has become a firm conviction and a reason for action, the principle of loyalty demands that he make that conviction known to his commander. It is possible that such a response to the situation will trigger some appropriate accommodation. If discussion with his commander produces no results, Captain White is back in his original choice situation. The daily patrol requirement makes a rapid decision imperative and unavoidable.

Consideration of the professional military ethic itself sheds little light. Upon first consideration, duty requires obedience to legal orders, which are in conflict with considerations of subordinate welfare. Both the performance of duty requirement and the principles of loyalty and truth telling weigh heavily against any deception such as false reporting of his company's activities. Larger issues of national security, civilian authority, politics, and the laws of war are not relevant to the situation. The moral principles manifested in the Constitution, which Captain White is sworn to defend, do not appear to direct a choice of one course over another.

If Captain White is to analyze his professional responsibility fully, he must also consider whether the boundary condition established by the American value system eliminates one of his possible courses of action. The value of freedom, given the restrictions of military service and the combat situation, provides only general constraints. If the objectives of participation in the conflict are justified in terms of the values of American society, the professional officer has a strong obligation to be loyal and to obey legal orders. In doing so he is defending the value of freedom. The orders in this case are legal under existing criteria.

The requirement to safeguard the welfare of subordinates reflects another moral value of American society. It is the value of individual personality, which attributes intrinsic worth to each individual. This value supports a refusal to continue to order persons to undertake fatal missions that are also futile. Defending the value of freedom noted in the preceding paragraph suggests that obeying the orders is appropriate. The value of individual personality suggests that it is not. Thus, the values of freedom and individual personality considered together do not appear to point in the same direction.

The most telling moral principle in this situation is perhaps that of individual rights, however, which derives from the broad values of freedom and individual personality. The principle of individual rights is a formulation of the fundamental moral concept of the Constitution. In considering his own men, Captain White might decide that their rights as human beings preclude the use of his authority to send them into Area B-7. To continue to do so, given Captain White's understanding of the situation, would be to decide that their right to determine their own lives—which they surrendered only to the extent of contributing to the achievement of justified objectives in the conflict—could be justly overridden. Since Captain White believes that the Cemetery missions do not contribute to that goal, and that they are also destroying morale and discipline within his unit, the moral argument for refusing to carry out the B-7 patrol missions appears to outweigh the demand of obedience to orders. The moral requirement in this situation may well result in a truncated military career for Captain White.

Applying the moral values that are implicit in or related to the professional military ethic is quite difficult in a case such as this. Acting in accordance with moral conclusions may also be exceedingly difficult. Both, however, are part of the professional obligation inherent in the professional role. They are also necessary if Captain White is to preserve his integrity.

The difficulty of such obligations emerges in a reminiscence reported by Colonel Harry Summers. He relates a 1977 conversation between a retired general and General Harold K. Johnson, who was the Army's Deputy Chief of Staff for Operations during the Vietnam years and later Army Chief of Staff. To the question, "If you had your life to live over again, what would you do differently?" General Johnson responded:

> I remember the day I was ready to go over to the Oval Office and give my four stars to the President and tell him, "You have refused to tell the country they cannot fight a war without mobilization; you have required me to send men into battle with little hope of their ultimate victory; and you have forced us in the military to violate almost every one of the principles of war in Vietnam. Therefore, I resign and will hold a press conference after I walk out of your door."[8]

But, of course, General Johnson did not do so, and, "with a look of anguish," he reportedly said, "I made the typical mistake of believing I could do more for the country and the Army if I stayed in than if I got out. I am now going to my grave with that burden of lapse of moral courage on my back." Following the morally correct alternative is sometimes more than even exceptional men can accomplish, though they fail at the cost of their honor.

One fact is quite clear. The professional role requires that decisions be made and that the moral factors involved in professional decisions be considered as fully as possible. Within the context of the role of the American professional soldier, the morally correct choice is also professionally correct.

Case 7: The Ranger

Situation. Captain Black commands a U.S. Army Ranger company. His unit is conducting winter warfare training in the northwest, where a snowstorm has just swept into the training area. The training program the company is following includes strenuous mountain climbing under hazardous conditions. During the previous day, two men were seriously injured in training accidents resulting from the inclement weather and the precipitous mountains in which the company is working. Captain Black is considering whether to curtail training. The serious injuries to his men have been a grim shock.

One of the combat missions that Captain Black's unit could be assigned involves operations in mountainous terrain. He recognizes that it is essential in terms of combat effectiveness for his unit to learn how to function effectively under extremely adverse conditions. Should they be given a combat mission, they quite possibly would have to operate in conditions as bad or worse that those they are now experiencing. Further, this is an annual training exercise and thus a once-a-year opportunity to develop critical expertise.

Given the weather conditions, however, further accidents would be almost inevitable. Captain Black is extremely reluctant to order his men into a training exercise that will almost certainly result in injuries that could be fatal. Captain Black's higher headquarters, geographically far removed, has given him the authority to make the decision.

Discussion. The obligation to protect the welfare of the individual soldier is a basic principle of the American professional military ethic that applies even to Rangers. Problems similar to this one—frequently encountered by military commanders—pose troubling questions in some circumstances. In this instance, the obligation to protect the welfare of individual soldiers appears to be in conflict with Captain Black's mission to produce and maintain a capable, experienced combat unit that is prepared as well as possible for its primary function—combat.

As a professional officer and as a commander responsible to superiors, Captain Black has the obligation to produce the best-trained and best-prepared unit possible given his resources. His company has the opportunity to learn how to function in extremely adverse conditions if the training program is continued. Such training could one day be critical to combat success. The question faced by Captain Black is whether such readiness justifies the risk of training casualties.

Needless to say, the activities of soldiers in armed conflict are exceedingly hazardous, but one could argue that given that obvious fact, unnecessary exposure to injury and death can hardly be justified in peacetime. On the other hand, the failure to prepare a military unit as thoroughly as possible for the hazards of war also appears inexcusable, in terms of both the professional's responsibility to society and his responsibility to his men.

In this instance, the principle of the welfare of the individual soldier is not necessarily in conflict with the objective of maximizing training effectiveness. The inability of the unit to cope with the rigors of mountainous terrain under adverse weather conditions could eventually be more detrimental to individuals than the current training program. From a professional point of view, so long as the training develops critical skills, risks of injury can justifiably be accepted. At some point damage to unit confidence and morale, in addition to physical risk, will overbalance the tangible training benefits that can be gained from continuing such an exercise. Commanders should take all possible safety precautions in the form of training support, but they can accept a significant degree of risk without ethical misgivings. In situations involving critical skills, commanders *should* accept such risk. After winning the North African campaign in World War II but suffering some severe setbacks, General Eisenhower realized that one of the commander's primary responsibilities to subordinates, as well as to the nation, is to ensure that soldiers are prepared for the rigors of battle. In *Crusade in Europe*, he reflects: "Until world order is an accomplished fact and universal disarmament the logical result, it will always be a crime to excuse men from the types and kinds of training that will give them a decent chance to survive in battle."[9]

Case 8: The Readiness Report

Situation. Captain Verde must report the readiness status of his unit to his commander. Captain Verde knows that his commander will write his efficiency report next week; that report will go into his military records in time for consideration by a promotion board about to meet. Verde very much wants to be promoted to major, but he recognizes that promotions are far from a sure thing in a downsizing military. Verde's commander has said he will accept *no excuses* for the failure of his subordinates to meet his announced readiness goals. A failure would almost certainly mean a bad efficiency report.

Verde's problem is that his unit does not meet the announced readiness standard because of one aircraft. Verde knows that the aircraft should be operational tomorrow, but the report reflects the status of his unit at the close of business today. The aircraft in question is on a special mission in Central America. If Verde reports that he meets readiness standards, no one will know that the report is not quite accurate. The aircrew is oblivious to the reporting issue, and no one else knows of the operational problem.

Clearly, a false report appears to be in Verde's immediate self-interest. Although Verde is aware of the importance of accurate reporting so that the Army has a reasonably clear picture of current capabilities and readiness issues, he also knows that a report that will satisfy his commander will accurately reflect reality—a day later.

Discussion. At first glance, this situation appears to present a conflict between personal self-interest—Verde's pursuit of promotion—and accuracy in formal reporting. The professional military ethic provides clear guidance on each point. An honorable officer of integrity will not lie. Most particularly, he or she will not lie on an official document that affects military operations. Officers are to subordinate their personal interests to the requirements of their professional function. In this case, accurate data in the readiness report clearly are professionally required. Captain Verde's personal interests have a lower priority than adherence to established standards in readiness reporting.

On the other hand, Captain Verde may reason that readiness reports are supposed to provide a snapshot of actual readiness, of actual capabilities available to military commanders. Using that information, commanders can make operational and logistics decisions that will serve ongoing and expected missions. Since the aircraft will be operational the next day, identifying it as operational on this report will actually provide a more accurate picture than a technically accurate report. In addition, Captain Verde knows that the status of one aircraft will not make any difference to the overall readiness condition of the Army. On the other hand, his promotion will make a long-term difference to the Army. If he is passed over, he knows that his future will probably not involve wearing an Army uniform.

Such reflections suggest the seductiveness of rationalization about matters that affect personal interests. The motivation to do what in one's own interests will always be strong. That is one reason the professional ethic emphasizes the importance of subordinating one's interests to professional requirements. Another fundamental reason is that effective professional performance depends upon individual honor and character. Military professionals can meet functional requirements only if they are consistently honest. If an officer chooses when to be truthful, chooses duty over self-interest on a variable basis, other members of the profession will not be able to depend upon the accuracy of reports and statements concerning operational matters. The resulting lack of trust would undermine all professional activity and render all undertakings more difficult and less efficient. In terms of the professional military ethic, there can be no justification of dishonest reporting in the routine activity of a military professional.

Senior Leaders

Case 9: The Brigade Commander

Situation. Colonel Amber is the commander of an infantry brigade in Vietnam. The year is 1968, shortly after the Tet Offensive. Colonel Amber's brigade is assigned a large area of operations within which he is to destroy both main force enemy units and the Viet Cong infrastructure.

Since the Tet Offensive in January, the American command in Saigon has been under intense pressure to produce positive results and to demonstrate thereby that the battle against the VC and the North Vietnamese is being won. Colonel Amber's division commander has informed his subordinate commanders that while vital U.S. national interests are at stake in Vietnam, Congress is being pushed by public sentiment to require withdrawal of U.S. forces. That sentiment, he feels, is fueled by both communist propaganda and a perception that the American military effort is nonproductive and futile. Higher command and the current administration each contend that the public sentiment is dangerously misguided. The division commander has repeatedly emphasized that it is vital to achieve a record of successful operations against the enemy during the current period of doubt at home.

With these points in mind, Colonel Amber finds himself in a dilemma. He has just finished sitting in on a briefing presented by the division commander to the commander of all American forces in

Vietnam (COMUSMACV). The division commander has told COM-USMACV that in an operation that Colonel Amber's brigade has just completed—one resulting in heavy casualties to one of Colonel Amber's battalions—over 400 enemy soldiers were killed. Earlier this day, Colonel Amber, having joined his engaged forces toward the end of the battle and having walked the area and talked after the engagement with the units involved, had briefed the division commander on the details of the operation. Colonel Amber told him that only forty enemy bodies were found, though supporting artillery and air bombardment of the enemy had been heavy. Since Colonel Amber's companies had suffered over one hundred fifty casualties, including fifty-three dead, the verifiable "kill ratio" had been quite unfavorable even though the enemy unit had been driven from the area. The figures reported by the division commander to COMUSMACV in the afternoon briefing were patently false.

Colonel Amber is a career Army officer. He has private doubts about the effectiveness of current U.S. combat operations in Vietnam, but the most effective remedy in his view is an extension of the ground war into North Vietnam and Laos, which provide essentially secure bases for operations against the American and South Vietnamese forces. As Colonel Amber sees it, the North Vietnamese enjoy all the strategic offensive options, while the Americans and South Vietnamese forces remain restricted to a strategic defensive posture. Colonel Amber accepts the importance of the U.S. role in the Vietnamese struggle, believing that the fall of the South Vietnamese government would be unacceptable in terms of U.S. interests. As a military professional, Colonel Amber is not sure about what he should do in this instance. He recognizes his duty to be loyal to his commander and to do all he can to bring about the success of the overall mission.

Discussion. Colonel Amber has a professional responsibility to report truthfully. He has done so. However, the purpose of truthful reporting in a military context is in large part provided by the need for accurate information in making responsible decisions. Superiors will hardly make effective decisions concerning the application of force and the use of resources if the decisions are based upon false or inaccurate data. Colonel Amber knows that the division commander's report is inaccurate. He should also recognize that the objective act of false reporting is morally wrong in itself, though the wrongness could be ameliorated by the subjective factor of intent.

Colonel Amber has a number of options. Among them:

1. He can keep silent and do his own job to the best of his ability.
2. He can keep silent but request a transfer out of the division.
3. He can discuss the matter with the division commander and express his views.
4. He can attempt to correct the false report.
5. He can resign his commission in protest and publicize his reasons.

This set of alternatives presents Colonel Amber with a difficult choice. If he decides to keep silent and continue carrying out the immediate responsibilities of his command position, he recognizes that the false report of which he is aware will probably be uncorrected. His unit will certainly hear of the inflated casualty report. Many members, privy to only a small part of the battle, may assume that actions of which they were unaware produced the enemy casualties. A number will know, however, that the figures are drastically inflated. Colonel Amber realizes that a logical conclusion will be that he himself is the source of the erroneous reporting. If that perception were to become widespread, Colonel Amber's integrity in the eyes of his command would be severely tarnished. The most obvious interpretation of such an action would be one that categorized Colonel Amber as a highly ambitious and apparently unprincipled officer seeking to protect and enhance his own reputation. Besides undermining his effectiveness, such a result would also feed the inevitable cynicism about "higher headquarters." That series of events would clearly be undesirable.

Any attempt to inform his command of the source of the false report would only make matters worse. It would only be natural for some of his subordinates to question Colonel Amber's word, and shifting responsibility one level higher would hardly moderate cynical response. Colonel Amber is also concerned about the effect within his unit that reporting the false casualty figures may produce. The principle of truth telling is obviously weakened if soldiers perceive that higher headquarters are going to alter statistics for their own purposes regardless of the reports received. They may conclude that falsification of their own reports is expected.

The second alternative—keeping silent but requesting a transfer—is obviously not a viable solution. While it might remove Colonel Amber from a difficult position in one sense, but the problems of principle would remain for the division and the Army, which is Colonel Amber's primary concern from a professional point of view. While one false report will, in itself, hardly affect major strategic or even significant tactical decisions, a pattern of false reporting would be a serious failing that could lead to misinformed decisions of great consequence. The effects on the soldiers and professionals under Colonel Amber's command could also be telling in the long run, conceivably even to the extent of undermining the entire American effort to assist the South Vietnamese government.

The third alternative—discussing the matter with the division commander—will be personally difficult. Whereas it may reveal some logical reason for the false report, it will probably result in the division commander's animosity. He may tell Colonel Amber that the reason for the greatly inflated figures on enemy casualties is a determination to avoid providing ammunition for those who misguidedly seek to curtail American military involvement in Vietnam. While such an intent might be understandable, it would hardly be supportable in Colonel Amber's view. The army's responsibility is to carry out assigned missions and to provide accurate professional reporting, analysis, and evaluation to superiors, not to determine national policy decisions. If the division commander were motivated in some sense such as this, he would be advocating substituting the military's view of what was best for the country in place of the civilian leadership and society in general.

The division commander might also direct Colonel Amber to leave such matters to him and to run his brigade. On the other hand, the general might decide to avoid such incidents in the future if he knew that Colonel Amber was strongly opposed on principle to his actions. If the division commander condones violations of the principle of truth telling for reasons of expediency, and simply misjudged Colonel Amber's reactions, a serious problem would remain. Colonel Amber should recognize that the division commander is high enough in the military hierarchy to provide a far reaching and deleterious example if he does not adhere to the principle of truth telling. Further, he is in a position to "contaminate" the information upon which significant tactical decisions are made.

If Colonel Amber attempts to correct the false report outside the regular channel through division headquarters, he will be violating the principle of loyalty in a dramatic fashion. Such an effort may result in controversy and doubt rather than clarification. In any case, it would probably be disastrous for Colonel Amber's career. Though he should recognize that as a personal rather than a strictly professional interest, it is a consideration that would nonetheless loom large in anyone's mind. However his attempt to correct the record turned out, his motives would be misinterpreted and his judgment severely questioned. Most professionals at a distance, firmly convinced of the necessity for loyalty in military organizations, would conclude that there must have been more appropriate ways to handle such a situation.

The last alternative—to resign in protest and make the reasons known—is a traditionally accepted response to superiors' policies or orders that are unacceptable to the individual professional. Weighing against this choice is the possibility of misinterpretation, which can obscure the purpose of the act of resignation. Colonel Amber realizes that little attention would be given to the resignation of one colonel as a result of what could well be seen as a personality conflict between a subordinate and his superior rather than a resignation on principle.

An additional empirical factor to consider is the extent to which false reporting is actually the case and the extent to which such false reporting is tolerated. If it is tolerated, bypassing the division headquarters will not be effective. Transfer to another organization would not even help Colonel Amber's personal situation if falsification for command purposes is generally condoned. If the division commander's report is an isolated instance, discussion with him that reveals Colonel Amber's professional concern may be sufficient to rectify the situation, though it will hardly improve relations between Colonel Amber and his commander. If the practice is pervasive and is subtly and indirectly condoned, Colonel Amber may not be able to find a clear basis for choosing among the alternatives. If such practices are indeed widespread, the officer corps and the society it serves have a serious problem.

The issues in a case such as this, however, revolve about the principle of truth telling. The duty principle requires that Colonel Amber take action in opposing fundamentally misguided decisions by his commander that are clearly detrimental to the protection of national interests. If the difference is one of professional judgment concerning functional requirements, then the superior's views prevail. If the difference involves a violation of professional ethics, however, Colonel Amber has an obligation to do what is necessary to uphold the principle of truth telling. To do so appears to serve not only that principle but also the principle of subordination to civilian control, the exigencies of the profession, and the national interest.

Case 10: The Imam[10]

Situation. During a visit to a training center where his some of his units are preparing for deployment on a peacekeeping mission, Colonel Silver observes a training scenario that involved a lynching. In the scenario, a company commander, with his troops in Bradleys, has stopped in a village because the road through the village center is blocked. When he came forward, he found a television news team, complete with camera, filming a clash between two ethnic groups. Both are reportedly highly suspicious of the U.S. presence in their country. The captain finds himself before the camera talking to an aggressive reporter. The captain has been told that he is not to take any action that would favor one ethnic group over the other, that no backup is readily available if he encounters problems, and that force protection has a high priority.

As he talks with the reporter, he sees a makeshift scaffold in the village square. Two men carrying rifles push a third man, hands tied, toward the scaffold. A large crowd has assembled and appears to be cheering the action. The reporter explains that the local citizenry has assembled to watch the hanging of a local Imam who has been captured by an armed group that has declared itself the security force for the village. The reporter asks the captain, "How do you feel about lynching, and are you going to do anything about it?"

The director of the exercise in turn turns to Colonel Silver and asks him, "How do you want your people to respond to a situation like this one?"

Discussion. If we assume that the mission of the peacekeeping force is to maintain stability and the conditions for progress in returning the area concerned to a peaceful state, Colonel Silver will probably conclude that the force must intervene in some manner. An actual lynching of a religious leader would inflame relations between the two ethnic groups. At the same time, the peacekeepers must both maintain neutrality to the extent possible and use only the amount of force necessary to prevent the death of the Imam. Any excessive use of force will undermine the peacekeeping mission. Appearing to favor one of the two ethnic groups over the other will have the same result.

Another judgment that the captain must make quickly concerns the danger to members of his unit. The physical features of the area concerned, the size and attitude of the crowd, the weaponry he is likely to face, and the capabilities of his soldiers must all be part of his considerations of courses of action. A show of force with his Bradleys may be all that will be necessary. Colonel Silver should recognize that his company commander needs to reason in the same manner in this training scenario to prepare for operational missions. The officers in the peacekeeping assignment need to understand the cultural beliefs and attitudes of the two ethnic groups if they are to be successful; that knowledge will help in identifying appropriate responses in training scenarios such as this one. Stress in the training scenarios will make considered judgment more likely in actual situations that add the weight of danger and responsibility.

Case 11: The Base Commander

Situation. Captain Gray commands a naval facility that provides the home port for a number of fleet vessels that rotate from duty in Southeast Asian waters where they support the war effort. In recent months, there has been increasing unrest among the sailors under Captain Gray's command. An underground newsletter that makes its way onto the base has been conducting a virulent campaign against the claimed exploitation of the poor and minorities in America through military service. Captain Gray is aware that a group of African American sailors meets regularly and criticizes American participation in the conflict in Southeast Asia. His staff has advised him that the rate of disciplinary actions has been increasing over recent weeks, particularly among African American sailors. The staff attributes the increase primarily to opposition to American policies concerning Southeast Asia that has been spread by the apparently organized group of African American sailors, though such a conclusion is admittedly speculative at this point.

The legal staff of the base has advised Captain Gray that the meetings of the African American sailors, though they have not been clandestine or secretive, constitute conspiracy to foster disloyalty and insubordination. The lawyers believe that there is sufficient basis to institute court martial proceedings. The available evidence makes it quite clear that the African American sailors have contended that American participation in the war is morally wrong because they believe that the United States is intervening in a civil war in the pursuit of its own interests. They have pointed out that minorities and the poor constitute a much larger percentage of the military services than they do of the population in general, which they claim is a deliberate policy of the government. The purpose of that policy, they have contended, is to use only the unneeded and unwanted elements of society to fight the country's wars. In addition, the African American sailors have encouraged others to bring complaints and grievances to their group and to allow it to intercede with the chain of command in correcting injustices. The African American committee has also requested a meeting with Captain Gray to voice its dissatisfaction and opposition.

Captain Gray is satisfied that, in light of recent court decisions, the leaders of the rebellious group have taken actions that may well be held criminal in a court martial. Both the Supreme Court and the Court of Military Appeals have established that the military institution, which is directly responsible for the military security of the United States, cannot permit speech and rhetoric that is detrimental to the accomplishment of assigned missions. The courts have upheld restrictions of First Amendment rights, including both censorship and prior restraint. The courts also have upheld suppression of speech in the military if such speech threatens the military subordinate–superior relationship, creates an adverse impact on morale and discipline, or constitutes an immediate danger to national security interests.

Because the African American sailors are members of various units, Captain Gray (rather than a subordinate) is considering whether to press charges under the *Uniform Code of Military Justice.* He is sincerely concerned with the question of fairness. The African American sailors apparently have not advocated the overthrow of the government. No evidence exists indicating they have even advocated disobeying orders, though that seems to be implied. Captain Gray has reviewed their files and found that they all apparently perform their duties adequately. Only a few minor disciplinary actions mar their records. By the Navy's standards, they are competent sailors.

As a professional, Captain Gray is keenly aware of the moral end served by the American military: the preservation of fundamental rights and liberties. He recognizes that in situations such as this he has an obligation to evaluate the moral as well as the legal status of taking action against sailors, who, in their view, may be exercising what they consider to be the right of free speech.

Discussion. The legal merits of this situation are not the central issue. If the only question were legality, the most reasonable action would be to refer the matter to the court for decision. The primary issue is the resolution of professional obligations. In upholding the Constitution, Captain Gray is necessarily involved with what Chief Justice Earl Warren termed "the vertical reach of the Bill of Rights within the military."[11]

As a professional, Captain Gray is obligated to take the actions he deems necessary in the performance of his immediate duties. If the conduct of his subordinates contributes to the weakening of morale and discipline or directly endangers national security interests, he should counter the effects of such conduct and take action to prevent its continuation. His warrant for action, however, is limited to those measures that are not contrary to the values of American society and the moral principles reflected in the Constitution. The protection of individual rights and liberties (among them the right of free speech) is a protection of such values. Thus, Captain Gray must determine whether the suppression of free speech in this instance is in fact justified. Disagreement with the policies of the government would appear to be a legitimate exercise of free speech, one consistent with the equal exercise of such a right by others. Soldiers remain persons in the sense of autonomous moral entities capable of rational choice. As such, they retain the right to exercise fundamental freedoms unless such exercise endangers the equal exercise by others.

In a military context, advocacy of mutiny, disobedience, or revolution would usually fall into a class of actions unacceptable under this criterion. All such activity causes physical or political violence that endangers the exercise of basic rights by the members of society. Unless such advocacy was a response to sustained institutional or political wrongs, it would be unacceptable and thus the legitimate object of sanctions.

In this case, have the black sailors taken actions that are unacceptable in these terms? They have expressed disagreement with government policies, but they have apparently stopped short of advocating disobedience or mutiny. Disagreement does not constitute disloyalty in the legal sense. There is no clear evidence of an attempt to undermine the chain of command. On the contrary, the African American sailors apparently intend to make use of the chain of command to air their grievances and complaints. They have requested the opportunity to express their views to the commander, Captain Gray.

Given the limited information presented in this case, the most reasonable course of action for Captain Gray to follow appears to be one in which he grants the request for a meeting with the disaffected sailors. While listening to their views, Captain Gray should present to them the perspective in which he views their actions and make clear the criteria under which their actions will be evaluated. Among those criteria is the actual effect of their meetings and the expression of their views. To the extent that the results constitute a "clear and present danger" to national security interests (ambiguous as such wording is), the conduct of the African American sailors will be actionable, both legally and morally. If, after such a meeting and subsequent counseling by the chain of command, the actions of the sailors result in the deterioration of morale and discipline or in a threat to specific missions or functions, Captain Gray can and should take action against them as a part of his professional duties.

Several assumptions surface in this discussion. One is that, in Captain Gray's evaluation, American participation in the war in question is not immoral in terms of national values, either in reference to the issues involved in the war or to the conduct of the war itself. Another is that the government is not pursuing unjust and immoral domestic policies. Were either assumption not the case, Captain Gray's position would be more challenging to assess. The issues of concern in this case, however, are those of individual rights and command responsibility for combat readiness. In the circumstances described, legal action does not yet appear warranted from a moral point of view.

Case 12: The Technical Expert

Situation. Lieutenant Colonel Brown is a career Air Force officer who currently works in research and development. Her project team is involved in developing and testing a robot aircraft possessing remarkable new capabilities that is to be added to the inventory of the Air Force. Lieutenant Colonel Brown is responsible for testing the performance of the weapons system in a variety of operational environments.

The development program is a controversial one. The Air Force sought approval and funding for the "integrated systems unmanned aerial vehicle" (ISUAV) system for several years before Congressional resistance was overcome. Several key members of Congress are still adamantly opposed to the continuation of the program and the eventual purchase of the system, which poses a direct threat to the role (and thus production) of future manned fighter and reconnaissance aircraft. The Air Force, with Pentagon backing, has long insisted that such a weapons system is essential to ensure that it is able to counter a variety of threats in future conflicts. Capable of performing both reconnaissance and attack roles, the weapons system that Lieutenant Colonel Brown is testing is the choice of the Air Force, which has invested heavily in its development. She believes that it will revolutionize aerospace capabilities.

Unfortunately, the ISUAV has failed to meet certain minimum requirements established by the Pentagon. When Lieutenant Colonel Brown first reported the difficulties to her project chief, the officer ordered her to run the tests again. She was also told that if the system, which had been developed at such cost, were to prove unsatisfactory, the possibility was great that Congress would terminate the entire program in the upcoming budget cycle. In the view of the Air Force, such a result would critically undermine its future capabilities. The project chief went so far as to say that even the President has agreed that the timely procurement of the weapons system is essential to national defense.

Although no specific directives have been issued, the project chief has implied that it is Lieutenant Colonel Brown's responsibility in this unusual case to ensure that the ISUAV meets the minimum requirements. She has identified certain deficiencies that can be corrected in time, but the process will require additional (and costly) development that cannot be accomplished quickly. The project chief has said informally that a flawed but perfectible system would be infinitely preferable to no system at all, but it seems clear that if the system does not meet minimum requirements, Congress will cut funding entirely in the upcoming budget process. The project chief has temporarily delayed publication of the test data, but he can resist pressure for only a limited time.

Lieutenant Colonel Brown agrees that procurement of the ISUAV is vitally important. She believes that it will both save the lives of pilots and add lethal capability to the Air Force inventory. In her view, it would be an extremely grave error to terminate the program and thus, at the very least, postpone acquisition of the system for the foreseeable future. At the same time, she is instinctively repelled by the thought of doctoring her test results in order to conceal the existing shortcomings of the ISUAV.

Discussion. To report the test results in a manner that would betray the purpose of the tests would be a blatant violation of the principle of truth telling. Arrayed against this clear-cut professional military ethic requirement is the more opaque one of determining what action will best serve the purpose of maintaining the security of the nation. While it seems unlikely that any one weapons system would actually be essential to the nation's security, it is certainly possible that someone should believe that to be the case. Lieutenant Colonel Brown may well believe that the congressmen opposed to the ISUAV system are simply misinformed or are acting from ulterior motives, and that if they clearly understood the situation or acted responsibly, they would have to admit that the program deserved support. She may consider the question of procurement to be one of professional judgment that is not properly decided by laymen. If acquisition of the weapons system is vital to the ability of the military services to perform their defensive function, much might be justified in achieving that goal.

To conceal the actual capabilities of the system as revealed by the tests, however, would be to subvert the principle of subordination to civilian leadership. In effect, Lieutenant Colonel Brown and her project chief would be deciding that they, not the elected representatives of the nation's citizens, should determine how the country should be defended and how it should allocate funds for doing so. From the point of view of professional ethics and constitutional authority, even if Lieutenant Colonel Brown and her project chief were correct in their beliefs concerning the need for obtaining the weapons system, it would nonetheless be better to report their results accurately and contribute as best they could to informed debate concerning the best course of action. Human judgment is indeed fallible, but in a representative democracy it should be the will of society as interpreted by elected representatives that proves to be in error, not the self-imposed judgments of a few who decide they know better than all others what "should" be done. If such a view gained currency among those trusted to serve society, democracy would assume a most tenuous existence. Needless to say, such actions in the long run would undermine rather than "support and defend" the Constitution.

The commitment of the professional officer corps is to support and defend the Constitution. That can hardly be accomplished in any coherent fashion by subverting the constitutional process, however urgent the need may appear to be.

Case 13: The Court Martial

Situation. Colonel Slate faces an Article 32 investigation, which could lead to a court martial. An Article 32 investigating officer examines available evidence on behalf of a commander and recommends for or against proceeding with a court martial. Colonel Slate had commanded the only armor brigade in U.S. forces deployed in a small Middle Eastern country, Irabat. Forces of Sindonia, a hostile state to the north, invaded Irabat three days ago, sweeping south across the border and achieving complete surprise. American forces were held in reserve until eight hours after the invasion, when their positions were attacked by two enemy divisions. For the next two hours, U.S. forces conducted a delaying action on the north side of the Khyler River as they tried to stem the rout of Irabati units that threatened the Irabati capital just thirty miles to the south. For all involved, the Khyler River became critical. The Khyler is a major tributary, more than half a mile across.

The UN condemned the invasion, and forces from other NATO countries as well as U.S. reinforcements were preparing for movement. If the Sindonian forces could get across the Khyler, they could drive south rapidly and conquer Irabat before help arrived. Colonel Slate began to move his units across a highway bridge on the river, the only one for many miles east and west. The bridge had been prepared for demolition, and Colonel Slate was to blow the bridge as soon as his forces were across. Both the Irabati high command and Colonel Slate's superiors had made clear that he must destroy the bridge so that the enemy would be halted long enough to reorganize Irabat's forces in defense of the capital. In addition, the U.S. commander emphasized that Slate must preserve his tanks for the battle south of the river if the allied force were to have a prayer of succeeding.

When Colonel Slate's last two tank battalions tried to reach the bridge, they found that the refugee flood fleeing the invaders had become uncontrollable. Masses of men, women, and children blocked the bridge and the approaches to it. Horns, loudspeakers, even machine gun fire over the heads of the panicked crowds made no impression. Sindonian forces were in sight on the horizon, pressing toward the crossing site.

Colonel Slate, knowing he had to get his tanks across and blow the bridge, ordered his units to drive into the packed masses of people. When they did so, many civilians were killed. As soon as the tanks were across, he ordered the engineers to blow the bridge, even though it was still crowded with refugees. The next day, heavy air strikes began destroying the Sindonian divisions massed on the north side of the river. Irabat was saved—and Colonel Slate faced a court martial for war crimes because of the death of Irabati civilians.

Discussion. The professional military ethic identifies service to country as a military professional's primary duty. In this case, success in the assigned mission—destroy the bridge and save his unit for subsequent missions—appears to have been Colonel Slate's primary duty. The measures necessary to achieve that two-fold mission would then appear to have been militarily necessary. Military necessity, however, is not a blank check. As the U.S. Army's guidance on the law of war states, "Military necessity has generally been rejected as a defense for acts forbidden by the customary and conventional laws of war inasmuch as the latter have been developed and framed with consideration for the concept of military necessity."[12] The field manual discussion establishes that military necessity can seldom be used as justification for violating the laws of war, and of course intentionally killing civilian noncombatants appears to be such a violation. The 1949 Geneva Conventions (specifically the Geneva Convention Relative to the Protection of Civilian Persons in Time of War, Article 147) prohibit intentionally killing civilian noncombatants—and in this case the noncombatants are the very people whose country the American units are fighting to protect.

In the last chapter we discussed the professional military ethic of the Israeli Defense Forces. It states that "the obligations to fulfill the mission and be victorious in war will be the compass guiding any effort to balance the system of values and basic principles of *The Spirit of the IDF*."[13] A soldier following that code who faced a conflict between values or principles would look for the alternative that would secure victory. Actions necessary to military victory would appear to be the appropriate choice in most circumstances. For those adhering to the American professional military ethic, success in war remains the touchstone, but not success at any cost. Actions that are functionally necessary are circumscribed first by the laws of war and finally by the values of American society. In this instance, the laws of war protect noncombatants. In the constraints established by American society, the value of individualism limits the power of the state when the fundamental rights of American citizens are concerned. The principle is one that does not allow the weight of numbers to override the fundamental rights of the individual. If we carry that reasoning into this situation, we would expect Colonel Slate to have searched for alternatives to that of killing civilian noncombatants.

One course of action would have been to establish a defensive position around the end of the bridge on the enemy side. In a short period it might have been possible to stem the tide of refugees and begin a withdrawal across the long bridge. The forces on the enemy side would have been at serious risk, but some situations require such risk in war. A defensive position on the far side of the bridge would have given engineers more time to prepare for bridge demolition and more time for the number of civilians on the bridge to diminish before the bridge had to be blown.

Applying the doctrine of double effect would appear to justify blowing the bridge while some civilians remained on it more readily than the doctrine would support driving tanks over the bodies of civilian noncombatants fleeing the battle area. The good effect of preventing enemy movement across the bridge—and thus preventing enemy victory in the war—appears to far outweigh the good effect of saving the tanks and men in the two battalions. Although there is an argument that the good effect of saving Colonel Slate's units for further combat may outweigh the bad effect of killing noncombatants, it is certainly not as strong as the argument that one can marshal for blowing the bridge.

The killing of noncombatants in considerable numbers should not be a decision taken except in the most unusual and critical circumstances. Legal as well as moral considerations apply. Because that is so, the court martial of Colonel Slate should proceed. Once the court determines the legal status of his actions, the moral aspect will come into play. One would expect that moral factors will have a role in mitigation and extenuation, and thus in any sentence the court might pronounce.

In the press of combat, leaders assess their situations and make decisions. Choices made in the attempt to do what is right merit respect, but leaders must also accept responsibility for those choices. Colonel Slate's case presented stark alternatives. The professional military ethic and the values that underlie it provide guidance in "the hardest place."

Case 14: The Joint Chiefs

Situation. After a fiercely fought political campaign, a charismatic politician became President. During her first year, she replaced the Secretary of Defense, the secretaries of the military departments, and the Chairman of the Joint Chiefs of Staff. As the country struggles to climb out of a ruinous depression that has decimated the American economy, the president begins issuing presidential decrees aimed at rejuvenating American industry, relieving the financial hardships of the poor and unemployed, and providing support for what she terms "core structure businesses."

At the same time, a populist senator leads a political crusade based on creating a more effective government. The senator gains widespread support for his call for change, saying that to pull itself out of the hole it is in, the country must have a more powerful central government with broad authority to direct domestic affairs. He explains tirelessly that only a managed economy will restore prosperity to the nation. After three years of economic collapse and the continuing disintegration of everything from roads to schools to the reliability of Internet access, people across the country are desperately seeking a change of course for the nation.

Mid-term election campaigns begin. The senator advocates the establishment of what he calls the Office of the Controller, for which special legal authority would be created. With that authority, the office would be able to set aside federal court rulings and override executive orders in the process of directing both public agencies and private organizations to ensure national survival and revival. Polls indicate that the senator's Radical Reform Party will win a large majority of seats in the House and Senate unless some change occurs. With such a majority, the senator may well be able to pass the radical legislation he supports. Constitutional amendments appear entirely possible.

The President calls in the chairman of the Joint Chiefs of Staff and the chiefs of the military services. She explains that a crisis is at hand: the future of American democracy is at risk. She has no doubt about who the controller will be if the senator is successful. In her view, the one pillar of support that would ensure the senator's success would be the armed forces. The controller would have operational control of military units under the senator's proposals. She asks the military to announce support publicly for the administration and to denounce the senator's plans. Because the military remains one of the most highly respected institutions in society, the President is confident that such support would rally many votes, certainly enough to prevent the three-quarter majority required to pass Constitutional amendments.

Discussion. The professional military ethic states that military professionals conform strictly to the principle that subordinates the military to civilian authority. Under that principle, the military leaders of American forces take orders from their civilian superiors. In this case, the president has "requested" that the military leaders make public statements and provide public commentary presenting their opposition to the legislation that would establish the Office of the Controller. The difficulty here is that the civilian authority principle has always been focused on keeping the military *out* of domestic politics and *out* of the process of establishing national priorities. The principle is a manifestation of the "man on horseback" syndrome that retains a healthy skepticism about any person in uniform who seeks power in the political affairs of the state. Such men historically have not been supporters of democracy. In conforming to the principle of subordination, members of the military have traditionally avoided any involvement in domestic politics beyond the exercise of basic civil rights. Before World War II, some military professionals felt it was inappropriate even to vote. Today, all men and women in uniform are encouraged to vote, but the public does not expect any activity beyond that action in domestic politics.

If the members of the Joint Chiefs of Staff were to take public positions on this particular political issue, they would be establishing a precedent that would allow them to take such actions in the future. Although the objections to the controller legislation would appear to be reasonable ones in light of the values of democracy and freedom, a president one day might well encourage the military leadership to take political actions that might not be consistent with American values.

In this case, the President has not issued what could be construed as an illegal order. Military regulations require service members to disobey illegal orders, but the President's request does not ask the leaders of the services to do anything overtly illegal. She has asked them, however, to take actions that violate the professional military ethic. At least one purpose of the provision of the professional military ethic that forbids political involvement is to ensure that the American values of freedom and democratic constitutionalism endure. A military leader who attained political power through military force would not be a friend of democracy. To the extent that military leaders take part in domestic politics, the temptation to generate political change using military power will grow.

One might counter, however, that the President is asking the

Joint Chiefs of Staff to help preserve democratic institutions and individual freedoms and that supporting the President's domestic political agenda appears to be the best way to do just that. Staying out of domestic politics, one could argue, is admirable and desirable so long as America's core values are not at stake, but that restraint in the face of challenges to those values is no virtue.

Institutional neutrality nonetheless appears to be appropriate in this instance. So long as domestic peace and constitutional processes are not threatened, the military as an institution should remain politically neutral. If the armed forces become publicly aligned with one political party or publicly opposed to one, the democratic principle will be more seriously at risk than it will be by any radical political program on which members of the public will vote in accordance with constitutional principles. I would argue that the members of the Joint Chiefs of Staff should not accede to the wishes of the President in this situation.

Chapter Ten

Epilogue

Men and women who find themselves in combat fight to survive. But beyond that instinctive drive, they fight for their fellows—some of them close friends, some mere acquaintances, but all of them confederates—bonded together by common circumstance. Seldom do they fight for causes or for abstract values, though they will fight for a strong leader whom they know well. Military professionals, however, serve with a concept of commitment to an institution, which they describe variously and roughly, usually with some discomfort when the subject comes up in a personal context. Americans possessing both dedication and strong character serve in accordance with the professional military ethic. We have many dedicated people in our military services, and they take their professional commitment seriously.

It is mainly for them that I have tried to delineate the moral structure that girds and illuminates the American professional military ethic. To clarify some of the relationships that determine the guidelines for conduct by members of the American military, I have employed the concept of role-differentiated behavior. My discussion has presented a justification for the military ethic in terms of the value and function of the military institution within American society. As Chapter 1 made clear, I accept Elizabeth Anscombe's position, which claims that the military and the police are essential elements in contemporary human affairs: "For society is essential to human good; and society without coercive power is generally impossible."[1] By applying the concept of role differentiation, I have attempted to show that the professional military ethic limits the use of the military's coercive power in important ways.

Analytical devices other than role differentiation could be employed, of course, to include an examination of virtues or an analysis of conduct from the point of view of particular moral theories. Role differentiation provides advantages, however, in that the issue of justification is neatly circumscribed in ways that reflect our thinking about professional conduct. In addition, the perspective I have employed avoids some of the traditional (and unresolved) questions concerning moral truth. If I had answers to those questions, I would have written a much different book.

I have concluded that functional requirements necessitate a partially differentiated role for military professionals—one in which professional considerations alter the balance of moral judgments in ways that would be inappropriate for individuals outside the profession. Such differentiation, however, finds justification in the core values of society, which place distinct limits on morally acceptable, professional conduct. My examination claims, in broad terms, that the American professional military ethic is a synthesis of the functional requirements of the profession of arms, the principles underlying the prescriptions of the laws of war, and the moral implications generated by the enduring values of American society.

Some may disagree with the model of ethical relationships I have presented, but I hope that exploring their disagreement clarifies and reinforces their own ethical positions. To those who maintain that in war one does whatever is necessary to win, I must respond that they have no ethic at all: without moral purpose war is simply the exercise of destructive power against other human beings in the pursuit of self-interest. From the American perspective, war without moral purpose is always wrong. I remain convinced that the strength of our military leadership and thus our military forces as a whole lies in our commitment to a coherent and stable military ethic.

In the aftermath of Vietnam, the U.S. Army was subjected to painful scrutiny, both from within and from without—for good reason. We had lost a war that we apparently could have won. Among other analyses, that of Richard A. Gabriel and Paul L. Savage found fault with the leadership of the officer corps and traced that shortcoming to an institutional failing: "It has been the failure of the Army as an organization to develop an institutional sense of ethics that is supportive of individual notions of integrity, to ensure that individual officers are trained in a sense of what the ethics of the military institution are."[2]

The Army changed for the better in the decade that passed after Gabriel and Savage presented their analysis, and by 1991 American military forces were superbly prepared for conventional combat, as the First Gulf War demonstrated. In the decade following that triumph, however, we found that the central role of ethics in military professionalism still needed to be stressed. To fulfill their obligations, military professionals must understand the moral framework within which they operate and the military ethic that is to be applied within that framework. Successful military operations in the twenty-first century require greater flexibility and a wider range of capabilities than ever before, as we saw in our return to Iraq in 2003. They also continue to require men and women of character committed to their profession.

America's overwhelming military power in this new century makes ethical considerations and ethical constraint even more significant. A recent article focused on the extraordinary capabilities of U.S. forces: "The American military is now the strongest the world has ever known, both in absolute terms and relative to other nations: stronger than the Wehrmacht in 1940, stronger than the legions at the height of Roman power."[3] With such dominance comes great responsibility.

To be morally and logically consistent in applying their professional ethic, members of the military must be able to evaluate problematic situations and develop reasonable conclusions about possible responses. Difficult choices arise frequently in military life, as our case studies indicate. We all know that character weaknesses sometimes lead to wrong actions despite a clear grasp of the ethical dimensions of a situation, but recognizing the morally appropriate choice remains the necessary starting point for moral conduct.

In those hard cases involving warfare, the first step in deciding what to do is to recognize what is functionally required to accomplish the mission. The second step is to apply the provisions of the professional military ethic, which include the restrictions imposed by the laws of war. To be consistent in resolving troublesome situations, one needs to recognize the role of the laws of war in limiting acceptable courses of action that are available to fulfill any particular military mission. Members of the American armed forces, by virtue of their commitment to defend the Constitution, are morally and legally obligated to adhere to the laws of war, as we have discussed in considerable detail. The third major step is to recognize the restriction on possible responses imposed by the fundamental values of American society, which can be described by the terms freedom, equality, individualism, and democracy. These three steps help filter out courses of action that are morally inappropriate.

In this nation, the four fundamental social values undergird the military profession and the ethic that guides the activities of its members. Because the armed forces exist to defend and preserve the social realization of those values, the military cannot systematically violate them yet succeed in its overall purpose.

Understanding the nature of the professional military ethic and the normative context in which it is applied can make our military leaders more capable and more reliable. Those objectives have motivated my reflection. One question that obviously arises in relation to my discussion, a question I have not directly addressed, is whether the American military would be well served by the publication of a formal codified ethic. Perhaps a military service should have several specific codes: one for officers, one for enlisted men, one for combat, and one for POWs such as we now have in the *Code of Conduct*.[4] My own view is that a variety of codes would de-emphasize the importance of each, a result that would not serve well the purposes of the military.

A further question is whether each military service should have its own formal ethical code, or whether one code should apply to all components of the armed forces. Does the U.S. Air Force have special requirements that would dictate a somewhat different code from one appropriate for the Navy or one appropriate for the Army? Should a broad set of principles apply to all the services, published perhaps by the Department of Defense, with each individual service then promulgating its own supplemental guidance? Or is it the case either that the services' level of conduct is such that no steps for improvement need be taken (a position difficult to maintain) or that a formally codified ethic would not contribute appropriately to attempts at improvement? We have not ignored such questions in the past, but they need more attention in this era of joint operations.

Properly applying the professional military ethic, formally codified and published or not, will always require judgment, education, training, and experience—the more the better. Military leaders will continue to face hard cases in the future. Adhering to the ethic under difficult conditions will require both competent leadership and strong character. Most members of the profession of arms would agree with those claims, I suspect, and perhaps with one additional conviction as well: without those qualities among its members, neither the military nor the society it defends is likely to succeed.

Appendix: Universal Declaration of Human Rights

PREAMBLE

Whereas recognition of the inherent dignity and of the equal and inalienable rights of all members of the human family is the foundation of freedom, justice and peace in the world,

Whereas disregard and contempt for human rights have resulted in barbarous acts which have outraged the conscience of mankind, and the advent of a world in which human beings shall enjoy freedom of speech and belief and freedom from fear and want has been proclaimed as the highest aspiration of the common people,

Whereas it is essential, if man is not to be compelled to have recourse, as a last resort, to rebellion against tyranny and oppression, that human rights should be protected by the rule of law,

Whereas it is essential to promote the development of friendly relations between nations,

Whereas the peoples of the United Nations have in the Charter reaffirmed their faith in fundamental human rights, in the dignity and worth of the human person and in the equal rights of men and women and have determined to promote social progress and better standards of life in larger freedom,

Whereas Member States have pledged themselves to achieve, in cooperation with the United Nations, the promotion of universal respect for and observance of human rights and fundamental freedoms,

Whereas a common understanding of these rights and freedoms is of the greatest importance for the full realization of this pledge,

Now, therefore,

The General Assembly,

Proclaims this Universal Declaration of Human Rights as a common standard of achievement for all peoples and all nations, to the end that every individual and every organ of society, keeping this Declaration constantly in mind, shall strive by teaching and education to promote respect for these rights and freedoms and by progressive measures, national and international, to secure their universal and effective recognition and observance, both among the peoples of Member States themselves and among the peoples of territories under their jurisdiction.

ARTICLE 1
All human beings are born free and equal in dignity and rights. They are
endowed with reason and conscience and should act towards one another in a
spirit of brotherhood.

ARTICLE 2
Everyone is entitled to all the rights and freedoms set forth in this Declaration, without distinction of any kind, such as race, colour, sex, language,
religion, political or other opinion, national or social origin, property, birth or
other status.
Furthermore, no distinction shall be made on the basis of the political,
jurisdictional or international status of the country or territory to which a
person belongs, whether it be independent, trust, non-self-governing or under any other limitation of sovereignty.

ARTICLE 3
Everyone has the right to life, liberty and security of person.

ARTICLE 4
No one shall be held in slavery or servitude; slavery and the slave trade
shall be prohibited in all their forms.

ARTICLE 5
No one shall be subjected to torture or to cruel, inhuman or degrading
treatment or punishment.

ARTICLE 6
Everyone has the right to recognition everywhere as a person before the
law.

ARTICLE 7
All are equal before the law and are entitled without any discrimination to
equal protection of the law. All are entitled to equal protection against any
discrimination in violation of this Declaration and against any incitement to
such discrimination.

ARTICLE 8
Everyone has the right to an effective remedy by the competent national
tribunals for acts violating the fundamental rights granted him by the constitution or by law.

ARTICLE 9
No one shall be subjected to arbitrary arrest, detention or exile.

ARTICLE 10
Everyone is entitled in full equality to a fair and public hearing by an
independent and impartial tribunal, in the determination of his rights and
obligations and of any criminal charge against him.

ARTICLE 11

1. Everyone charged with a penal offence has the right to be presumed innocent until proved guilty according to law in a public trial at which he has had all the guarantees necessary for his defence.

2. No one shall be held guilty of any penal offence on account of any act or omission which did not constitute a penal offence, under national or international law, at the time when it was committed. Nor shall a heavier penalty be imposed than the one that was applicable at the time the penal offence was committed.

ARTICLE 12

No one shall be subjected to arbitrary interference with his privacy, family, home or correspondence, nor to attacks upon his honour and reputation. Everyone has the right to the protection of the law against such interference or attacks.

ARTICLE 13

1. Everyone has the right to freedom of movement and residence within the borders of each State.

2. Everyone has the right to leave any country, including his own, and to return to his country.

ARTICLE 14

1. Everyone has the right to seek and to enjoy in other countries asylum from persecution.

2. This right may not be invoked in the case of prosecutions genuinely arising from non-political crimes or from acts contrary to the purposes and principles of the United Nations.

ARTICLE 15

1. Everyone has the right to a nationality.

2. No one shall be arbitrarily deprived of his nationality nor denied the right to change his nationality.

ARTICLE 16

1. Men and women of full age, without any limitation due to race, nationality or religion, have the right to marry and to found a family. They are entitled to equal rights as to marriage, during marriage and at its dissolution.

2. Marriage shall be entered into only with the free and full consent of the intending spouses.

3. The family is the natural and fundamental group unit of society and is entitled to protection by society and the State.

ARTICLE 17

1. Everyone has the right to own property alone as well as in association with others.

2. No one shall be arbitrarily deprived of his property.

ARTICLE 18

Everyone has the right to freedom of thought, conscience and religion; this right includes freedom to change his religion or belief, and freedom, either alone or in community with others and in public or private, to manifest his religion or belief in teaching, practice, worship and observance.

ARTICLE 19
Everyone has the right to freedom of opinion and expression; this right includes freedom to hold opinions without interference and to seek, receive and impart information and ideas through any media and regardless of frontiers.

ARTICLE 20
1. Everyone has the right to freedom of peaceful assembly and association.
2. No one may be compelled to belong to an association.

ARTICLE 21
1. Everyone has the right to take part in the government of his country, directly or through freely chosen representatives.
2. Everyone has the right to equal access to public service in his country.
3. The will of the people shall be the basis of the authority of government; this will shall be expressed in periodic and genuine elections which shall be by universal and equal suffrage and shall be held by secret vote or by equivalent free voting procedures.

ARTICLE 22
Everyone, as a member of society, has the right to social security and is entitled to realization, through national effort and international co-operation and in accordance with the organization and resources of each State, of the economic, social and cultural rights indispensable for his dignity and the free development of his personality.

ARTICLE 23
1. Everyone has the right to work, to free choice of employment, to just and favourable conditions of work and to protection against unemployment.
2. Everyone, without any discrimination, has the right to equal pay for equal work.
3. Everyone who works has the right to just and favourable remuneration ensuring for himself and his family an existence worthy of human dignity, and supplemented, if necessary, by other means of social protection.
4. Everyone has the right to form and to join trade unions for the protection of his interests.

ARTICLE 24
Everyone has the right to rest and leisure, including reasonable limitation of working hours and periodic holidays with pay.

ARTICLE 25
1. Everyone has the right to a standard of living adequate for the health and well-being of himself and of his family, including food, clothing, housing and medical care and necessary social services, and the right to security in the event of unemployment, sickness, disability, widowhood, old age or other lack of livelihood in circumstances beyond his control.

2. Motherhood and childhood are entitled to special care and assistance. All children, whether born in or out of wedlock, shall enjoy the same social protection.

ARTICLE 26

1. Everyone has the right to education. Education shall be free, at least in the elementary and fundamental stages. Elementary education shall be compulsory. Technical and professional education shall be made generally available and higher education shall be equally accessible to all on the basis of merit.

2. Education shall be directed to the full development of the human personality and to the strengthening of respect for human rights and fundamental freedoms. It shall promote understanding, tolerance and friendship among all nations, racial or religious groups, and shall further the activities of the United Nations for the maintenance of peace.

3. Parents have a prior right to choose the kind of education that shall be given to their children.

ARTICLE 27

1. Everyone has the right freely to participate in the cultural life of the community, to enjoy the arts and to share in scientific advancement and its benefits.

2. Everyone has the right to the protection of the moral and material interests resulting from any scientific, literary or artistic production of which he is the author.

ARTICLE 28

Everyone is entitled to a social and international order in which the rights and freedoms set forth in this Declaration can be fully realized.

ARTICLE 29

1. Everyone has duties to the community in which alone the free and full development of his personality is possible.

2. In the exercise of his rights and freedoms, everyone shall be subject only to such limitations as are determined by law solely for the purpose of securing due recognition and respect for the rights and freedoms of others and of meeting the just requirements of morality, public order and the general welfare in a democratic society.

3. These rights and freedoms may in no case be exercised contrary to the purposes and principles of the United Nations.

ARTICLE 30

Nothing in this Declaration may be interpreted as implying for any State, group or person any right to engage in any activity or to perform any act aimed at the destruction of any of the rights and freedoms set forth herein.

Notes

Chapter One. The Hardest Place

1. Charles R. Kemble, *The Image of the Army Officer in America* (Westport, CT: Greenwood Press, 1973), 202.
2. Harry Redner, *Ethical Life: The Past and Present of Ethical Cultures* (New York: Rowman & Littlefield, 2001), 9.
3. Ibid., 13.
4. "US Military Expenditures," website of the Nuclear Age Peace Foundation, available at <http://www.wagingpeace.org/articles/01.04/usmilitary expenditures.html>, accessed January 2, 2002.
5. Gregg Easterbrook, "American Power Moves Beyond the Mere Super," *New York Times,* 27 April 2003 (Section 4), 5.
6. The "rogue states," Russia, and China together will spend less than a third of the U.S. military budget in 2003—a startling observation. See "World Military Expenditures," Center for Defense Information, available at <http://www.cdi.org/issues/wme/>, accessed 2 January 2002.
7. The officer's oath of office appears in Title 10, USC, and the oath of the enlisted soldier appears in Title 5.
8. James R. McDonough, *Platoon Leader* (New York: Bantam Books, 1985), 139.
9. Omar N. Bradley, *A Soldier's Story* (New York: Henry Holt, 1951), 330. Bradley tells the story of Operation COBRA on pp. 330–49.
10. Walzer, *Just and Unjust Wars,* 317–19.
11. Bradley, *A Soldier's Story,* 344.
12. Richard Wasserstrom, "Lawyers as Professionals: Some Moral Issues," *Human Rights* 5 (1975): 3.
13. For the clarification provided by this sentence, I am indebted to an unknown reviewer for the University Press of Kansas.
14. As related by C. E. Harris, Jr., *Applying Moral Theories* (Belmont, CA: Wadsworth, 1986), 114–15.
15. Ibid., 115.
16. British philosopher Thomas Hobbes (1588–1679) imagined a state of nature, without any organized society or state, in which every person was pitted against every other in the struggle for scarce resources necessary to sustain life. In that state, he said that morality and rights would not exist: only the struggle to survive would have meaning. To escape that war of all

against all, which would be the essential characteristic of the state of nature, Hobbes claimed that reason dictated that men join to form a society and agree to a contract that would provide mutual and collective security.

17. As I will discuss later, a variety of publications, many of them military manuals and pamphlets, express and explain various aspects of the American professional military ethic even though there is no formal, comprehensive code for any particular service or the military as a whole. The American professional military ethic, then, is a set of moral guidelines for practice perpetuated by many informal mechanisms as well as through formal training and schooling within the military system. Anyone attempting to present a comprehensive articulation of the professional military ethic must draw upon a wide variety of sources.

Chapter Two. The Military as a Profession

1. Andrew Abbott. *The System of Professions: An Essay on the Division of Expert Labor* (Chicago: University of Chicago Press, 1988), 1.

2. Alan Goldman, *The Moral Foundations of Professional Ethics* (Totowa, NJ: Rowman & Littlefield, 1980), 18.

3. Abbott, *The System of Professions*, quoting A. P. Carr-Saunders and P. A. Wilson, *The Professions* (Oxford: Oxford University Press, 1933), 4.

4. That military service qualifies as a professional activity is widely accepted. William M. Sullivan implies as much when he says: "The traditional professions of pre-modern Europe—the church, the law, medicine, and state and military service—were highly honorific because of their perceived centrality to the social and moral order of society. At their best, they were callings to serve the common good" ("Calling or Career: The Tensions of Modern Professional Life," in *Professional Ideals*, ed. Albert Flores [Belmont, CA: Wadsworth, 1988], 41). Sullivan also emphasizes the importance of the idea of service to society in the concept of a profession. One reason for examining the concept in some detail in this chapter, despite the largely noncontroversial nature of the claim that the military constitutes a professional group, is that doing so tells us much about the nature of military service.

5. Abbott, *The System of Professions*, 7.

6. See James Burk, "Expertise, Jurisdiction, and the Legitimacy of the Military Profession," in Don M. Snider and Gayle Watkins, *The Future of the Army Profession* (New York: McGraw-Hill, 2002), 19–38, for a succinct discussion of current perspectives.

7. Samuel S. Huntington, *The Soldier and the State* (Cambridge, MA: Belknap Press of Harvard University Press, 1957), 8. In this book, Huntington states that "the modern officer corps is a professional body and the modern military officer a professional man" (p. 7). He refers to this statement as perhaps the "fundamental thesis" of his book.

8. Samuel S. Huntington, "The Soldier and the State in the 1970's," in *The Changing World of the American Military*, ed. Franklin D. Margiotta (Boulder, CO: Westview Press, 1978), 16.

9. Samuel S. Huntington, *The Soldier and the State*, 8.

10. By "norm" I mean a rule or guideline regarding what an individual

ought to do under certain conditions; a norm is "an idea that a given behavior is expected because it is right, proper, moral, wise, efficient, technically correct or otherwise defined as desirable" (Frederick L. Bates and Clyde C. Harvey, *The Structure of Social Systems* [New York: Gardner Press, 1975], p. 77). Norms are passive possessions until the agent encounters conditions in which they apply. The conditions may arise from material events in the agent's environment, from social interactions with other agents, or from internal conative or cognitive activity.

11. Roger H. Nye, *The Challenge of Command* (Wayne, NJ: Avery, 1986), 31.

12. Ibid., 33.

13. Paul L. Miles, as quoted in Nye, *Challenge of Command*, 136.

14. Thomas Pakenham, *The Boer War* (New York: Random House, 1979), xxi–xxii, 521–24. Also see Edgar Holt, *The Boer War* (London: Putnam, 1958), Chapter 21.

15. "The World at War," Center for Defense Information, available at <http://www.cdi.org/issues/World_at_War/wwar00.html>, accessed 7 January 2003. The Center defines a war as an armed conflict in which at least 1,000 soldiers and civilians have been killed.

16. This view is shared by Glossup, *Confronting War: An Examination of Humanity's Most Pressing Problem* (Jefferson, NC: McFarland & Co. 1983), 4.

17. Michael Ignatieff, "The Burden," *New York Times Magazine*, 5 January 2003, 27. Ignatieff presents a discussion that examines the burdens of military power and global responsibility for the United States in the first decade of the new century.

18. Don Snider and Gayle Watkins, *The Future of the Army Profession* (New York: McGraw Hill, 2002), 7.

19. For a brief but clear discussion of this point, see Lewis R. Sorley, "Competence as an Ethical Imperative," *Army* 34 (August 1982): 42–48.

20. For a review of the history of the changes in Army jurisdiction, see Leonard Wong and Douglas V. Johnson II, "Serving the American People: A Historical View of the Army Profession," in Snider and Watkins, *The Future of the Army Profession*, 59–75.

21. Huntington, *The Soldier and the State*, 16.

22. Some analysts identify three military professions: army, maritime, aerospace. For some purposes such a division is useful since the military services do have different cultures, but all three groups have features in common. Those commonalities are the focus in the discussion that follows in this text. See Don Snider and Gayle Watkins, *The Future of the Army Profession*, 7f.

23. Abbott, *The System of Professions*, Chapter 1.

24. James Burk, "Expertise, Jurisdiction, and the Legitimacy of the Military Profession," in Don M. Snider and Gayle Watkins, *The Future of the Army Profession* (New York: McGraw-Hill, 2002), 23.

25. Snider and Watkins, *The Future of the Army Profession*, 6–7. The authors claim that "[a]lthough they appear static, modern professions also have a hidden, dynamic, and occasionally indecorous side. They are continuously engaged in fierce competitions for control over the jurisdictions in which they apply their expertise" (7).

26. Bernard Barber, "Some Problems in the Sociology of Professions," in

Kenneth S. Lynn, ed., *The Professions in America* (Boston: Houghton Mifflin, 1965), 18.

27. The term most clearly applies to career officers in the combat arms and career officers whose functions are unique to military activity.

28. David K. Hart, "Self-Serving Power and Noblesse Oblige: George C. Marshall and J. Edgar Hoover," paper delivered at the Annual Conference, American Society for Public Administration, Portland, Oregon, 19 April 1988.

29. John Adams, "Dissertation on the Canon and the Feudal Law," [1765] in *The Selected Writings of John and John Quincy Adams* (New York: Knopf, 1946), 18. Professor David K. Hart brought this quotation to my attention in his unpublished paper, "Self-Serving Power and Noblesse Oblige: George C. Marshall and J. Edgar Hoover."

30. I am again indebted to David K. Hart, who cites Hanoch Bartow, *Dado: 48 Years and 20 Days,* trans. I. Friedman (Israel: Ma'ariv Book Guild, 1981), p. 34, as the source for this information.

31. Albert Flores, ed. *Professional Ideals* (Belmont, CA: Wadsworth, 1988), 1.

32. This is true even of the lower, perhaps less than fully professional ranks. U.S. Army Training Circular 22-9-1, *Military Professionalism (Platoon and Squad Instruction)* (May 1986, p. 10) notes that members of the military "are unique in that we are expected to follow higher standards of conduct than civilians are expected to follow." Whether this is so or not, the U.S. Army teaches its members that it is the standard, which is my point at the moment.

33. Ernest Greenwood, "Attributes of a Profession," in *Man, Work, and Society,* ed. Sigmund Nosow and William H. Form (New York: Basic Books, 1962), 207.

34. Ibid., 215.

35. Ibid.

36. Allan R. Millett, *Military Professionalism and Officership in America* (Columbus, OH: Mershon Center, 1977), 18. For a succinct summary of the historical development of professional armed forces, see Bengt Abramsson, *Military Professionalism and Political Power* (Beverly Hills, CA: Sage, 1972), 21–23.

37. Ibid., 2.

38. Everett C. Hughes, "Professions," in *The Professions in America,* ed. Kenneth S. Lynn (Boston: Houghton Mifflin, 1965), 10.

39. Abbott, *The System of Professions,* 40.

40. Burk, 21.

41. Burk, 23.

42. Oliver L. North, testimony before the Select Committee of the House and Senate, in *Taking the Stand* (New York: Pocket Books, 1987), 236–45, 251–54, 293–94.

43. Morris Janowitz, *The Professional Soldier: A Social and Political Portrait* (Glencoe, IL: Free Press, 1960), 6.

Chapter Three. The Nature of Professional Ethics

1. Let me make clear that by a code of professional ethics I mean just this: the set of rules and standards that govern the conduct of members of a profes-

sion. A code may be formal, that is, it may be written down, acknowledged, and published. A code may also be informal and unpublished yet recognized and adhered to by members of the profession. Informal codes have the character of customs for the group concerned. Needless to say, deeply entrenched customs often have a much more dominating effect on behavior than would a formally published code. In the discussion following, I will use "professional ethic" to refer to the actual set of rules and standards governing conduct within a profession, whether they have been written down in a formal document or not, and I will use "formal code" or name a particular published document when I refer to a formally propagated written code. The professional military ethic is the implicit or explicit set of rules and standards accepted by military professionals, taught to entering soldiers with varying degrees of complexity based upon rank and experience, and generally held up as the model for professional conduct. The American professional military ethic has not been formally codified, but it plays a dominant role in professional activity.

2. Ernest Greenwood, "Attributes of a Profession," in *Man, Work, and Society,* ed. Sigmund Nosow and William H. Form (New York: Basic Books, 1962), 6.

3. See American Institute of Certified Public Accountants, *Professional Standards,* vol. 2 (Chicago: Commerce Clearing House, 1977) and AICPA, *Rules of Conduct, Bylaws* (New York: AICPA, Inc., 1978).

4. Rena A. Gorlin, *Codes of Professional Ethics* (Washington, DC: BNA Books, 1994), 87–92. See also the discussion of the engineer code in *Ethical Problems in Engineering,* ed. Robert Baum and Albert Flores (Troy, NY: Center for the Study of Human Dimensions of Science and Technology, Rennselaer Polytechnic Institute, 1978).

5. American Medical Association, *Principles of Medical Ethics of the A.M.A.* (Chicago: American Medical Association, 1970).

6. The first two purposes are discussed by Bengt Abrahamsson in *Military Professionalism and Political Power* (Beverly Hills, CA: Sage, 1972), 69.

7. From *The Trial of Queen Caroline,* vol. 2, ed. J. Nightingale (London: Albion Press, 1821), p. 8, as quoted by Charles Fried, *Right and Wrong* (Cambridge, MA: Harvard University Press, 1978).

8. Sam C. Sarkesian, *The Professional Army Officer in a Changing Society* (Chicago: Nelson-Hall, 1975), 240–41.

9. Sam C. Sarkesian, "Empirical Reassessment of Military Professionalism," in *The Changing World of the American Military,* ed. Franklin D. Margiotta (Boulder, CO: Westview Press, 1978), 43.

10. Samuel S. Huntington, *The Soldier and the State* (Cambridge, MA: Belknap Press of Harvard University Press, 1957), 73.

11. See Edward Sherman, "Free Speech and the Military," *Update* 5 (Winter 1981): 25–27, 33–34.

12. U.S. Army War College, *Study on Military Professionalism* (Carlisle Barracks, PA: U.S. Army War College, 1970), 30–31.

13. Huntington, *The Soldier and the State,* 61.

14. Huntington, *The Soldier and the State,* 60.

15. For further discussion of the "military mind," see Maury Feld, "Professionalism, Nationalism and the Alienation of the Military," in *Armed Forces and Society,* ed. Jacques van Doorn (The Hague: Mouton, 1968), 55–70;

Morris Janowitz and Roger W. Littel, *Sociology and the Military Establishment*, revised ed. (New York: Russell Sage Foundation, 1965), 20–27, 31–76; Jacques van Doorn, "Ideology and the Military," in *On Military Ideology*, ed. Morris Janowitz and Jacques van Doorn (Rotterdam, The Netherlands: Rotterdam University Press, 1971), xv–xxix.

16. Abrahamsson, *Military Professionalism*, 64–65.

17. Huntington, *The Soldier and the State*, 65.

18. Ibid., 68.

19. Abrahamsson, *Military Professionalism*, 111.

20. Richard Falk, *Human Rights Horizons: The Pursuit of Justice in a Globalizing World* (New York: Routledge, 2000), 18.

21. Ibid., 76–79 in particular. See also the results of the 1999 survey of the American military by the Center for Strategic and International Studies in *American Military Culture in the Twenty-first Century* (Washington, DC: The CSIS Press, 2000).

22. "Effective" is a relative term, needless to say. Expressions such as this refer to an ideal level of effectiveness. History is replete with examples of armed forces seriously deficient in such characteristics that were nonetheless victorious in a given battle or conflict.

Chapter Four. The American Professional Military Ethic

1. Thomas Hobbes, *Leviathan* (London: Penguin Books, 1985), 186.

2. As quoted by Mark Mattox in "The Ties That Bind: The Army Officer's Obligations" in Snider and Watkins, *The Future of the Army Profession* (New York: McGraw-Hill, 2002), 301.

3. Ibid.

4. The book by Don Snider and Gayle Watkins, *The Future of the Army Profession*, explores in detail the complexity of professional activity in the U.S. Army at the beginning of the twenty-first century.

5. The analysis of the practice of being a commissioned Army leader in terms of these four identities originated at the United States Military Academy in the late 1990s as the staff and faculty developed concepts for the education and development of future officers. The possibility of basing professional socialization on this approach subsequently spread to the Army education system under the title of "officership."

6. Several studies reveal this to be the case. These include the following: U.S. Army War College, *Study on Military Professionalism* (Carlisle Barracks, PA: U.S. Army War College, 1970); John N. Moellering, "Future Civil-Military Relations: The Army Turns Inward?" *Military Review* 53 (July 1973); Bruce M. Russett, "Political Perspectives of U.S. Military and Business Elites," *Armed Forces and Society* 1 (Fall 1974); and Franklin D. Margiotta, "A Military Elite in Transition: Air Force Leaders in the 1970's," *Armed Forces and Society* 2 (Winter 1976).

7. The concept of interpreting the Constitution for application to changing social, political, and economic circumstances is strongly criticized by some legal scholars. Strict constructionists have long argued that an interpretive view of the Constitution is fundamentally in error, that the creation of new standards and new law without a clear textual reference in the Consti-

tution violates the very concept of constitutionality. In their view, the Constitution is a specific, unchanging document that is to be applied as written. Needless to say, if one accepts their view, my contention that there are certain fundamental, unchanging principles reflected in the Constitution gains even more support.

8. Leonard W. Levy, *Judgments: Essays of American Constitutional History* (Chicago: Quadrangle Books, 1972), 71.

9. Jethro K. Lieberman, *Understanding Our Constitution* (New York: Walker, 1967), 14. Fundamentally, I contend that this is true for the principles identified in this discussion. It would be both naive and erroneous, however, to fail to recognize that a broadly stated principle can have radically different characters depending upon application in practice. Thus, "never give up" in some situations may be considered an injunction that appeals to the tenacious, courageous, essentially noble fire of the human spirit. Stalingrad, however, was an inhumane example of the capacity of human nature to produce suffering and barbarism. For a caustic view of the fate of the Bill of Rights in judicial application, see William O. Douglas, "The Bill of Rights Is Not Enough," in *The Great Rights*, ed. Edmund Cahn (New York: Macmillan, 1963). Nonetheless, in considering the ideal standards of the professional military ethic, certain broad moral principles that have not changed do seem to be identifiable in the Constitution.

10. James L. Elston, "The Warren Court and Civil Rights: Era of Positive Constitutionalism and Egalitarianism," *Journal of Thought* 8 (January 1973), 30.

11. Though, admittedly, the extension of the concept of who is included among the equal right-holders has indeed changed. One need only remember that many of the primary authors of the Declaration of Independence were slave owners in order to realize that ethnic discrimination has always belied the rhetoric that proclaimed that all human beings possess natural rights. In this sense, the Civil War era and the middle twentieth century can be seen as dramatic changes in the concept of equality. I would argue, however, that the moral principle of equality itself did not change; rather, the extension of the principle in social application changed. More critically, American society has slowly and unevenly moved toward the full instantiation of such principles in practice in social institutions.

12. For a brief but illuminating discussion of the protection afforded individual rights by the Constitution, see Zechariah Chaffee, Jr., *How Human Rights Got Into the Constitution* (Boston: Boston University Press, 1952).

13. Sotiros A. Barber, *On What the Constitution Means* (Baltimore: Johns Hopkins Press, 1984), 127.

14. Clinton Rossiter, *Seedtime of the Republic* (New York: Harcourt, Brace, 1953), 375.

15. David A. J. Richards, "Reverse Discrimination and Compensatory Justice: Constitutional and Moral Theory," in *The Value of Justice*, ed. Charles A. Kelbley (New York: Fordham University Press, 1979), 104–5. For a scholarly discussion of this issue, see Leonard W. Levy, *Judgments: Essays in American Constitutional History*, particularly "The Fourteenth Amendment and the Bill of Rights" and the essays of Part II and Part III.

16. Arthur E. Sutherland, *Constitutionalism in America* (New York: Blaisdell, 1965), 469.

17. Michael Walzer, *Just and Unjust Wars* (New York: Basic Books, 1977), Chapter 4.

18. Ibid., 89.

19. Ibid., 53.

20. I intend here a broad sense of the "rule of law" concept. The fundamental issue is that all governmental agencies and officials are subordinate to the law, particularly the most powerful, such as the military services and the office of the president. In referring to the power of the Court in this context, I do not mean to invoke the controversial issue of judicial review.

21. Richards, "Reverse Discrimination," 105–6.

22. Ibid., 107.

23. Ibid.

24. Ibid.

25. For a specific declaration of the rights held under the doctrine of natural rights during this period in America, see the Virginia Declaration of Rights, 1776, which can be found, among other places, in F. N. Thorpe, *Federal and State Constitutions, Colonial Charters, and Other Organic Laws*, vol. 7 (Washington, DC: GPO, 1909), 3812–14.

26. U.S. Army War College, *Study on Military Professionalism*, 28–29.

27. For a thorough discussion of such problems, see *American Military Culture in the Twenty-first Century*, published by The Center for Strategic and International Studies (Washington, DC: The CSIS Press, 2000).

28. In the CSIS study, a survey of thousands of service members provided the following results to questions about trust: only 35 percent agreed that "[w]hen my Service's senior leaders say something, you can believe it is true," and only 36 percent agreed that "an atmosphere of trust exists between leaders and their subordinates." For details, see *American Military Culture in the Twenty-first Century*, published by The Center for Strategic and International Studies (Washington, DC: The CSIS Press, 2000), 72.

29. Rear Adm. John T. Natter, Lt. Alan Lopez, and Lt. Doyle K. Hodges, "Listen to the JOs—Why Retention is a Problem." Proceedings (October 1998), as quoted in *American Military Culture in the Twenty-first Century*, The Center for Strategic and International Studies (Washington, DC: The CSIS Press, 2000), 34.

30. Department of Defense, *The Armed Forces Officer*, DoD GEN-36 (Washington, DC: GPO, 1975), 3.

31. Charles R. Kemble, *The Image of the Army Officer in America* (Westport, CT: Greenwood Press, 1973), 24–25.

32. Sir John Winthrop Hackett, *The Professions of Arms* (London: Times Publishing Co., 1962), 38.

33. U.S. Army War College, *Study of Military Professionalism*, iii. The authors of the War College study found it difficult to articulate the implications of this motto. An unusually perceptive examination is presented by James R. Golden, "The Future Demands of Military Professionalism: The Views of an Army Major," in *The Changing World of the American Military*, ed. Franklin D. Margiotta (Boulder, CO: Westview Press, 1978), 395–412.

34. Sam C. Sarkesian, "Empirical Reassessment of Military Professionalism," in *The Changing World of the American Military*, ed. Franklin D. Margiotta (Boulder, CO: Westview Press, 1978), 48.

35. Golden, "Future Demands," 398.

36. Melville A. Drisko, Jr., *An Analysis of Professional Military Ethics: Their Importance, Development, and Inculcation* (Carlisle Barracks, PA: U.S. Army War College, 1977), 4.

37. Golden, "Future Demands," 404–5.

38. Ibid., 409.

39. Lewis S. Sorley, "Competence as Ethical Imperative: Issues of Professionalism," in *Military Ethics and Professionalism: A Collection of Essays,* ed. James Brown and Michael J. Collins (Washington, DC: National Defense University Press, 1981), 42.

40. Morris Janowitz, *The Professional Soldier: A Social and Political Portrait* (Glencoe, IL: Free Press, 1960), 233.

41. See Charles H. Coates and Roland J. Pellegrin, *Military Sociology* (University Park, MD: Social Science Press, 1965); Samuel S. Huntington, *The Soldier and the State* (Cambridge, MA: Belknap Press of Harvard University Press, 1957); Sam C. Sarkesian, *The Military-Industrial Complex: A Reassessment* (Beverly Hills, CA: Sage, 1972); John M. Swomley, Jr., *The Military Establishment* (Boston: Beacon Press, 1964); Adam Yarmolinsky, *The Military Establishment* (New York: Harper & Row, 1971), pp. 8–15, Chapter 5, and especially Chapter 16.

42. Francis B. Catanzaro, *With the 41st Division in the Southwest Pacific: A Foot Soldier's Story* (Bloomington, IN: Indiana University Press, 2002), 93–94.

43. Within the UCMJ, however, there is a well-known provision, Article 133, which provides for punishment of "conduct unbecoming to an officer and a gentleman." While this provision is as vague in statement as any punitive article is likely to be, the courts have long upheld its validity, primarily because they have recognized that there is a distinct, traditional military ethic that is established and accepted for military officers. Thus, while the UCMJ is not part of the professional military ethic, it certainly recognizes the binding quality of the American professional military ethic and the existence of a separate set of standards.

44. The *Joint Ethics Regulation* can be accessed on-line at <http://www.defenselink.mil/dodgc/defense_ethics/ethics_regulation />.

45. *Joint Ethics Regulation* (Washington, DC: Department of Defense, 30 August 1993). Paragraph 1-100.

46. *Joint Ethics Regulation* (Washington, DC: Department of Defense, 30 August 1993). Paragraph 12-300.

47. *Joint Ethics Regulation* (Washington, DC: Department of Defense, 30 August 1993). Paragraph 12-501.

48. Harry Redner, *Ethical Life: The Past and Present of Ethical Cultures* (New York: Rowman & Littlefield, 2001), 10.

49. Note that the Navy indicates links directly to the oath of enlistment.

50. "Navy Core Values," U.S. Navy; available at <http://www.worldsfinestnavy.com/corevalues.html> and at <http://www.chinfo.navy.mil/navpalib/traditions/html/corvalu.html>, accessed 10 January 2003.

51. "U.S. Air Force Core Values," U.S. Air Force, 1 January 1997; available at <http://www.usafa.af.mil/core-value/cv-mastr.html>, accessed 10 January 2003.

Chapter 5. Human Rights and the Just War Tradition

1. Brian Orend, *Human Rights: Concept and Context* (Peterborough, Ontario, Canada: Broadview Press, 2002), 24.

2. Brian Orend, *War and International Justice: A Kantian Perspective* (Waterloo, Ontario, Canada: Wilfrid Laurier University Press, 2000), 91–92.

3. Gary B. Herbert, *A Philosophical History of Rights* (New Brunswick, NJ: Transaction Publishers, 2002), xviii.

4. Michael J. Meyer, *The Constitution of Rights: Human Dignity and American Values*, eds. Michael J. Meyer and William A. Parent (Ithaca, NY: Cornell University Press, 1992), 1–2.

5. Alan Gewirth, "Human Dignity as the Basis of Human Rights," in Michael J. Meyer and William A. Parent, eds., *The Constitution of Rights: Human Dignity and American Values* (Ithaca, NY: Cornell University Press, 1992), 10.

6. Meyer, 4.

7. William A. Parent, "Constitutional Values and Human Dignity," in Michael J. Meyer and William A. Parent, eds., *The Constitution of Rights: Human Dignity and American Values* (Ithaca, NY: Cornell University Press, 1992), 70.

8. Parent, 65.

9. Herbert, xviii.

10. Ibid., 40.

11. *Justinian's Institutes*, trans. Peter Birks and Grant McLeod (Ithaca, NY: Cornell University Press, 1987), I.2.1, as quoted by Herbert, *A Philosophical History of Rights*, 42.

12. See Herbert, Chapter 2, for a full discussion of the struggle between the Pope and the Franciscan order.

13. Herbert, *A Philosophical History of Rights*, 192–93.

14. Ibid., 179.

15. Ibid., 260. Bentham articulated the view of later utilitarians on this point, though John Stuart Mill resuscitated rights for utilitarians to a degree when he argued in *On Liberty* (Chapter 4) that respecting rights can have utilitarian value. Jeremy Bentham, "Anarchical Fallacies," in *The Works of Jeremy Bentham*, ed. John Bowring (Edinburgh: Simpkin, Marshall, & Co., London, 1843), vol. 2, 500, as quoted by Herbert, *A Philosophical History of Rights*, 260. John Stuart Mill. *On Liberty*, ed. Elizabeth Rapaport (Indianapolis, IN: Hackett Publishing Co., 1978).

16. See Herbert, *A Philosophical History of Rights*, Chapter 5, for an extended discussion of Hegel's views.

17. Herbert, 274.

18. Karl Marx, "On the Jewish Question," in *The Marx-Engels Reader*, ed. Robert C. Tucker (New York: W.W. Norton, 1972), 40–41.

19. Thomas W. McShane, "Blame It on the Romans: Pax Americana and the Rule of Law," *Parameters*, vol. xxxii, no. 2 (Summer 2002), 59.

20. Shi Yinhong and Shen Zhixiong, "After Kosovo: Moral and Legal Constraints on Humanitarian Intervention" (Lanham, MD: Lexington Books, 2002), 251.

21. Universal Declaration of Human Rights, available on-line at <http://www.un.org/Overview/rights.html>, accessed 22 March 2003.

22. Mary Robinson, *Oxfam Exchange*, Winter 2003, 7.

23. Brian Orend, *Human Rights*, 28.

24. Yinhong and Zhixiong, 252.

25. Herbert, *A Philosophical History of Rights*, xvii.

26. Michael Ignatieff, *Human Rights as Politics and Idolatry* (Princeton: Princeton University Press, 2001), xi.

27. Ignatieff, xx. Gutman argues that we do not need a single grounding for the fundamental set of human rights. Plural foundations will make human rights more acceptable to people around the globe.

28. Ibid., 11.

29. Ibid., 14.

30. David Luban, "The Legacy of Nuremberg," *Philosophy and Public Policy*, vol. 6, No. 1 (Winter 1986), 9–12.

31. Ibid., 10.

32. Robert O. Keohane, "Political authority after intervention: gradations in sovereignty," in J. L. Holtzgrefe and Robert O. Keohane, eds., *Humanitarian Intervention: Ethical, Legal, and Political Dilemmas* (Cambridge: Cambridge University Press, 2003), 282.

33. Note that among other results, the Peace of Westphalia established the supreme position of secular authority. The Church no longer could proclaim a law superior to that of the sovereign.

34. Michael Walzer, *Just and Unjust Wars* (New York: Basic Books, 1977), 82n.

35. Robert O. Keohane discusses these issues in useful detail in "Political authority after intervention: gradations in sovereignty." This chapter (276–98) and others in J. L. Holtzgrefe and Robert O. Keohane, *Humanitarian Intervention: Ethical, Legal, and Political Dilemmas*, provide many insights concerning the issue of sovereignty in the context of humanitarian intervention.

36. Leon Friedman, ed., *The Law of War: A Documentary History* (New York: Random House, 1972), 3.

37. Sidney Bailey, *Prohibitions and Restraints in War* (Oxford: Oxford University Press, 1972), 4–7.

38. Bailey, 9.

39. For a detailed, careful examination of the concept of pacifism, see Jenny Teichman, *Pacifism and the Just War: A Study in Applied Philosophy* (Oxford: Basil Blackwell, 1986).

40. The history of the development of just war theory is presented clearly in James Turner Johnson, *Just War Tradition and the Restraint of War: A Moral and Historical Inquiry* (Princeton: Princeton University Press, 1981).

41. *The Convention on the Prevention and Punishment of the Crime of Genocide*, adopted by the United Nations in 1948, has been in effect since 1951. One hundred twenty-seven nations have ratified the treaty; the United States did so in 1988. The convention defines genocide as the committing of certain acts with intent to destroy, wholly or in part, a national, ethnic, racial, or religious group and deems it a crime under international law, whether committed in war or peace.

42. Walzer, *Just and Unjust Wars*, 53–54.

43. The estimates of noncombatant deaths in World War II exceed thirty-two million (see "Source List and Detailed Death Tolls for the Twentieth Cen-

tury Hemoclysm" online at <http://users.erols.com/mwhite28/warstat1 .htm>, accessed 26 February 2003.

44. Martin Shaw, "Risk-Transfer, small massacres and the historic legitimacy of war," available at <http://www.theglobalsite.ac.uk/press/205shaw .htm>, accessed 26 February 2003.

45. "Experts differ on America's resolve if war goes badly," *Times Herald-Record*, 10 March 2003, 12.

46. Dennis Cauchon, "Why U.S. casualties were low," *USA Today*, 21 April 2003, 2A.

Chapter Six. The Moral Character of the Laws of War

1. In an opinion that has not been questioned by civilized nations, and has been supported in the actions of the United Nations, the International Military Tribunal at Nuremberg following World War II declared that "the conventions Hague and Geneva were merely declaratory of pre-existing and well-established laws 'recognized by all civilized nations,' and that the laws of war are binding on all, irrespective of whether a particular government has signed a particular convention" (Marjorie M. Whiteman, *Digest of International Law*, Department of State Publication 8367, vol. 11 [Washington, DC: GPO, 1968], 886). The point merits attention since the United Nations Charter restricts armed conflict only between signatory nations.

2. The International Criminal Court (ICC), established in 2002, has jurisdiction over serious crimes, with one notable exception: the United States does not accept the court's authority. The treaty creating the ICC has been ratified by most of the major nations of the world.

3. Under Article VI, Clause 2 of the U.S. Constitution, treaties relating to the laws of war to which the United States is a signatory have a force equal to that of laws passed by Congress. As early as 1900, the U.S. Supreme Court ruled in *The Paquette Habana*, 175 US 677, that international law is in fact the law of the United States.

4. Part V of Department of Defense (DoD) Directive 5100.17, 5 November 1974, the current official document concerning the DoD Law of War Program, 1–8.

5. Carl von Clausewitz, *On War*, ed. Anatol Rapoport (Baltimore, MD: Penguin Books, 1968), 101.

6. Marjorie M. Whiteman, *Digest of International Law*, vol. 10 (Washington, DC: GPO, 1968), 288.

7. U.S. Army, *The Law of Land Warfare*, FM 27-10 (Washington, DC: 1956), 7.

8. A. Pearce Higgins, *The Hague Peace Conferences and Other International Conferences Concerning the Laws and Usages of War: Texts of Conventions with Commentaries* (Cambridge, MA: Cambridge University Press, 1909), 256.

9. Telford Taylor, "Foreword," in *The Law of War: A Documentary History*, ed. Leon Friedman (New York: Random House, 1973), 6.

10. Richard I. Miller, *The Law of War* (Lexington, MA: DC Heath, 1975), 6.

11. Morris Greenspan, *The Modern Law of Land Warfare* (Berkeley: University of California Press, 1959), 11.

12. GWS, Article 149; GWS Sea, Article 50; GPW, Article 129; GC, Article 146.

13. A further form of sanction has been developing since World War II. The European Court of Human Rights, while not specifically concerned with war crimes, is a forum in which abuses of civilized behavior in armed conflict can be identified and dealt with in an international forum. An Inter-American Court of Human Rights, a special organ of the Organization of American States, entered into force in 1978. Such regional courts of an international nature may develop as an effective source of sanctions in addition to the cooperative actions possible through the United Nations. See Carlos Alberto Dunshee de Abranches, "The Inter-American Court of Human Rights" and Thomas Burgenthal, "The American and European Conventions on Human Rights: Similarities and Differences," *American University Law Review* 30 (Fall 1980).

14. Bert A. Röling, "Aspects of Criminal Responsibility for Violations of the Laws of War," in *The New Humanitarian Law of Armed Conflict*, ed. Antonio Cassese (Napoli, Italy: Editoriale Scientifica, s.r.l., 1979), 227n.

15. Sidney Bailey, *Prohibitions and Restraints in War* (Oxford: Oxford University Press, 1972), 62.

16. Greenspan, *The Modern Law of Land Warfare*, 4.

17. As quoted by Bailey, *Prohibitions and Restraints*, 65.

18. As quoted by Greenspan, *The Modern Law of Land Warfare*, 6.

19. Greenspan, *Prohibitions and Restraints*, 7–8.

20. Ibid., as quoted, 8.

21. U.S. Department of the Air Force, *International Law—The Conduct of Armed Conflict and Air Operations,* AF Pamphlet 110-31 (Washington, DC, 19 November 1976), 11-1. Nations have adopted the practice of formally acceding to international treaties with reservations, that is, with stipulations about their understanding of possibly ambiguous wording or with qualifications about their acceptance of specific provisions of treaties otherwise accepted as binding.

22. As of December 1986, of the 171 nations in the international community, 22 had ratified Protocol I and 44 more had acceded to it; 20 states had ratified Protocol II and 40 had acceded to it. Neither the United States nor the USSR have ratified either, though both were signatories. In 1987, President Reagan called on the U.S. Senate to ratify Protocol II.

23. Article 1, Hague Convention III, 1907.

24. The first public announcement of this policy occurred at West Point's graduation exercises, 1 June 2002, when President George W. Bush stated that America must be prepared to launch pre-emptive strikes against terrorist groups and those who might use weapons of mass destruction against the United States. The enormity of the threat to national security presented by weapons of mass destruction, he argued, allows the extension of just war principles to include pre-emptive war when the choice of not taking action places the nation at unacceptable risk.

25. The British, West German, and U.S. military manuals that address the laws of war all declare that nuclear weapons are not prohibited in the existing laws of war. Their use, nonetheless, would be governed by the general laws of war, a fact none dispute. The uses of nuclear weapons planned by the nuclear powers would involve noncombatants in ways that would appear to violate

the laws. While Protocol I to the Geneva Conventions of 12 August 1949 is not moving from the status of "being considered" to that of being ratified by the states of international society, the movement is steady. Including declarations, seventy-three states have formally accepted the Protocol, Part IV of which essentially prohibits all attacks on the civilian population and threats of violence intended to terrorize civilians. So long as the use of nuclear weapons remains indiscriminate, the provisions of Protocol I would appear to prohibit their employment—and perhaps even the threat of their employment. For a detailed discussion, see Tony Carty, "Legality and Nuclear Weapons: Doctrines of Nuclear War Fighting," in *Ethics and Defence*, ed. Howard Davis (Oxford: Basil Blackwell, 1986).

26. Article 22, Hague Regulations, 1907.

27. U.S. Army, FM 27-10, 18.

28. In any consistent application of the laws of war, the use of nuclear weapons would appear to be a violation, though I will not argue the point here.

29. Relatively few nations have as yet ratified the Protocols. As I noted in the text, the United States, though a signatory to the Protocols in 1977, has not yet formally ratified the documents and filed the ratification in Geneva.

30. Friedman, *The Law of War*, vol. I, 161.

31. Immanuel Kant, "Perpetual Peace," in *Kant's Political Writings*, ed. Hans Reiss, trans. H.B. Nisbet (Cambridge: Cambridge University Press, 1977), 32.

32. U.S. Army, FM 27-10, 22.

33. Ibid., 23.

34. Ibid., 22.

35. Ibid.

36. Friedman, *The Law of War*, vol. 1, 595.

37. U.S. Army, FM 27-10, 178.

38. Ibid., 180.

39. So called in recognition of the Russian jurist F. F. Martens, President of the 1899 Hague Conventions.

40. Friedman, *The Law of War*, vol. 1, 309.

41. U.S. Air Force, AFP 110-31, 1–6.

42. Ibid., 1–6.

43. Ibid., 11–4.

44. Greenspan, *The Modern Law of Land Warfare*, 22.

45. This point is presented forcefully in the Preamble to Hague Convention No. IV (1907).

46. U.S. Army, FM 27-10, para. 85, p. 35.

47. U.S. Air Force, AFP 110-31, para. 13-2, p. 13-1.

48. Military necessity is not a fourth type of necessity to be added to Leibniz's three categories: logical, physical, and moral. If the action required by military necessity is not accomplished, no logical, physical, or moral law is violated. In any technical sense, the term "military necessity" is a misnomer, for it concerns neither a necessary proposition nor a state of affairs that cannot be other than it is. The notion implicit in this term is that of a necessary condition.

One can identify two broad contexts in which the term "necessity" is used in connection with warfare: that of military necessity and that of the necessity of self-preservation. The sense of necessity is not the same in both. Military necessity connotes indispensability. If, in the conditional proposition, "If A, then B," A is defined as a state of affairs in which the war is won, the objective is achieved, or the enemy is defeated, then B is an act or state of affairs that constitutes a necessary condition for the realization of A. Needless to say, that B is a necessary condition is, in practice, a matter of more or less reliable judgment. At best, that B is a necessary condition is a conclusion based on a process of induction involving a very narrow and incomplete database.

The sense of necessity in the necessity of state self-preservation also carries the idea of conditionality, but it adds a very important notion that changes the sense of the term: the notion of inevitability. When necessity is used in this context, if the action required is not taken, a law is claimed to have been violated. The laws involved in such cases are moral laws or rules. Just as individuals are sometimes held to have not only a right but also an obligation to preserve themselves (consider John Locke, *Two Treatises of Government*, Book II, Chapter I), states as corporate entities are held to have an absolute moral obligation to act in self-preservation, or to be so constituted that they can act in no other way when their existence is threatened. When necessity is used in this sense, the clear implication is that no other action is possible, from either a moral or literal point of view—hence the notion of inevitability. This sense is quite different from the hypothetical sense that is appropriate with respect to the term "military necessity." The indiscriminate use of the term "necessity" sometimes confuses discussions of the laws of war.

49. HP2, applied directly to actions, functions just as the Happiness Principle (or Pleasure Principle) functions in "act utilitarian" theory. Minimizing suffering is merely the converse of maximizing happiness, so that if HP2 were the sole basis for deciding what to do in situations involving moral choice in warfare, we would be concerned with a particular application of utilitarianism. However, our discussion has shown this not to be the case. Further, if HP2 were the principle from which all the laws of war were derived, we would be concerned with a form of "rule utilitarianism," with the laws of war being the rules that, all things being considered, best served HP2. (Such a situation would be the ideal, that is, though it certainly has not been achieved in practice.) This is not the case, for HP1 appears to have priority over HP2 when the two principles conflict. While we have not examined all such cases (nor would that be possible), the representative cases presented make this a reasonable conclusion. The point argued here is that analysis of the current laws of war reveals that HP1 has priority over HP2 in the formulation of such laws.

50. Richard B. Brandt, "Utilitarianism and the Rules of War," *Philosophy and Public Affairs* 1 (Winter 1972): 145–65.

51. Adopting a rule to be followed without exception could be the result of rule utilitarian reasoning, which is probably the position Brandt would take concerning HP1.

52. U.S. Air Force, AFP 110-31, 1–10.

53. Dietrich Schindler, ed., *The Laws of Armed Conflict* (Geneva: Henry Dunant Institute, 1973), 133.

54. U.S. Army, FM 27-10, 20.

55. Ibid., 19.

56. Schindler, *The Laws of Armed Conflict*, 142.
57. Ibid., 142.
58. Article 26, Hague Regulations, 1907.
59. U.S. Army, FM 27-10, 20.
60. Under Protocol I of the Protocols to the Geneva Conventions of 1949, the bombing mission would appear even more clearly illegal. Article 51(4) prohibits "indiscriminate attacks," defined as those employing a method that cannot be directed at a specific military objective. The B-52 strike appears, in these circumstances, to be such an attack. Article 51(5) goes further, declaring an "indiscriminate attack" to be one that treats as a single military objective a number of clearly separate and distinct military objectives located in the same area.

Chapter Seven. The Values of American Society

1. Barbara Crossette, "Culture, Gender, and Human Rights," in Michael J. Meyer and William A. Parent, eds., *The Constitution of Rights: Human Dignity and American Values* (Ithaca, NY: Cornell University Press, 1992), 178.
2. William C. Mitchell, *The American Polity* (New York: Free Press of Glencoe, 1962), 105.
3. David Hume, *Essays Moral, Political, and Literary*, ed. T. H. Green and T. H. Grose, vol. 1 (London: Longmans, 1882), 248.
4. Mitchell, *The American Polity*, 376.
5. Robin M. Williams, Jr., "Values and Modern Education in the United States," in *Values in America*, ed. Donald Barrett (Notre Dame, IN: University of Notre Dame Press, 1961), 63.
6. Seymour M. Lipset, *The First New Nation* (New York: Basic Books, 1963), 123.
7. Ronald Ingelhart, "Culture and Democracy," in Michael J. Meyer and William A. Parent, eds., *The Constitution of Rights: Human Dignity and American Values* (Ithaca, NY: Cornell University Press, 1992), 80.
8. Robin M. Williams, Jr., for example, in *American Society: A Sociological Perspective* (New York: Alfred A. Knopf, 1958), says that values are "modes of organizing conduct—meaningful, affectively invested pattern principles that guide human action" (375).
9. Gerald E. Critoph, "The Contending Americas," in *Values in America*, 18.
10. Ralph Barton Perry, *Realms of Value* (New York: Greenwood Press, 1968 reprint), 273.
11. Ibid., 285.
12. Ibid., 286.
13. Williams, *American Society*, 436–37.
14. Ibid., 419.
15. The specific references I have in mind are the Reconstruction Amendments (13–15) and the 25th Amendment granting women the right to vote.
16. Lipset, *The First New Nation*, 101.
17. Perry, *Realms of Value*, 286.
18. Williams, *American Society*, 415.
19. John Locke, *Two Treatises of Government*, ed. Peter Laslett (New York:

New American Library, 1960), pp. 374–75. For an extended discussion of the pervasive influence of individualism, see Elizabeth Wolgast, *The Grammar of Justice* (Ithaca, NY: Cornell University Press, 1987), Chapter 1.

20. Williams, *American Society*, 433.

21. Perry, *Realms of Value*, 273.

22. Eugene Kamka, ed., *Nationalism* (Canberra: Australian National University Press, 1973), 15.

23. Williams, *American Society*, 429.

24. This particular trait has been commented on extensively by many people, to include De Tocqueville, James Bryce, Harold Laski, Gunnar Myrdal, and Margaret Mead.

25. Williams, *American Society*, 399f.

26. See Milton Rokeach, Part 2, "Values in American Society," in *The Nature of Human Values* (New York: Free Press, 1973) and Norman Feather, *Values in Education and Society* (New York: Free Press, 1975).

27. U.S. Air Force, AFP 110-31, 11-4.

Chapter Eight: Justifying Military Decisions

1. Maxwell D. Taylor, "A Do-It-Yourself Professional Code for the Military," *Parameters* 10 (Dec 1980): 11.

2. Ibid., 11.

3. Ibid., 13.

4. Ibid., 14.

5. Alan Goldman, *The Moral Foundations of Professional Ethics* (Totowa, NJ: Rowman & Littlefield, 1980), 24.

6. See D. Clayton James, *The Years of MacArthur* (Boston: Houghton Mifflin, 1970); William Manchester, *American Caesar* (Boston: Little, Brown, 1978); or Trumbull Higgins, *Korea and the Fall of MacArthur* (New York: Oxford University Press, 1960).

7. Marjorie M. Whiteman, *Digest of International Law*, vol. 10, Department of State Publication 8367 (Washington, DC: GPO, 1968), 308.

8. Goldman, *The Moral Foundations*, 49.

9. Ibid., 57.

10. Ibid.

11. Civilians, as noncombatants who possess certain rights *because* they are noncombatants, may not participate in combat operations during wartime unless they are directly defending their homes and their state against invasion. If they take up arms "spontaneously" for that purpose, they are entitled to POW status if captured and cannot be tried for crimes against the invading force, as a civilian could otherwise be tried if he bore arms and used them against a military force without being a member of an organized military unit.

12. Goldman, *The Moral Foundations*, 90.

13. Ibid., 117.

14. Ibid., 112–37.

15. Ibid., 120.

16. Ibid., 122.

17. The literal translation is as follows: "Reasons of war go before the manners of war." The doctrine maintains that the needs of war take precedence over the laws and customs of warfare.

18. See the discussion of this point in James L. Narel, "Values and the Professional Soldier," *Parameters* 11 (December 1981): 76.

19. I contend that this is so, and that any comprehensive examination of the American professional military ethic reveals that it is so, despite the functional explanation provided in the primary Army document concerning the subject, FM 100-1, *The Army* (August 1986). The discussion there captures just one aspect of the duty principle under the professional military ethic, which is that of accomplishing assignments as effectively as possible. In doing so, the passage is somewhat misleading.

Duty is obedience and disciplined performance, despite difficulty or danger. It is doing what should be done when it should be done. Duty is a personal act of responsibility manifested by accomplishing all assigned tasks to the fullest of one's capability, meeting all commitments, and exploiting opportunities to improve oneself for the good of the group. Duty requires each of us to accept responsibility not only for our own actions, but also for the actions of those entrusted to our care. (p. 22)

20. Military necessity refers to the rationale justifying actions that must be taken if military objectives are to be achieved with minimum loss of time, life, and resources. Proportionality refers to the moral limitation on action that requires that the injury and cost incurred by the means employed to achieve an objective be proportional to the importance of that objective.

21. Even strong defenders of rights sometimes compromise in this regard. For a case in point, see Michael Walzer, *Just and Unjust Wars* (New York: Basic Books, 1977). Walzer argues throughout most of his book for adherence to guidance for conduct based on the claim that "life and liberty are something like absolute values" (xvi). But when national survival is at stake he accepts the concept of "supreme emergency," under which agents of the state may justifiably do whatever is necessary to avoid defeat (see Chapter 16).

22. William Frankena, *Ethics* (Englewood Cliffs, NJ: Prentice-Hall, 1963), 98.

23. This argument does not deny that in some situations, certain rights *override* others. In our society, the principle of taxation, the exercise of eminent domain, and the policy of military conscription are but a few of many examples. But numbers alone are not the explanation for such cases.

24. "The Ethical Code of the IDF," Jewish Army, available at <http://www .ahavat-israel.com/ahavat/eretz/army.asp.>, accessed 14 January 2003.

25. "Doctrine," Israeli Defense Force, available at <http://www.idf.il/ english/doctrine/doctrine.stm>, accessed 14 January 2003.

26. Under the American value system, fundamental rights can be justly overridden only on the basis of a principle such as that of greatest equal liberty. The principle of greatest equal liberty, long a staple of the classic liberal positions and now the libertarian view, states that all persons have a right to the greatest liberty in their actions consistent with equal liberty for all others.

27. Most of these considerations come from Jean Maria Arrigo, "A Consequentialist Argument against Torture Interrogation of Terrorists," a paper

presented at the Joint Services Conference on Professional Ethics in Spring-field, VA, on 31 January 2003. Available on-line at <http://www.usafa.af.mil/jscope>.

Chapter Nine. Making Choices: Case Studies

1. As noted in Chapter 8, see the United Nations Convention Against Torture and Other Cruel, Inhuman, or Degrading Treatment or Punishment, which entered into force in 1987. Available on-line at <http://193.194.138.190/html/menu3/b/h_cat39.htm>.
2. Colonel Anthony Harriman provided the idea for this scenario, which is similar to an incident Colonel Harriman's forces faced in Bosnia.
3. ROE gained prominence in the Vietnam War and have been employed in every conflict and peacekeeping operation since. ROE establish the conditions under which the use of military force is permissible. The usual purpose is to limit risk to noncombatants.
4. The use of nonlethal chemical weapons remains controversial. Some claim that the 1925 Geneva Protocol forbids any such weapons. The Protocol prohibits "asphyxiating, poisonous, or other gasses and . . . biological warfare." The Chemical Weapons Convention of 1983 is also open to interpretation. I place "nonlethal" in quotation marks because it has become that standard category label even though all recognize that in some circumstances any chemical incapacitating agent can be lethal. The category "nonlethal" refers to weapons designed to minimize the likelihood of death.
5. Michael Walzer, *Just and Unjust Wars: A Moral Argument with Historical Illustrations* (New York: Basic Books, 1977), 155.
6. This case is largely the product of Joseph Cox, who produced it for academic purposes at the United States Military Academy.
7. Geneva Convention Relative to the Protection of Civilian Persons in Time of War, Article 147.
8. Harry G. Summers, Jr., "Palmer, Karnow, and Herrington: A Review of Recent Vietnam War Histories," *Parameters* 15 (Spring 1985): 81.
9. *Crusade in Europe,* Vol. II, "The Sands Shift in North Africa," produced by Richard De Rochemont (New Line Home Video, 1993).
10. Colonel Anthony Harriman provided the idea for this scenario, which he encountered during military training in Germany.
11. Earl Warren, "The Bill of Rights and the Military," in *The Great Rights,* ed. Edmund Cahn (New York: Macmillan, 1963), 95.
12. Department of the Army, *The Law of Land Warfare* (Washington, DC: U.S. Government Printing Office, 1956), 4.
13. "The Ethical Code of the IDF," Jewish Army, available at <http://www.ahavat-israel.com/ahavat/eretz/army.asp>, accessed 14 January 2003.

Chapter Ten. Epilogue

1. Elizabeth Anscombe, "War and Murder," in *War, Morality, and the Military Profession,* 2d ed., ed. Malham Wakin (Boulder, CO: Westview Press, 1986), 288.

2. Richard A. Gabriel and Paul L. Savage, *Crisis in Command: Management in the Army* (New York: Hill and Wang, 1978), 104.

3. Gregg Easterbrook, "American Power Moves Beyond the Mere Super," *New York Times*, 27 April 2003, section 4, 1.

4. Nicholas Fotion and Gerard Elfstrom, *Military Ethics* (London: Routledge & Kegan Paul, 1986), Chapter 3, suggest that the military needs several different formal, short, easily comprehended sets of rules for its members that would apply in appropriate contexts.

Bibliography

Abbott, Andrew. *The System of Professions: As Essay on the Division of Expert Labor.* Chicago: University of Chicago Press, 1988.

American Bar Association. *Code of Professional Responsibility.* Chicago: American Bar Association, 1969.

American Medical Association. *Principles of Medical Ethics of the A.M.A.* Chicago: American Medical Association, 1970.

Bailey, Sidney. *Prohibitions and Restraints in War.* Oxford: Oxford University Press, 1972.

Barber, Bernard. "Some Problems in the Sociology of the Professions." In *The Professions in America,* ed. Kenneth S. Lynn. Boston: Houghton Mifflin, 1965.

Barrett, Donald, ed. *Values in America.* Notre Dame, IN: University of Notre Dame Press, 1961.

Bentham, Jeremy. "Anarchical Fallacies." In *The Works of Jeremy Bentham,* ed. John Bowring. Edinburgh: Simpkin, Marshall, & Co., London, 1843, vol. 2, 500.

——. "An Introduction to the Principles of Morals and Legislation." In *British Moralists, 1650–1800,* ed. D. D. Raphael. Oxford: Clarendon Press, 1969.

Bledstein, Burton J. *The Culture of Professionalism.* New York: W. W. Norton, 1976.

Bradley, Omar N. *A Soldier's Story.* New York: Henry Holt, 1951.

Brandt, Richard B. "Utilitarianism and the Rules of War." *Philosophy and Public Affairs* 1 (Winter 1972): 145–65.

Braun, William N. *An Ethical Army Leadership—Real or Wanting?* Individual Study Project. Carlisle Barracks, PA: U.S. Army War College, 1988.

Brierly, J. L. *The Law of Nations,* 6th ed. New York: Oxford University Press, 1963.

Brown, James, and Michael J. Collins, eds. *Military Ethics and Professionalism: A Collection of Essays.* Washington, DC: National Defense University Press, 1981.

Cassese, Antonio, ed. *The New Humanitarian Law of Armed Conflict.* Napoli, Italy: Editoriale Scientifica, s.r.l., 1979.

Catanzaro, Francis B. *With the 41st Division in the Southwest Pacific: A Foot Soldier's Story.* Bloomington, IN: Indiana University Press, 2002.

Cauchon, Dennis. "Why U.S. Casualties Were Low." *USA Today,* 21 April 2003, 1A.

The Center for Strategic and International Studies. *American Military Culture in the Twenty-first Century.* Washington, DC: The CSIS Press, 2000.

Clausewitz, Carl von. *On War.* Ed. Anatol Rapoport. Baltimore: Penguin Books, 1968.

Coates, Charles H., and Roland J. Pellegrin. *Military Sociology.* University Park, MD: Social Science Press, 1965.

Coppieters, Bruno, and Nicholas Fotion, eds. *Moral Constraints on War: Principles and Cases.* Lanham, MD: Lexington Books, 2002.

Cramer, Walter E. *The Year of Values.* Individual Study Project. Carlisle Barracks, PA: U.S. Army War College, 1986.

Crocker, Lawrence. *The Army Officer's Guide.* Harrisburg, PA: Stackpole Books, 1979.

Crusade in Europe. Produced by Richard De Rochemont. New Line Home Video, 1993.

Department of Defense. *The Armed Forces Officer,* DoD GEN-36. Washington, DC: Government Printing Office, 1975.

Department of Defense. *Standards of Conduct,* DoD Directive 5500.7. Washington, DC: Government Printing Office, 1987.

Downey, Robert S. *Roles and Values.* London: Methuen, 1971.

Downey, William G., Jr. "The Law of War and Military Necessity." *American Journal of International Law* 47 (1953): 251–62.

Drisko, Melville, Jr. *An Analysis of Professional Military Ethics: Their Importance, Development, and Inculcation.* Carlisle Barracks, PA: U.S. Army War College, 1977.

Dunbar, N. C. H. "Military Necessity in War Crimes Trials." *British Textbook of International Law* 29 (1952).

——. "The Significance of Military Necessity in the Law of War." *Judicial Review* 67 (1955): 201–12.

Dworkin, Ronald. *Taking Rights Seriously.* Cambridge, MA: Harvard University Press, 1977.

Dyck, Arthur J. "Ethical Bases of the Military Profession." *Parameters* 10 (March 1980): 39–46.

Elston, James L. "The Warren Court and Civil Rights: Era of Positive Constitutionalism and Egalitarianism." *Journal of Thought,* 8 (Summer 1977): 19–39.

Falk, Richard A. *Law, Morality, and War in the Contemporary World.* New York: Frederick A. Praeger, 1963.

——. "The Shimoda Case: A Legal Appraisal of the Atomic Attacks on Hiroshima and Nagasaki." In *International Law in the Twentieth Century,* ed. Leo Gross. New York: Appleton-Century-Crofts, 1969.

——. *Human Rights Horizons.* New York: Routledge, 2000.

Feather, Norman. *Values in Education and Society.* New York: Free Press, 1975.

Feld, Maury. "Professionalism, Nationalism, and the Alienation of the Military." In *Armed Forces and Society,* ed. Jacques van Doorn. The Hague: Mouton, 1968.

——. *The Structure of Violence: Armed Forces as Social Systems.* Beverly Hills, CA: Sage, 1977.

Flores, Albert, ed. *Professional Ideals.* Belmont, CA: Wadsworth, 1988.

Fotion, Nicholas, and Gerard Elfstrom. *Military Ethics: Guidlelines for Peace and War*. Boston: Routledge & Kegan Paul, 1986.

Frankena, William. *Ethics*. Englewood Cliffs, NJ: Prentice Hall, 1963.

Fried, Charles. *Right and Wrong*. Cambridge, MA: Harvard University Press, 1978.

Friedman, Leon, ed. *The Law of War: A Documentary History*. New York: Random House, 1972.

Gabriel, Richard A. *To Serve with Honor*. Westport, CT: Greenwood Press, 1982.

Gerke, Teitler. *The Genesis of the Professional Officer's Corps*. Beverly Hills, CA: Sage, 1977.

Goldman, Alan. *The Moral Foundations of Professional Ethics*. Totowa, NJ: Rowman and Littlefield, 1980.

Gorlin, Rena A. *Codes of Professional Responsibility*. Washington, DC: BNA Books, 1994.

Greenspan, Morris. *The Modern Law of Land Warfare*. Berkeley: University of California Press, 1959.

Greenwood, Ernest. "Attributes of a Profession." In *Man, Work, and Society*, ed. Sigmund Nosow and William H. Form. New York: Basic Books, 1962.

Hackett, Sir John Winthrop. *The Profession of Arms*. London: Times Publishing, 1962.

Handy, Rollo. *Value Theory and the Behavioral Sciences*. Springfield, IL: Charles C. Thomas, 1969.

Harris, C. E. *Applying Moral Theories*. Belmont, CA: Wadsworth, 1986.

Hartjen, Raymond C., Jr. *Ethics in Organizational Leadership*. Individual Study Project. Carlisle Barracks, PA: U.S. Army War College, 1984.

Hartle, Anthony E. "A Military Ethic in an Age of Terror." *Parameters* 17 (Summer 1987): 68–76.

———. "Humanitarianism and the Laws of War." *Philosophy* 235 (1986): 109–16.

Herbert, Gary B. *A Philosophical History of Rights*. New Brunswick, NJ: Transaction Publishers, 2002.

Higgins, A. Pearce. *The Hague Peace Conferences and Other International Conferences Concerning the Laws and Usages of War: Texts of Conventions with Commentaries*. Cambridge: Cambridge University Press, 1909.

Holzgrefe, J. L., and Robert O. Keohane, eds. *Humanitarian Intervention: Ethical, Legal, and Political Dilemmas*. Cambridge: Cambridge University Press, 2003.

Hughes, Everett C. "Professions." In *The Professions in America*, ed. Kenneth S. Lynn. Boston: Houghton Mifflin, 1965.

Hume, David. *Essays Moral, Political, and Literary*. T. H. Green and T. H. Grose, eds. London: Longmans, 1882.

Huntington, Samuel. *The Soldier and the State*. Cambridge, MA: Belknap Press of Harvard University Press, 1957.

Ignatieff, Michael. "The Burden." *The New York Times Magazine*, 5 January 2003, 22–27, 50–54.

———. *Human Rights as Politics and Idolatry*. Princeton: Princeton University Press, 2001.

Inlow, Gail M. *Values in Transition: A Handbook*. New York: John Wiley & Sons, 1972.

Janowitz, Morris. *The Professional Soldier: A Social and Political Portrait.* Glencoe, IL: Free Press, 1960.

Janowitz, Morris, and Jacques van Doorn, eds. *On Military Ideology.* Rotterdam, The Netherlands: Rotterdam University Press, 1971.

Janowitz, Morris, and Roger W. Littel. *Sociology and the Military Establishment.* Rev. ed. New York: Russell Sage Foundation, 1965.

Johnson, James T. *Can Modern War Be Just?* New Haven, CT: Yale University Press, 1984.

Johnson, James Turner. *Just War Tradition and the Restraint of War: A Moral and Historical Inquiry.* Princeton: Princeton University Press, 1981.

Kalish, Richard A., and Kenneth W. Collier. *Exploring Human Values: Psychological and Philosophical Considerations.* Monterey, CA: Brooks/ Cole, 1981.

Kalshoven, Frits. *The Law of Warfare.* Geneva: Henry Dunant Institute, 1973.

Kamka, Eugene. *Nationalism.* Canberra: Australian National University Press, 1973.

Kant, Immanuel. In *Kant's Political Writings.* Trans. H. B. Nisbet and ed. Hans Reiss. Cambridge: Cambridge University Press, 1977.

Kelley, Hugh A. *A Proposal for the United States Army Ethic.* Unpublished individual study project. Carlisle Barracks, PA: 1984.

Kemble, Charles K. *The Image of the Army Officer in America.* Westport, CT: Greenwood Press, 1973.

Kriete, Charles F. "Ethical Presuppositions of the Army's Professional Slogans." *Parameters* 10 (September 1980): 86–89.

Levy, Leonard W. *Judgments: Essays on American Constitutional History.* Chicago: Quadrangle Books, 1972.

Lieberman, Jethro K. *Understanding Our Constitution.* New York: Walker, 1967.

Lillich, Richard B., and John N. Moore. *International Law Studies.* Newport, RI: Naval War College Press, 1980.

Lipset, Seymour. *The First New Nation.* New York: Basic Books, 1963.

Littel, Roger W. *Sociology and the Military Establishment.* New York: Russell Sage Foundation, 1965.

Locke, John. *Two Treatises of Government.* Ed. Peter Laslett. New York: New American Library, 1960.

Luban, David. "The Legacy of Nuremberg." *Philosophy and Public Policy* 6 (Winter 1986): 9–12.

Lynn, Kenneth S. *The Professions in America.* Boston: New American Library, 1965.

Margiotta, Franklin D., ed. *The Changing World of the American Military.* Boulder, CO: Westview Press, 1978.

Marqua, Francis C. *A Code of Ethics for Air Force Officers. Individual Study Project.* Maxwell Air Force Base: U.S. Air Command and Staff College, 1974.

Marx, Karl. "On the Jewish Question." In *The Marx-Engels Reader,* ed. Robert C. Tucker. New York: W.W. Norton, 1972.

Mavrodes, George I. "Conventions and the Morality of War." *Philosophy and Public Affairs* 4 (Winter 1980).

McDonough, James R. *Platoon Leader.* New York: Bantam Books, 1985.

McIntyre, J. W., ed. *The Writings and Speeches of Daniel Webster*. Boston: Little, Brown, and Company, 1903.

McShane, Thomas W. "Blame It on the Romans: Pax Americana and the Rule of Law." *Parameters* xxxi (Summer 2002): 57–72.

Meyer, Michael J., and William A. Parent, eds. *The Constitution of Rights: Human Dignity and American Values*. Ithaca, NY: Cornell University Press, 1992.

Military Ethics. Washington, DC: National Defense University Press, 1987.

Mill, John Stuart. *On Liberty*. Ed. Elizabeth Rapaport. Indianapolis, IN: Hackett Publishing Co., 1978.

Miller, Richard I. *The Law of War*. Lexington, MA: DC Heath, 1975.

Millett, Allan R. *Military Professionalism and Officership in America*. Columbus, OH: Mershon Center, 1977.

Mitchell, William C. *The American Polity*. New York: Free Press of Glencoe, 1962.

Moore, Wilbert E. *The Professions: Roles and Rules*. New York: Russell Foundation, 1976.

Murray, Richard N. *Ethics and the Army Officer: An Assessment and Recommendations for the Future*. Individual Study Project. Carlisle Barracks, PA: U.S. Army War College, 1984.

Narel, James. "Values and the Professional Soldier." *Parameters* 11 (December 1981): 74–79.

North, Oliver L. *Taking the Stand: The Testimony of Lieutenant Colonel Oliver L. North*. Ed. Daniel Schorr. New York: Pocket Books, 1987.

Nussbaum, Arthur. *A Concise History of the Law of Nations*. New York: Macmillan, 1954.

Orend, Brian. *Human Rights: Concept and Context*. Peterborough, Ontario, Canada: Broadview Press, 2002.

Osgood, Robert E., and Robert W. Tucker. *Force, Order, and Justice*. Baltimore, MD: Johns Hopkins Press, 1967.

Perry, Ralph Barton. *Realms of Value*. New York: Greenwood Press, 1968.

Pictet, Jean. *The Principles of International Humanitarian Law*. Geneva: International Committee of the Red Cross, 1966.

Pojman, Louis. *Global Political Philosophy*. New York: McGraw-Hill, 2003.

Potts, Robert E. *Professional Military Ethics: Are We on the Right Track?* Individual Study Project. Carlisle Barracks, PA: U.S. Army War College, 1986.

Rawls, John. *A Theory of Justice*. Cambridge, MA: Belknap Press of Harvard University Press, 1971.

Redner, Harry. *Ethical Life: The Past and Present of Ethical Cultures*. New York: Rowman & Littlefield, 2001.

Reese, Thomas H. "An Officer's Oath." *Military Law Review* 25 (July 1964): 1–41.

Richards, David A. J. "Reverse Discrimination and Compensatory Justice: Constitutional and Moral Theory." In *The Value of Justice*, ed. Charles A. Kelbley. New York: Fordham University Press, 1979.

Rokeach, Milton. *The Nature of Human Values*. New York: Free Press, 1973.

Rossiter, Clinton. *Seedtime of the Republic*. New York: Harcourt, Brace, 1953.

Sarkesian, Sam C. *The Professional Army Officer in a Changing Society*. Chicago: Nelson-Hall, 1975.

Schindler, Dietrich, ed. *The Laws of Armed Conflict*. Geneva: Henry Dunant Institute, 1973.

Schwander, Jeffrey L. *A Functional Army Officer Code of Ethics*. Individual Study Project. Carlisle Barracks, PA: U.S. Army War College, 1988.

Shaw, Martin. "Risk-transfer Militarism, Small Massacres and the Historic Legitimacy of War." *International Relations*, 16 (December 2002): 343–60.

Sherman, Edward. "Free Speech and the Military." *Update* 5 (Winter 1981): 25–27, 33–34.

Snider, Don, and Gayle Watkins. *The Future of the Army Profession*. Ed. Lloyd Matthews. New York: McGraw Hill, 2002.

Sorley, Lewis R. "Competence as an Ethical Imperative." *Army* 34 (August 1982): 42–48.

Stockholm International Peace Research Institute. *The Law of War and Dubious Weapons*. Stockholm: Almqvist and Wiksell, 1976.

Sutherland, Arthur E. *Constitutionalism in America*. New York: Blaisdell, 1965.

Taylor, Maxwell D. "A Do-It-Yourself Professional Code for the Military." *Parameters* 10 (December 1980): 10–15.

——. "A Professional Ethic for the Military?" *Army* 28 (May 1978): 18–21.

Taylor, Robert L., and William F. Rosenbach. *Military Leadership: In Pursuit of Excellence*. Boulder, CO: Westview, 1984.

Taylor, Telford. *Nuremberg and Vietman: An American Tragedy*. Chicago: Quadrangle Books, 1970.

Teichman, Jenny. *Pacifism and the Just War: A Study in Applied Philosophy*. Oxford: Basil Blackwell, 1986.

Tucker, Robert W. *The Just War*. Baltimore, MD: Johns Hopkins Press, 1960.

Ulmer, Walter F., Jr. "The Army's New Senior Leadership Doctrine." *Parameters* 17 (December 1987): 10–17.

U.S. Air Force. *Commander's Handbook on the Law of War*. AF Pamphlet 110-34. Washington, DC, 1980.

U.S. Air Force. *International Law—The Conduct of Armed Conflict and Air Operations*, AF Pamphlet 110-31. Washington, DC: 1976.

U.S. Air Force. "U.S. Air Force Core Values." 1 January 1997. Available online at <http://www.usafa.af.mil/core-value/cv-mastr.html>. Accessed 10 January 2003.

U.S. Army. *The Army*, FM 100-1. Washington, DC: 1986.

——. *Fundamentals of Military Law*, ROTC Manual 145-85. Washington, DC: 1980.

——. *The Law of Land Warfare*, FM 27-10. Washington, DC: 1956.

——. *Leadership and Command at Senior Levels*, FM 22-103. Washington, DC: 1987.

——. *Military Leadership*, FM 22-100. Washington, DC: 1983.

——. *Military Professionalism, Battalion Instruction*, TC 22-9-3. Washington, DC: 1987.

——. *Military Professionalism, Company\Battery Instruction*, TC 22-9-2. Washington, DC: 1986.

——. *Military Professionalism, Platoon\Squad Instruction*, TC 22-9-1. Washington, DC: 1986.

——. *Protocols to the Geneva Conventions of 12 August 1949*, DA Pamphlet 22-1-1. Washington, DC: 1979.

——. *Selected Problems in the Law of War*, TC 27-10-1. Washington, DC: 1979.

U.S. Army War College. *Study on Military Professionalism*. Carlisle Barracks, PA: U.S. Army War College, 1970.

U.S. Navy. *Integrity and Efficiency Training Program*, SECNAV 5370. Washington, DC: 1985.

——. *The Law of Naval Warfare*, NWIP 10-2. Washington, DC: 1974.

——. "Navy Core Values." Available online at <http://www.worldsfinest navy.com/corevalues.html> and at <http://www.chinfo.navy.mil/navpa lib/traditions/html/corvalu.html. Accessed 10 January 2003.

——. *Standards of Conduct and Government Ethics*, SECNAV 5370.2H. Washington, DC: 1984.

Vollmer, Howard M., and Donald L. Mills, eds. *Professionalization*. Englewood Cliffs, NJ: Prentice Hall, 1966.

Wakin, Malham M., ed. *War, Morality, and the Military Profession*. 2d ed. Boulder, CO: Westview Press, 1986.

Walzer, Michael. *Just and Unjust Wars: A Moral Argument with Historical Illustrations*. New York: Basic Books, 1977.

Warren, Earl. "The Bill of Rights and the Military." In *The Great Rights*, ed. Edmund Cahn. New York: Macmillan, 1963.

Wasserstrom, Richard. "Lawyers as Professionals: Some Moral Issues." *Human Rights* 5 (1975): 1–24.

Whiteman, Marjorie M. *Digest of International Law*. Washington, DC: Government Printing Office, 1968.

Williams, M. Robin, Jr. *American Society: A Sociological Perspective*. New York: Alfred A. Knopf, 1958.

Wolgast, Elizabeth. *The Grammar of Justice*. Ithaca, NY: Cornell University Press, 1987.

Yarmolinsky, Adam. *The Military Establishment*. New York: Harper & Row, 1971.

Index